THE
SOUP BOOK

THE
SOUP BOOK

Editor-in-chief
SOPHIE GRIGSON

CONTENTS

SOPHIE GRIGSON

I have no hesitation in insisting that of all types of food, soup is the most universally relevant. Soup can be whatever you want it to be. It has the potential to make itself at home on any dining table or lap or rug laid out on the grass, no matter whether as part of a multi-coursed banquet for kings and queens, or the main nourishment for humble cash-strapped commoners. There are no eating occasions when a well-judged slurp of soup would not be welcome. Or at least none that I can think of.

This really is the joy of soup. It can be thick or thin, elegant or rustic, subtle or brassy, light or filling, vegetarian, meaty, fishy, vegan, dairy-free, wheat-free, hot or cold, health-giving, revitalizing, comforting, and many, many more fine, upstanding adjectives. The one blot on this cavalcade of praise is the poorly made soup, or worse still, the instant hot-water-'n'-mix sort of a soup that is sprinkled out of a packet with no regard for taste. For that, I have no time, and I hope, too, that with this book in hand, you will jettison such abominations.

Anyone can make a good soup. Yes, anyone. The simplest of soups, those that are an elementary assembly job of ingredients whizzed up in a liquidizer or processor, could be made by a six year old with minimal assistance, and still merit bags of praise. From there it is only a small step to that wonderful crowd of cooked and puréed vegetable soups. Once this technique is mastered, a vast world of possibilities opens up before you. As long as you make sure you start with good fresh ingredients (soup should never be just a dustbin job for the wrinkled remnants at the back of the vegetable rack), preferably organic or locally sourced, and you pay a gentle degree of attention to what you are doing, you can hardly go wrong. And in the unlikely event that you do, there may well be remedies (see pp34–35) to speedily restore your reputation as a fine soup-maker.

In this book you will find soups of every hue and texture, and complexity. Many of the most famous soups of the world have found their way here – starlets such as the hearty chowders of the Newfoundland fishermen, or warming Hungarian Goulash. There's Vichyssoise, the posh version of leek and potato soup, Minestrone, the Italian mama's favourite, Russian Borscht, and cool, Spanish Gazpacho, so invigorating on a searingly hot day. Scattered amongst these are swathes of lesser known, though equally satisfying, soups of many types, from a simple pumpkin and apple soup to Indian-inspired broths or more surprising fruit soups.

As well as the soups themselves, you will find a neat guide to garnishes great and small, and suggestions for bread accompaniments – from a straightforward crusty white loaf to golden American cornbread. In short, everything you'll ever need to know about soup is gathered here in *The Soup Book*.

INTRODUCTION

In our house, we look forward to soup on a Sunday afternoon. The whole family love it. Ask anyone about their childhood food memories and soup is likely to come up. Whether it's a humble cream of tomato, a delicate bone broth, or a peppery minestrone, there is a soup for all tastes.

At Food for Life we are striving for tasty, real food for everyone. Soup is a food that really encompasses this ethos. Responding to the seasons and using fresh ingredients available locally is a great way to make a meal with minimal impact on the environment. Meat can come from the local butchers and seasonal veg will often be in abundant supply and therefore cheaper. It's also a clever way of using up leftovers and ensuring the glut of leeks in the bottom drawer of the fridge don't go to waste.

Back in 2003, when Food for Life started, we wanted to see what could be achieved when a school, a kitchen, and the community worked together. We wanted kids to connect what they saw on the plate in front of them with the soil it was pulled from, or the animal it came from.

Today, Food for Life is ingrained in thousands of schools across the country. The programme has reached beyond schools, and Food for Life supports cooks and encourages them to take pride in the food they serve in care homes, hospitals, nursery schools, and beyond.

At Food for Life we want to make real, healthy food the easy choice for everyone, and what better way to make a healthy choice than a delicious bowl of soup?

Jeanette Orrey MBE,
Co-founder of Food for Life

We would like to thank the following for kindly donating recipes:
Darina Allen • Dan Barber • Raymond Blanc • Sally Clarke • Jeff Cox • Monty Don
Josephine Fairley • Livia Firth • Skye Gyngell • Shaun Hill • Juliet Kindersley
Daphne Lambert • Allegra McEvedy • Clodagh McKenna • Jeanette Orrey
Arthur Potts Dawson • Thane Prince • Sarah Raven • Rosemary Shrager
Geetie Singh • Rebecca Sullivan • Eric Treuille • Alice Waters

TECHNIQUES

MAKING STOCK

The cornerstone of many soups is a well-made stock and, though the ingredients for it may seem humble and the preparation simple, the contribution it makes is vital.

The four stocks most commonly called for in soup-making are brown stock, vegetable stock, fish stock, and chicken stock. Made from bones and/or common vegetables and flavourings, they are easy to prepare and freeze well for up to three months. If produced from meat bones, stock is clear and relatively fat-free, though it will be gelatinous enough to set when cold. Vegetable stock is lighter and requires a careful balance of ingredients to make it flavoursome. Stocks should not be seasoned with salt – they are one of the building blocks for a soup, not a dish in their own right.

SELECTION OF STOCKS

Brown stock (see p14) is so called because it is produced from meat bones that have been "browned" by cooking in fat. It jellies when cold.

Vegetable stock (see p15) can be given extra depth by the addition of mushrooms, potato, and tomatoes that will offset the sweetness of the other vegetables.

Fish stock (see pp16–17) is quick to make, ideally from the bones and heads of salmon or mild-flavoured white fish, especially flat fish like sole and plaice.

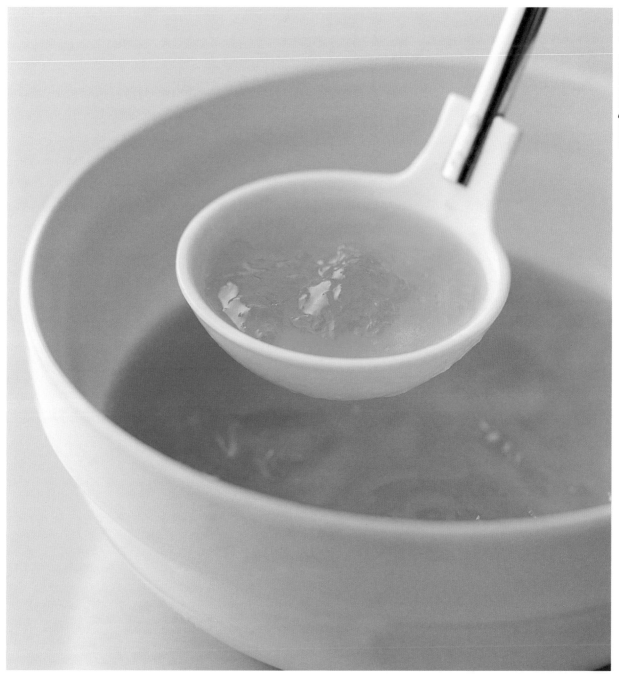

Chicken stock (see pp18–19) serves
as the base for many a fine soup. Some raw
or cooked chicken bones and a few standard
aromatics are all that's required to produce
a rich, gelatinous stock.

MAKES **2.5 LITRES (4½ PINTS)**
PREP **10 MINS**
COOK **3½–4½ HRS**
FREEZE **3 MONTHS**

BROWN STOCK

For a rich meat-based stock, use either beef or lamb bones, but never a mixture of the two. If you have any bacon rinds or vegetable trimmings to hand, pop them in the pot too.

1.35kg (3lb) raw or cooked beef or lamb bones

2–3 onions, halved

2–3 carrots, halved

1 bouquet garni (see p24)

2.5–3 litres (4½–5¼ pints) cold water

1 tsp black peppercorns

1 If you're using raw bones, roast them with the onions and carrots in an oven preheated to 200°C (400°F/Gas 6), turning them frequently, for 30 minutes or until browned. If you're using cooked bones, start the stock from step 2.

2 Put all the ingredients into a large pan, bring to the boil, then skim off any foam that rises to the surface with a slotted spoon. Lower the heat, cover with a lid, and simmer for 3–4 hours. Strain the stock through a sieve, pressing the ingredients against the sides of the sieve to extract all the liquid. Leave to cool, then chill in a covered container for up to 3 days. Before use, remove any solidified fat from the surface with a slotted spoon, then bring the stock to the boil.

MAKES 1 LITRE (1¾ PINTS)
PREP **5 MINS**
COOK **35 MINS**
FREEZE **3 MONTHS**

VEGETABLE STOCK

This is an excellent stock, with a good balance of flavours. The potato means it will not be clear, but since it is being used in a soup, that doesn't matter.

1 leek, thickly sliced

1 large carrot, thickly sliced

2 celery stalks, thickly sliced

1 onion, roughly chopped

75g (2½oz) button, chestnut, or
    open-cup mushrooms, quartered

1 medium potato, thickly sliced

1 tomato, quartered

3 parsley stalks

2 bay leaves

4 sprigs thyme

1.5 litres (2¾ pints) cold water

1 Put all the ingredients into a large pan. Bring to the boil, then lower the heat, cover with a lid, and simmer very gently for 30 minutes.

2 Strain the stock through a fine sieve, pressing the ingredients well against the sides of the sieve to extract all the liquid. Leave to cool completely, then chill in a covered container for up to 3 days before use.

MAKES 1.5 LITRES (2¾ PINTS)
PREP 5 MINS
COOK 30 MINS
FREEZE 2 MONTHS

FISH STOCK

Ask the fishmonger for the bones when getting fish filleted, and check if they have any extra that they can give you. Fish bones will freeze, well-wrapped, for up to two months.

675g–1kg (1½–2¼lb) salmon or white fish bones, heads, and skin (don't use those from dark, oily fish such as mackerel, herring, and sardines – they will give the stock an unpleasant flavour)

6 black peppercorns

1 sprig of thyme

1 bay leaf

2 parsley stalks

2 small carrots

1 onion

2 celery stalks

1 generous glass of dry white wine

1.7 litres (3 pints) cold water

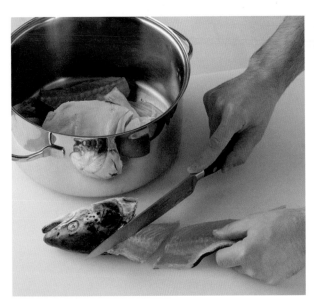

1 Put the fish heads and bones into a large pan, breaking or cutting them up with a knife to fit. Add the black peppercorns, thyme, bay leaf, and parsley.

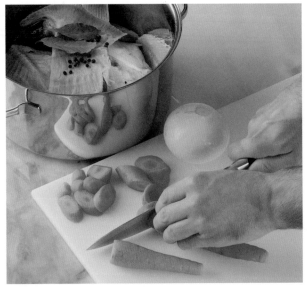

2 Roughly chop the vegetables and add to the pot with the wine. Place the pan over a moderate heat and let the wine bubble for 3 minutes. Add the water and bring to the boil.

3 Lower the heat and simmer the stock, uncovered, for 20–25 minutes – no longer or the stock may begin to develop a bitter taste. Skim off any scum from time to time with a slotted spoon.

4 Strain the stock through a fine sieve into a bowl, pressing the solids against the side of the sieve to extract all the liquid. Leave to cool completely, then chill in a covered container for up to 3 days.

5 The finished stock should be thin in texture, with a delicate flavour. It will make an excellent base for all kinds of fish soup.

MAKES 1.5 LITRES (2¾ PINTS)
PREP 5 MINS
COOK 3 HRS
FREEZE 3 MONTHS

CHICKEN STOCK

This recipe gives an ideal list of ingredients, but as long as you have the chicken carcase, onion, carrot, and one or two of the herbs, you can turn out a fine stock.

1 raw or cooked chicken carcase, roughly broken into pieces

1 onion, quartered

1 carrot, quartered

1 leek, quartered

1 celery stalk, quartered

1 bay leaf

2 parsley stalks

1 sprig of thyme

8 black peppercorns

1.7 litres (3 pints) cold water

1 Put the chicken, vegetables, and all the flavourings into a large pan, cover with the water, and bring to the boil. Cover with a lid, lower the heat, and simmer for 2–3 hours, skimming off any foam from time to time.

2 Ladle the stock through a sieve into a clean bowl, pressing the ingredients firmly against the sides of the sieve with the back of the ladle to squeeze out as much liquid as possible.

3 If you're using the stock straightaway, remove any globules of fat from the surface by skimming the top of the stock with a piece of kitchen paper folded in two.

4 Otherwise, leave the stock to cool before chilling it in a covered container for up to 3 days. A layer of congealed fat will form on the surface. Scoop this off before use.

MICROWAVE CHICKEN STOCK

If you are short of time, you can also make chicken stock in a microwave. Put the broken-up chicken carcase into a large microwaveable bowl along with the onion, carrot, leek, and celery. Add the bay leaf, parsley, thyme and peppercorns, then cover with boiling water. Cover the bowl with cling film (roll it back at one edge to allow the steam to escape) and microwave on full power for 25 minutes. Leave to stand for a further 25 minutes, then strain.

PREPARING VEGETABLES

Careful preparation of vegetables is essential. Properly cut vegetables not only contribute to the finished appearance of a soup – they cook more evenly too.

Vegetables are best prepared just before cooking: washed, peeled, and cut ahead of time, they are left exposed to air and moisture, which can lead them to deteriorate and lose their vitamins. Most often vegetables can be cut by hand, so a good sharp knife is vital. Use a large or small knife depending on the vegetable you're cutting. Here's how to prepare those most commonly used in soups.

CHOPPING OR CRUSHING GARLIC

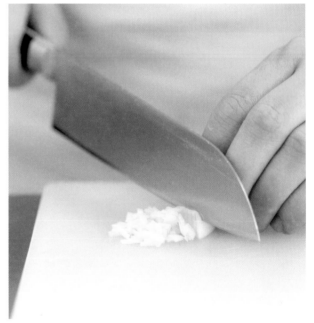

1 Lay the clove of garlic on a chopping board with the blade of a large knife on top of it. Strike the blade with the heel of your hand to break the skin of the clove, but don't press down so hard that you smash the garlic.

2 Peel off the skin, then chop off the ends of the garlic. Chop the garlic roughly, then sprinkle it with a little salt to stop it sticking to the blade. You can then chop it finely or crush smooth with the flat blade.

CHOPPING ONIONS

1 Cut the onion in half lengthways with a chef's knife. Peel away the skin, but leave the root intact – it will help keep the halves together as you chop.

2 With the onion flat side down on the chopping board, make two or three horizontal slices, cutting up to – but not through – the root.

3 Now, slice the onion finely vertically, taking care once again to cut up to but not through the root.

4 Turn the onion through 90 degrees and slice across to make even-sized dice. Discard the root when you get to it.

SKINNING AND DESEEDING TOMATOES

1 With a sharp knife, cut an "X" in the base of the tomato.

2 Immerse it in boiling water for around 20 seconds or until the skin begins to split.

3 Remove the tomato with a slotted spoon and plunge it into iced water to cool it.

4 When it's cool enough to handle, use a paring knife to peel off the skin.

5 Slice the tomato in half, then squeeze the seeds into a bowl and discard.

6 Slice the tomato half first into strips and then into dice.

CLEANING AND CHOPPING LEEKS

1 With a large knife, trim off the root and some of the dark green leaf at the top, then slice the leek in two lengthways and fan it open.

2 Rinse the leek under cold running water to remove the soil that tends to collect between the layers, then pat it dry with kitchen paper.

3 Sit the halved leek on the chopping board and slice it into thick or thin strips, according to the recipe.

CHOPPING CARROTS

Peel the carrot, then slice it lengthways. Cut the lengths crossways, then stack them and cut into batonnets. Slice across the batonnets to make even-sized dice.

SWEATING VEGETABLES

Sweating chopped vegetables in oil or butter gives a soup a more pronounced flavour. Heat a little fat over a low heat, stir in the vegetables, then add a pinch of salt, cover, and cook for 5–10 minutes or until soft but not brown.

PREPARING HERBS

Chopped herbs release more of their flavour than whole, but before the leaves of some herbs like rosemary can be chopped, they need to be stripped from their woody stalks.

CHOPPING HERBS WITH TENDER STALKS

1 To chop the leaves of herbs with tender stalks like basil, roll them together into a tight bunch.

2 Holding the bunch of leaves steady with one hand, slice across them with a chef's knife.

3 Using the knife in a rocking motion, chop the leaves finely, turning them 90 degrees halfway through.

USING A MEZZALUNA

A mezzaluna makes light work of chopping herbs. Rock it from side to side across them until they're chopped to your liking.

REMOVING WOODY STALKS

To strip the leaves of herbs with woody stalks, run the thumb and forefinger of one hand along the stalk.

MAKING A BOUQUET GARNI

For a classic soup flavouring, tie a sprig of thyme and parsley with a bay leaf. You could also include sage or rosemary.

PREPARING SPICES

Spices lend an extra dimension to many soups and, whether you're using them fresh or dried, they usually require a little straightforward preparation.

BRUISING WHOLE SPICES

Before use, whole fresh spices like lemongrass are usually bruised with the blade of a heavy knife and your hand.

GRATING ROOTS

Roots like ginger can be finely chopped by hand, but it's often easiest to grate them. Peel off the skin beforehand.

DESEEDING CHILLIES

Scraping out the seeds from chillies lessens their heat. Wear a pair of rubber or plastic gloves to do it.

FRYING IN OIL

When spices are fried till lightly coloured, their flavour gets trapped in the oil. The oil is used along with the spices.

DRY-ROASTING

To dry-roast spices, place them in an oven preheated to 160°C (325°F/ Gas 3), or fry them in a dry pan, till lightly browned.

CRUSHING

Dried or dry-roasted spices can be crushed by hand in a pestle and mortar or by machine in a spice mill.

PREPARING PULSES

Dried beans, peas, and lentils are perfect for soup-making. Little effort is required to prepare them – all you need to do is think ahead.

The basic preparation of pulses is simple: first, you need to sort and rinse them; then (in nearly all cases) you need to soak them; finally, the pulses have to be cooked until tender. This can take anything from around half an hour to 3 hours. Once cooked, pulses are well-suited to puréeing, but they also work well left whole in soups.

SORTING AND RINSING

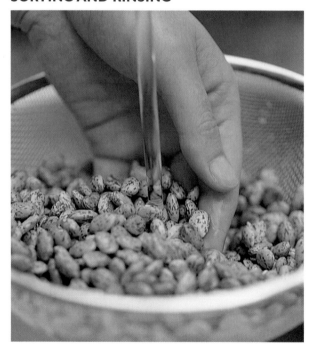

Whatever kind of pulse you're using, start by sorting and rinsing them. Place the pulses in a colander and carefully pick out any husks or pieces of grit, then rinse the pulses well under cold running water.

SOAKING

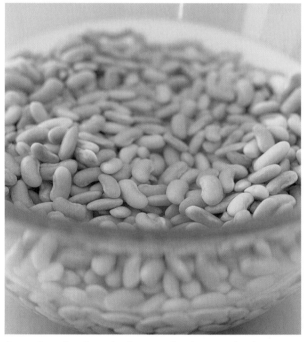

Apart from lentils and split peas, all pulses need to be soaked for at least 8 hours, and preferably overnight. Place them in a bowl, add three times their volume of cold water, then cover and place in the fridge.

ADDING FLAVOUR

The flavour of pulses can be rather bland, so it's usually a good idea to add some aromatics. A bouquet garni (see p24) or a sprig of herbs will do the trick: bay leaf, parsley, rosemary, or thyme all work well. A pinch of cumin, coriander, chilli, or caraway is another option, but you could also pop a carrot into the pan or an onion studded with cloves. Alternatively, you can cook pulses in a well-flavoured stock, but never season it with salt – it will prevent them from softening.

COOKING PULSES

Drain the soaked pulses, then place them in a large pan along with any flavourings. Pour in four times their volume of cold water and add 1 tbsp vegetable oil to stop them sticking. Bring rapidly to the boil, and boil hard for 10 minutes, skimming away any foam with a slotted spoon. Lower the heat, part-cover with a lid, and simmer until tender. The cooking time will depend on the variety of pulse (see right).

COOKING TIMES

Here are approximate cooking times for the pulses most commonly used in soups.

black beans	1 hour
black-eyed beans	1–1½ hours
borlotti beans	1–1½ hours
butterbeans	1–1½ hours
cannellini beans	1–1½ hours
chickpeas	2–3 hours
flageolet beans	1½ hours
haricot beans	1–1½ hours
lentils (split)	25 minutes
lentils (whole)	45 minutes
pinto beans	1–1½ hours
red kidney beans	1–1½ hours
split peas	45 minutes

PURÉEING

Among the easiest soups to prepare are those you whizz to a purée in a blender. The alternative is to use a food mill – this requires a little more effort, but the results are smoother.

The secret to success with puréed soups is thorough cooking, so that the starchy ingredients that give the soup its body can be blended to a smooth purée. For that reason, always cook root vegetables and dried beans till they are extremely tender, but never overcook potatoes, or they will become glutinous and gluey. There is also a range of semi-puréed soups, in which some of the ingredients are blended to thicken the broth, while the rest are left whole for interest.

USING A FOOD MILL

Working the ingredients through a food mill is particularly successful for soups that contain ingredients with skins and seeds, which blenders sometimes can't cope with.

SEMI-PURÉED SOUPS

To thicken a soup but keep some texture for interest, purée around half of it and then return it to the pan. Gently reheat the soup before serving.

IN A BLENDER

1 Before blending, test the ingredients are really tender with a knife – they are only ready to purée when completely soft.

2 Blend the soup until you have a smooth consistency with no lumps. Do it in batches so you don't overload the machine.

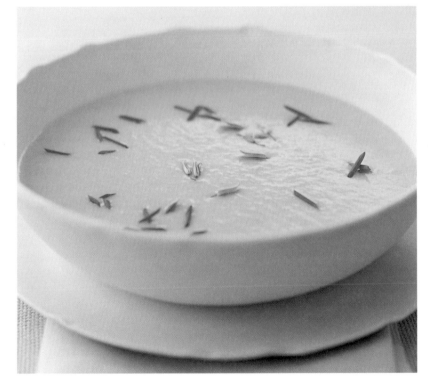

3 The consistency of a puréed soup will vary according to the ingredients used and the way in which they're processed. But, in general, it should be totally smooth and lump-free. To remove all traces of skins, seeds, and fibres, you may need to push the purée through a fine sieve.

ENRICHING

Butter or cream stirred into a soup at the last minute will greatly improve its character, adding body and shine. For interest, you can flavour the butter and serve it at the table.

Both cream and butter make a quick and simple garnish for individual servings of soup (see p36–39), but if you have another garnish in mind, you can add them to the soup to enrich it while it's still in the pan. Butters flavoured with herbs, nuts, or smoked fish are another way of enriching a soup, although these are best served separately, to be added to the soup by your guests.

WITH CREAM

Add the cream at the end of cooking and, in the case of a puréed soup, after blending. Stir it in well, then check the seasoning. If you've added a substantial amount, you may want to reheat the soup gently before serving.

WITH BUTTER

Cut a knob of chilled unsalted butter into cubes. Remove the pan from the heat and whisk it in a cube at a time – the soup should become glossy and smooth. Do not reheat the soup or the butter will separate.

WITH A FLAVOURED BUTTER

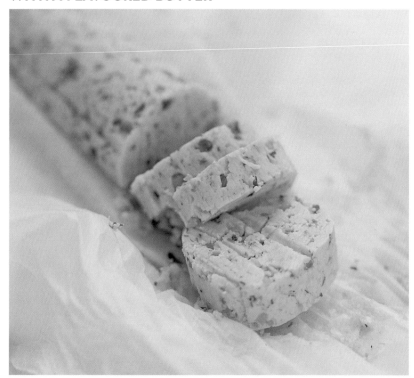

Flavoured butters are an ideal accompaniment to puréed soups and bisques. They are also easy to prepare and work well with a variety of ingredients. Blend the flavourings of your choice into the butter, then place the butter on a sheet of greaseproof paper and roll it tightly into a cylindrical shape. Chill it in the fridge or freezer until you're ready to dish up the soup, then simply slice it into rounds. You could also serve the butter at the table and allow your guests to help themselves. Here are recipes for two flavoured butters that are great with a whole range of soups.

Herb butter Mix 60g (2oz) softened butter with 6 blanched and finely chopped spinach leaves, 1 chopped shallot, 1 tsp each chopped parsley, chervil, and tarragon, and some salt and pepper. Roll in greaseproof paper and chill till needed.

Lemon and chilli butter Combine 60g (2oz) softened butter with 1 tsp finely grated lemon zest and ¼ tsp crushed dried chilli flakes (or more if you like your food quite spicy). Season to taste with salt.

THICKENING

A little butter or cream stirred into a soup just before serving will enrich it (see pp30–31), but there will be times when you want to thicken a soup rather more. Here's how to do it.

There are several quick and easy ways you can give body to a soup at the end of cooking. You could whisk egg yolk or a mixture of egg yolk and cream into the hot liquid. Another option is to use starch, in the form of cornflour, plain flour, or rice flour. Or you could make a paste from flour and butter and stir this into the soup before serving. But perhaps the oldest method of thickening a soup is with bread, either stirred into the broth at the last minute or incorporated into it earlier in the cooking process.

WITH STARCH

Mix a little cornflour, rice flour, or plain flour to a thin paste with some cold water. Stir the mixture into the pan of hot soup, bring back to the boil, and simmer, stirring all the time, for 1–2 minutes or until the soup thickens.

WITH FLOUR AND BUTTER

Combine two parts softened butter to one part flour. Gradually whisk small pieces of the paste into the hot soup at the end of cooking. Allow the flour to cook for 1–2 minutes, stirring all the time.

WITH EGG

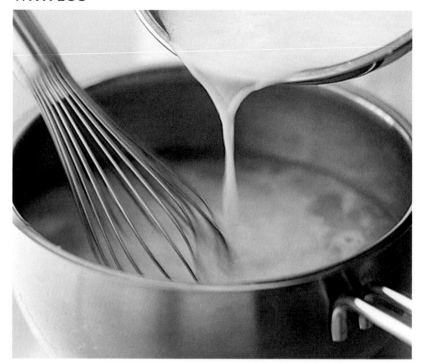

Added towards the end of cooking, egg yolk or a mixture of egg yolk and cream will thicken a hot soup and make it velvety. Remove the pan from the heat to incorporate the mixture, then reheat the soup gently, whisking until thick. Do not allow it to boil or it will curdle.

WITH BREAD

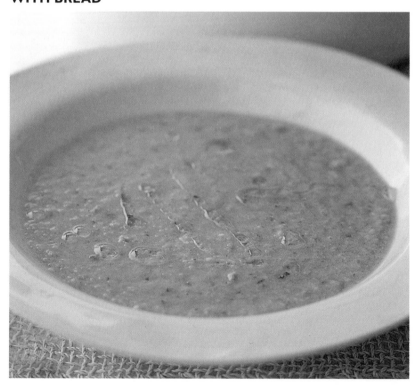

Bread has long been used to thicken country soups. For gazpacho (left), breadcrumbs are blended into the soup at an early stage. But bread can also be added to a broth at the last minute, and stirred until it breaks up and thickens the soup.

RESCUING

There's no need to worry if your soup hasn't turned out quite as you had intended – even the most accomplished cook occasionally produces a dish that's less than perfect.

Whether you are unhappy with the finished consistency or think the soup is too highly seasoned, here are some quick fixes to put things right.

TOO THIN

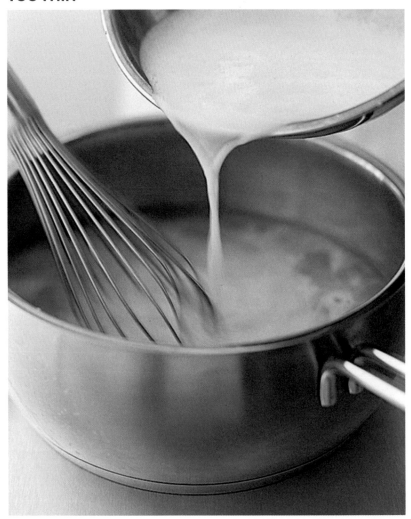

There are a number of ways you can thicken a soup that's too thin. You could whisk in a paste of butter and flour or a mixture of eggs and cream (as here). Or you could add some rice flour, cornflour, or plain flour blended with water (for more details, turn to pp32–33). Another option is to stir in a few instant potato flakes or instant oats.

TOO THICK

Depending on the liquid you've used to produce the soup, thin it with a little stock, milk, or water. Once the soup has reached the desired consistency, taste it, season, and reheat gently.

LUMPY OR STRINGY

Even a soup you've whizzed in a blender can turn out lumpy or stringy. Ladle it into a fine sieve, then use the back of the ladle, a wooden spoon, or a pestle to push the ingredients through. Reheat gently before serving.

TOO SALTY

If you only ever add salt towards the end of cooking and use home-made, unseasoned stock, the chances of your soup being too salty are slim. But if it is, there are a couple of things you can do. Add a couple of raw potatoes cut in half and simmer the soup gently until they're cooked, then remove and discard. Alternatively, add a little sugar and, if the soup is also too thick, some cream, milk, or water.

GARNISHING

From a single piece of seafood to a simple swirl of cream, a well-chosen garnish transforms a soup, adding extra colour, as well as texture and flavour.

For some soups, a garnish is an essential component – the soured cream stirred into Borscht, for instance, or the cheese-topped croûtes served with French onion soup. For others, a garnish is a way of introducing contrasting textures and flavours. Many ingredients can act as a garnish if they also complement the flavours of the soup, but here is a selection to suit almost every occasion.

WITH CREAM

Dolloped, swirled, or drizzled, cream makes an excellent garnish for thick puréed soups. Use single cream, double cream, whipped cream, soured cream, or crème fraîche. Yogurt is an alternative if you're counting the calories.

WITH HERBS

Fresh sage leaves or parsley fried in olive oil until crisp make a flavoursome garnish for gutsy soups, but a sprinkling of chopped parsley, chervil, or coriander instantly adds fragrance and colour to almost any soup.

WITH SHELLFISH

A whole prawn, crab claw, grilled scallop, or (as here) an oyster poached and served in its shell makes a spectacular garnish for a seafood soup. A wild garlic flower provides the finishing touch for this dish.

WITH OLIVE OIL

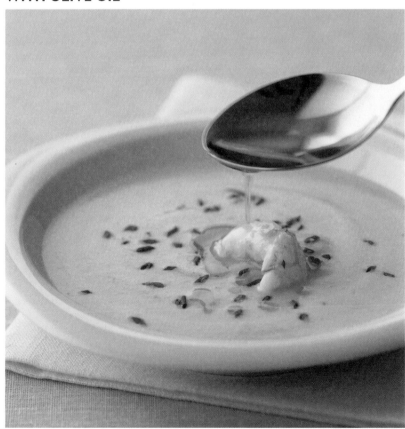

As much a condiment as a garnish, a drizzle of fragrant, full-bodied extra virgin olive oil brings a Mediterranean flavour to soups, while looking appetizing and glossy on the surface.

WITH VEGETABLES

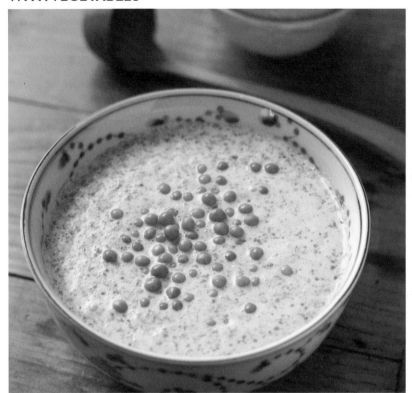

Raw or cooked, vegetables make eye-catching and healthy garnishes. If small, like peas, they can be served whole. Otherwise, slice them into decorative strips, dice, or rings.

WITH BACON

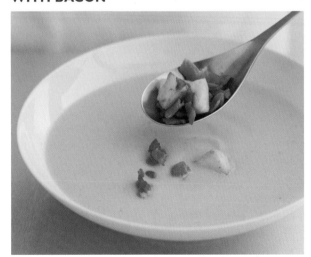

Grilled until crisp and then crumbled, bacon makes a tasty garnish that looks attractive floating on the surface of a pale puréed soup. Here it is accompanied by pieces of pan-fried scallop.

WITH SEEDS AND NUTS

Toasted seeds or nuts not only look pretty, they also add a satisfying crunch. Served with a vegetable soup, they are a good source of protein too.

WITH CROÛTONS

Small dice of fried bread are a classic garnish. For about 40 croûtons, cut four slices of day-old white bread (crusts removed) into 1cm (½in) dice. Heat 2 tbsp sunflower oil and 30g (1oz) unsalted butter in a large frying pan until hot, then fry the dice, stirring constantly, for 10 minutes or until golden. Drain on kitchen paper before serving. For extra flavour, stir in a finely chopped garlic clove a couple of minutes before the croûtons are due to be done.

WITH CROÛTES

Large croûtons are known as croûtes. To make them, cut a day-old baguette into 1cm (½in) slices, and toast until golden. Alternatively, place on a baking sheet and bake in an oven preheated to 180°C (350°F/Gas 4) for 15 minutes.

WAYS OF SERVING CROÛTES

Croûtes are a versatile garnish. Rubbed with garlic, then topped with cheese and flashed under the grill, they are perfect for French onion soup (above). For fish soups, spread them thickly with a garlicky rouille sauce.

SPRING

SPRING
SEASON'S BEST

Fresh tastes and sweetness mark the new crops of spring, from early peas to delicate asparagus and lettuce. These lend themselves to rich, creamy soups and pair well with flavours such as shellfish, rocket, and even fruity mango. The changeable weather means you'll sometimes still want something warming and hearty, such as a smoked cauliflower cheese soup or a wild salmon chowder, and there are also distinctly seasonal delicacies to try, such as wild garlic soup, or nettle soup made from the first new growth of the year.

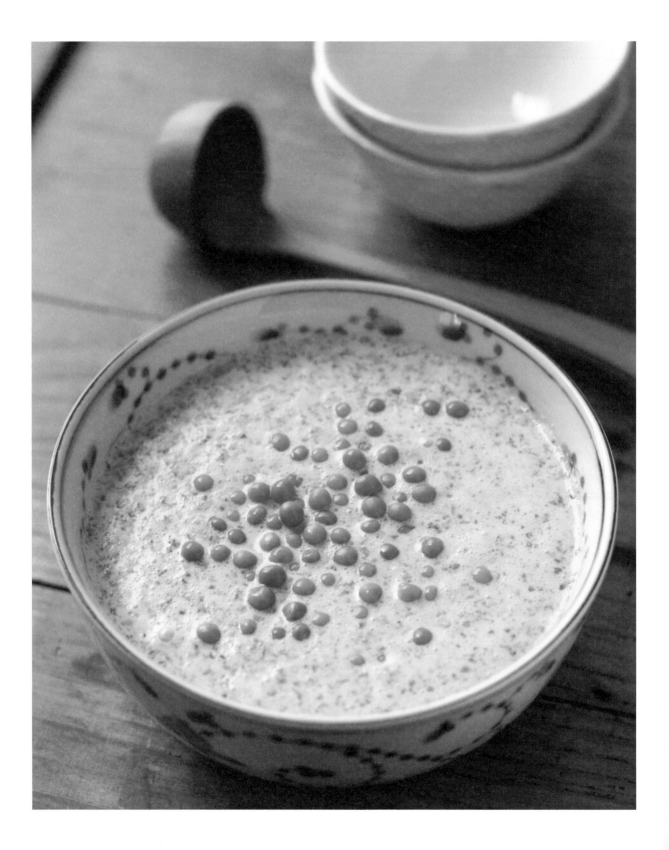

SERVES **4**
PREP **30 MINS**
PLUS 30 MINS CHILLING
COOK **NONE**
FREEZE **NOT SUITABLE**

125g (4½oz) peas (shelled weight)

1 small garlic clove

pinch of coarse salt

2 medium round lettuces (about 500g/1lb 2oz in total), cleaned, torn into pieces, and solid cores discarded

250ml (8fl oz) plain yogurt

2cm (¾in) piece fresh ginger, peeled and finely grated

handful of mint leaves

juice of ½ lemon

salt and freshly ground black pepper

RECIPE BY
CELIA BROOKES BROWN

LETTUCE SOUP WITH PEAS

Don't use lettuces that have bolted for this – they will have bitter cores. Some of the leaves may still be good to use, though. Have a taste first.

1 Bring a small amount of water to the boil in a pan, add the peas, and cook for 1 minute. Drain (reserving the cooking water), cool under cold running water, and refrigerate. Cut the garlic in half, and remove and discard any green at the centre. Crush the halves with a pinch of coarse salt.

2 Combine the garlic with all the other ingredients (except the peas) in a food processor or blender, adding just enough of the reserved cooking water to get the blades moving or until the desired consistency is achieved – this will vary according to the type of lettuce and the kind of machine you are using, but it is nice if you can get it fairly smooth, with a bit of texture.

3 Transfer the soup to a large bowl and chill for 30 minutes. When ready to serve, stir through the cooked peas, leaving a few to garnish.

SERVES **4**
PREP **20 MINS**
COOK **20 MINS**
FREEZE **UP TO 3 MONTHS**
SOUP AND PESTO SEPARATELY

2 tbsp olive oil

1 onion, chopped

2 celery sticks, halved
   lengthways, sliced

2 garlic cloves, chopped

4 slices prosciutto, chopped

pinch dried crushed chillies

handful basil leaves, shredded

900ml (1½ pints) vegetable
   or chicken stock

50g (1¾oz) spaghetti, broken
   into pieces

400g can butterbeans, drained

FOR THE PESTO

25g (scant 1oz) rocket, very
   finely chopped

2 tbsp very finely chopped basil

25g (scant 1oz) Parmesan
   cheese, grated

25g (scant 1oz) pine nuts,
   toasted and very finely
   chopped

1 small garlic clove, finely
   chopped

3 tbsp olive oil

salt and freshly ground
   black pepper

RECIPE BY
ANGELA NILSEN

BUTTERBEAN SOUP WITH ROCKET PESTO

A quick homemade version of pesto is spooned on top of this butterbean soup, giving it extra flavour, colour, and texture – perfect for serving at a supper party.

1 Heat the oil for the soup in a large saucepan. Add the onion and celery and fry for 4–5 minutes until the onion is soft but not brown. Add the garlic and fry for 1 minute. Stir in the prosciutto and chillies and fry another 1–2 minutes until the prosciutto is starting to go crisp. Stir in the basil, stock, and spaghetti. Bring to the boil. Simmer for about 10 minutes or until the spaghetti is al dente. Tip in the butterbeans and warm through.

2 Spoon 3 ladlefuls of the soup into a food processor or blender and whizz until smooth. Stir it back into the rest of the soup and season to taste.

3 Mix all the ingredients for the pesto together in a bowl or roughly chop in a small blender. Season it with pepper and a pinch of salt. Reheat the soup and serve with a spoonful of pesto on top.

SERVES **4**
PREP **10 MINS**
COOK **30 MINS**
FREEZE **UP TO 3 MONTHS**

RECIPE BY
CELIA BROOKS BROWN

ROCKET AND PARMESAN SOUP

This makes good use of peppery rocket that may have become
a bit leathery. If your rocket is in bloom, the flowers can add
a distinctive savoury flavour to the dish.

2 tbsp olive oil

2 medium onions, chopped

650g (1lb 7oz) potatoes,
  washed but not peeled,
  cut in 2cm (¾in) cubes

sea salt

4 small or 2 large garlic cloves,
  crushed

1 litre (1¾ pints) vegetable stock

1 Parmesan rind, about 3 x 9cm
  (1¼ x 3½in), cut into tiny dice

125g (4½oz) rocket leaves,
  roughly chopped

fresh Parmesan, to serve

rocket flowers, to serve
  (optional)

1 Heat the oil in a soup pan over a medium heat. Add the onions and cook, stirring frequently, until soft and translucent. Add the potatoes with a little salt, stir, cover, and cook for 5 minutes, stirring frequently.

2 Add the garlic and stir for a few seconds until fragrant, then pour in the stock. Bring to the boil, add the Parmesan rind, then simmer for about 10 minutes, stirring occasionally, until the potato is soft.

3 Add the rocket, stir and cook for 3–5 minutes, until tender but still bright green. Cool briefly, then purée the soup with a hand blender until smooth. Taste for seasoning. Serve each bowl with grated or shaved fresh Parmesan, and a few rocket flowers if you have them.

SERVES **4**
PREP **10 MINS**
COOK **40 MINS**
FREEZE **UP TO 3 MONTHS**
BEFORE EGG AND CREAM ADDED

CREAM OF ASPARAGUS SOUP

If you are a fan of puréed soups, you can whizz the mixture
in a blender at the end of cooking, then pass it through a fine
sieve and reheat gently before serving.

1 litre (1¾ pints) water

salt and freshly ground
    black pepper

60g (2oz) butter

500g (1lb 2oz) white or green
    asparagus, trimmed, peeled
    (reserve the trimmings), and
    cut into 2.5cm (1in) lengths

300ml (10fl oz) milk

30g (1oz) plain flour

pinch of caster sugar

pinch of freshly grated nutmeg

2 medium egg yolks

2 tbsp whipping cream

1½ tbsp chopped flat-leaf
    parsley

1 Put the water into a saucepan with 1 level tsp salt and 20g (¾oz) of the butter. Add the asparagus trimmings, bring to the boil, then cover and simmer for 15 minutes over a medium heat. Strain through a sieve (reserving the cooking liquid) and discard the trimmings.

2 Bring the cooking liquid to the boil and add the trimmed asparagus. Return to the boil, cover, and cook for 10–12 minutes or until al dente, then drain, reserving the cooking liquid. Add enough of the milk to the cooking liquid to make 1 litre (1¾ pints) in all.

3 Melt the remaining butter in a pan, add the flour, and cook over a low heat, stirring, for 2–3 minutes or until smooth. Gradually add the milk mixture, stirring vigorously with a whisk to make sure there are no lumps. Bring to the boil and cook, uncovered, over a low heat for 5 minutes, stirring occasionally. Add the sugar and nutmeg and season with salt and pepper.

4 Stir the egg yolks into the cream and slowly add the mixture to the soup, stirring carefully to get a smooth texture. Add the asparagus and reheat gently. Do not let the soup boil. Serve garnished with parsley.

SERVES **4**
PREP **15 MINS**
COOK **20 MINS**
FREEZE **NOT SUITABLE**

RECIPE BY
SHAUN HILL

ASPARAGUS AND MOREL SOUP

This soup is best made when asparagus first appears and when fresh morel mushrooms are in season. It should taste fresh and light, so cooking times are brief.

1.5 litres (2¾ pints) chicken stock

1 small potato, cut into 2cm (¾in) dice

1 small leek, trimmed and cut into 2cm (¾in) lengths

400g (14oz) asparagus, trimmed and cut into 5cm (2in) lengths

1 tbsp olive oil

1 tbsp crème fraîche

25g (scant 1oz) unsalted butter

salt and freshly ground black pepper

4 large fresh morels (or 4 dried morels soaked in lukewarm water for 30 minutes)

1 Heat the stock in a large saucepan, add the potato, and bring to the boil. Lower the heat and simmer for 5 minutes. Add the leek and asparagus and cook, uncovered, for 7–8 minutes. Pick out four attractive asparagus tips and reserve for garnishing. Transfer the contents of the pan to a blender and whizz until smooth. Add the olive oil, crème fraîche, and 20g (¾oz) of the butter, then season with salt and pepper.

2 Halve the morels lengthways and brush clean inside and out. Stew gently in a pan with the remaining butter for a few minutes until cooked. Meanwhile, reheat the soup. Serve garnished with the morels and reserved asparagus tips.

SERVES **4–6**
PREP **15–20 MINS**
COOK **40 MINS**
FREEZE **UP TO 1 MONTH**
WITHOUT CREAM OR BACON

2 tsp coriander seeds

40g (1½oz) unsalted butter

1 onion, diced

1 potato, diced

1 head cauliflower, finely
  chopped

500ml (16fl oz) vegetable stock

1 bay leaf

8 streaky bacon rashers,
  rinds removed

200ml (7fl oz) milk

100ml (3½fl oz) single cream

salt and freshly ground
  black pepper

RECIPE BY
ROOPA GULATI

CAULIFLOWER SOUP WITH TOASTED CORIANDER

Cauliflower is transformed when treated to gentle heat and aromatic spicing. For a vegetarian option, garnish this with croûtons and Parmesan cheese instead of bacon.

1 Heat a sturdy frying pan or small griddle and lightly roast the coriander seeds, stirring all the time, for about a minute. Grind the seeds to a coarse powder using a mortar and pestle and set aside.

2 Melt the butter in a large saucepan over a low heat. Add the onion and potato, cover and leave to soften for 10 minutes. Add the cauliflower and ground coriander, season well, cover, and continue cooking for a further 10 minutes.

3 Pour over the stock, add the bay leaf, cover, and simmer for about 15 minutes, until the cauliflower has softened. Meanwhile, cook the bacon rashers under a hot grill until crisp. Drain on kitchen paper, roughly chop, and set aside.

4 Remove the bay leaf and blend the soup to a purée with a stick blender or in a liquidizer. Stir in the milk and add the cream. Reheat and season again if necessary. Ladle the soup into bowls and scatter with the chopped bacon before serving.

SERVES **6**
PREP **15–20 MINS**
COOK **25–30 MINS**
FREEZE **UP TO 3 MONTHS**
BEFORE CHEESE IS ADDED

1 cauliflower, broken
    into florets

1 large onion, chopped

1 medium floury potato,
    cut into cubes

2 garlic cloves, sliced

1 bouquet garni (see p24)

30g (1oz) butter

1 litre (1¾ pints) hot vegetable
    or chicken stock

salt and freshly ground
    black pepper

100g (3½oz) coarsely grated
    smoked cheddar

a shake of cayenne pepper,
    freshly chopped parsley or
    chives, croûtons, or a dollop
    of soured cream, to garnish

RECIPE BY
SOPHIE GRIGSON

SMOKED CAULIFLOWER CHEESE SOUP

Make sure your cauliflower is impeccably fresh, and check that the cheese really is smoked, and not just laced with fake smoke flavouring as so many are.

1 Sweat the vegetables, garlic, and bouquet garni with the butter in a covered pan over a low heat for 10 minutes, stirring once or twice. Add the stock, a little salt, and loads of pepper, and bring to the boil. Simmer until the cauliflower and potato are just tender and no more. Remove the bouquet garni and whizz the soup in a blender until smooth, adding more stock or a little milk to thin it down as necessary.

2 Reheat the soup gently, but do not allow it to boil. Stir in two-thirds of the cheese, and taste, adding more cheese if needed. Taste one more time, then serve with the garnish of your choice.

SERVES **4–6**
PREP **30 MINS**
COOK **45 MINS**
FREEZE **NOT SUITABLE**

RECIPE BY
ALLEGRA MCEVEDY

SOUP OF THE FIRST AND LAST

TV chef and food writer Allegra McEvedy co-founded Leon, the healthy
and ethical restaurant chain. "A soup for early spring, using foods coming
in and going out of season."

10 oysters, opened, and
  with juice

1 tbsp butter

1 white onion, finely diced

2 garlic cloves, finely chopped

1 celery stalk, finely diced

salt and freshly ground
  black pepper

200ml (7fl oz) double cream

400ml (14fl oz) cold water

½ celeriac, peeled and
  finely diced

200g (7oz) Jersey royal
  potatoes, cut into thin slices

2 small–medium turnips, cut
  in two, then sliced into
  half-moons

200g (7oz) wild garlic leaves,
  roughly cut into 4cm (1¾in)
  pieces (you could use baby
  spinach and more garlic, but
  it won't be quite the same)

a handful of wild garlic flowers
  (optional)

1 Wash 4–6 oyster shells (one per serving) to remove any grit. Cover
with boiling water, to clean and keep warm. Heat the butter in a pan, add
the onion, garlic, celery, and a pinch of salt, cover with a lid, and sweat over
a low heat for 5 minutes or until soft. Add the cream, water, and celeriac,
and simmer, covered, for 10 minutes. Add the potatoes and cook for
10 minutes, then add the turnips and cook for a further 10 minutes.

2 Take off the heat and ladle half the soup into a blender. Add 4–6 oysters
(depending on how many you need to serve) and half the garlic leaves
and blend until smooth. Tip the mixture back into the pan, rinse the
blender out with 400ml (14fl oz) cold water, and add that to the pan
as well. Season with salt and pepper, add the rest of the garlic leaves,
then bring to a gentle simmer and cook for 5 minutes.

3 Meanwhile, put the remaining oysters and their juices in a pan with
2 tbsp water, and poach for 4 minutes or until firm. Turn halfway through.
Remove the oysters from the pan and set aside. Stir the warmed juices
into the soup, then check the seasoning and the consistency – add a little
hot water if the soup is too thick. Divide among 4–6 bowls. Drop a warm
oyster shell in each, fill with a reserved oyster, and garnish with wild garlic
flowers if you like.

SERVES **4–6**
PREP **10 MINS**
COOK **35 MINS**
FREEZE **UP TO 3 MONTHS**

RECIPE BY
DAPHNE LAMBERT

WILD GARLIC SOUP

Daphne Lambert runs Greencuisine at Penrhos Court in Herefordshire. There she teaches the benefits of organic, local, and wild foods.

6 large handfuls of wild garlic leaves

25g (scant 1oz) butter

3 medium potatoes, diced

1 large onion, diced

600ml (1 pint) hot vegetable stock

sea salt and freshly ground black pepper

1 Bring a pan of water to the boil and immerse the garlic leaves for 30 seconds. Remove with a slotted spoon (reserving the cooking liquid) and plunge into a bowl of cold water. Leave to cool, then drain and set aside.

2 Meanwhile, melt the butter in a saucepan over a medium heat. Add the potatoes and onion and cook gently for 15 minutes. Add the stock and 600ml (1 pint) of the reserved cooking liquid, bring to the boil, then lower the heat and simmer for 15 minutes or until the potatoes are soft.

3 Remove the pan from the heat and add the garlic leaves. Whizz the mixture in a blender until smooth, then return to the pan and reheat gently. Season with salt and pepper and serve.

SERVES **4**
PREP **10 MINS**
COOK **20 MINS**
FREEZE **UP TO 3 MONTHS**

RECIPE BY
CELIA BROOKS BROWN

NETTLE SOUP

A fantastic way to use this much maligned, fragrant weed – choose
young and tender specimens and wear a double layer of latex
gloves to handle them.

2 tbsp virgin rapeseed oil
   or olive oil

4 spring onions, sliced

3 leeks, roughly chopped

650g (1lb 7oz) potatoes,
   washed but not peeled,
   cut into 2cm (¾in) cubes

sea salt

1 litre (1¾ pints) vegetable
   stock

100g (3½oz) young nettles or
   nettle tips (about ¾ carrier
   bag full), washed

juice of half a lemon

freshly ground black pepper

plain thick yogurt, to serve

1 Heat the oil in a soup pan over a medium heat. Add the spring onions, leeks, and potatoes with a little sea salt. Stir, cover, and cook for 5 minutes, stirring frequently.

2 Add the stock and bring to the boil. Add the nettles, stir, and simmer for 10 minutes, or until the potato is soft. Cool briefly, then purée with a hand blender until completely smooth. Taste for seasoning, then squeeze in a little lemon juice and grind in some pepper. Serve each bowl with a dollop of thick yogurt and more pepper.

SERVES **6**
PREP **15 MINS**
COOK **25 MINS**
FREEZE **UP TO 3 MONTHS**

RECIPE BY
DARINA ALLEN

SPINACH AND ROSEMARY SOUP

Darina Allen of the world-class Ballymaloe Cookery School in Ireland says, "Add the greens at the last minute, otherwise they will overcook and the soup will lose its fresh taste."

50g (2oz) butter

110g (4oz) finely chopped onion

150g (5½oz) diced potato

salt and freshly ground black pepper

450ml (15fl oz) hot vegetable stock, chicken stock, or water

450ml (15fl oz) creamy milk (¼ cream and ¾ milk)

350g (12oz) spinach, destalked and chopped

1 tbsp chopped fresh rosemary

2 tbsp single cream, to garnish

sprig of rosemary or rosemary flowers, to garnish

1 Melt the butter in a heavy-bottomed pan. When it is starting to foam, add the diced onion and potato, and stir to coat well. Season well with salt and pepper, then cover the pan with a lid and sweat the vegetables on a gentle heat for 10 minutes.

2 Add the stock and milk, bring to the boil, then simmer for 5 minutes or until the potato and onion are completely cooked. Add the spinach and boil the soup with the lid off for 2–3 minutes or until tender. Do not overcook. Add the chopped rosemary, then whizz the soup in a blender until smooth. You may need to do this in batches. Return to the pan and reheat gently.

3 Serve in warm bowls garnished with a swirl of cream and a sprig of rosemary. If you have a rosemary bush in bloom, sprinkle a few flowers over the top for extra pzazz. This is good with crusty bread or cheese scones.

SERVES **4**
PREP **10 MINS**
COOK **15–20 MINS**
FREEZE **UP TO 3 MONTHS**
BEFORE PARMESAN IS ADDED

RECIPE BY
SKYE GYNGELL

SPINACH AND PARMESAN SOUP WITH CRÈME FRAÎCHE

Skye Gyngell is head chef at Spring restaurant, London, where she champions seasonal and local produce. "This soup is easy to make and sings of the garden."

300g (10oz) young spinach leaves

25g (scant 1oz) unsalted butter

2 banana shallots, finely sliced

1 garlic clove, finely chopped

sea salt and freshly ground black pepper

1 litre (1¾ pints) chicken stock

100ml (3½fl oz) crème fraîche

100g (3½oz) Parmesan cheese, grated

grated lemon zest, to garnish

1 Wash the spinach thoroughly, drain, and shake until almost dry. Place a large pan over a medium heat. Add the spinach, cover, and cook until it just wilts. Drain in a colander and set aside.

2 Rinse and dry the saucepan. Add the butter to the pan and melt over a low heat, then add the shallots and sweat for five minutes, or until softened and translucent. Add the garlic and cook for 1–2 minutes, then season with a little salt and some pepper.

3 Add the cooked spinach and stir once or twice. Pour in the stock and turn up the heat. Bring to a simmer then immediately remove from the heat. Purée the soup in a blender until smooth. Return it to the saucepan and stir in the crème fraîche. Add the grated Parmesan cheese and check the seasoning, then either reheat gently and serve warm, or allow to cool and enjoy at room temperature. Add a sprinkling of grated lemon zest before serving.

SERVES **4**
PREP **5 MINS**
COOK **NONE**
FREEZE **NOT SUITABLE**

RECIPE BY
SOPHIE GRIGSON

MANGO, CORIANDER, AND POMEGRANATE SOUP

This unusual chilled soup is extraordinarily good, bursting with health and vitality, and is made in seconds. What's not to like?

1 large or 2 small ripe mangoes

1 red chilli, seeded and roughly chopped

1cm (½in) fresh ginger, peeled and finely chopped

1 tbsp roughly chopped coriander leaves, plus extra to serve

juice of 1–1½ limes

300ml (10fl oz) pomegranate or cranberry juice

salt

a few pomegranate seeds, to serve (optional)

1 Peel the mango and cut off all the flesh. Drop into a blender or food processor along with the chilli, ginger, coriander, lime juice, pomegranate juice, and a little salt and blend to a purée. Taste and add a little more salt if needed.

2 Pour into small bowls or shot glasses, top with a little more chopped coriander and a few pomegranate seeds (if using) and serve at once.

SERVES **4**
PREP **15 MINS**
COOK **20 MINS**
FREEZE **UP TO 1 MONTH**
AT THE END OF STEP 3

RECIPE BY
ROOPA GULATI

MANGO AND CURRY LEAF SOUP

Alfonso mangoes, renowned for their fragrant flesh and creamy texture, have a short season from early April until the end of May. Other varieties work well too.

FOR THE GARNISH

small handful of curry leaves

vegetable oil for deep frying

FOR THE SOUP

4 ripe mangoes, Alfonso if in season, available from South Asian stores

2 tbsp vegetable oil

1 tsp black mustard seeds

handful of fresh curry leaves

1 red chilli, deseeded, finely chopped

2 tsp date palm sugar or dark muscovado sugar

½ tsp turmeric

2 tsp rice flour

300–400ml (10–14fl oz) vegetable stock

300ml (10fl oz) coconut milk

juice of 1 lime, to taste

salt and freshly ground black pepper

2 tbsp chopped fresh coriander leaves

1 First, make the garnish: deep-fry the curry leaves in hot oil until crisp – it only takes a few seconds. Drain on kitchen paper and set aside.

2 Roughly chop the flesh of 3 mangoes into small pieces and finely dice the fourth. Set aside. Heat the oil in a medium pan and, when hot, fry the mustard seeds for a few seconds before adding the curry leaves and chilli. Continue frying for 30 seconds, until the leaves stop spluttering.

3 Add the 3 roughly chopped mangoes to the pan, reserving the diced mango. Turn the heat down low and simmer the fruit until softened. Stir in the sugar and cook until the mango begins to caramelize. Sprinkle over the turmeric and rice flour and fry for 30 seconds, stirring all the time. Pour over 300ml (10fl oz) of the stock and simmer for 10 minutes.

4 Add the coconut milk and simmer for 2–3 minutes. Sharpen with lime juice, season with salt and pepper, and stir in the coriander leaves and diced mango. If the soup is too thick, add a little more hot vegetable stock. Divide the soup between the bowls and sprinkle with a few crisp-fried curry leaves.

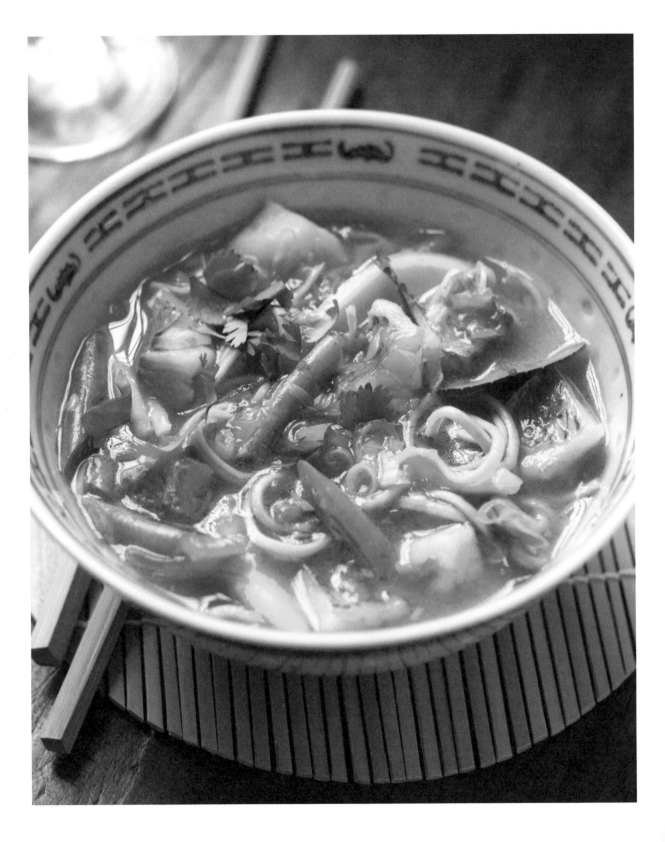

SERVES **4**
PREP **15 MINS**
PLUS 20 MINS MARINATING
COOK **15 MINS**
FREEZE **NOT SUITABLE**

1 tbsp light soy sauce

2 tsp fish sauce

1 tbsp toasted sesame oil

1 tbsp mirin

1 tsp sugar

juice of 1 lime

500g (1lb) red snapper
    fillets, skinless, cut into
    2.5cm (1in) cubes

2 stalks lemongrass,
    finely chopped

2 tbsp vegetable oil

4 bird's eye red chillies,
    finely sliced

4 spring onions, finely sliced

5cm (2in) fresh root ginger,
    finely shredded

4 garlic cloves, roughly chopped

4 small raw green mangoes, or
    under-ripe mangoes, peeled
    and finely chopped

2 tsp date palm sugar or dark
    muscovado sugar

2 tbsp rice wine vinegar

1 litre (2 pints) fish stock

8 lime leaves, torn in half

1 tbsp fish sauce

100g (4oz) medium egg noodles

100g (4oz) fine green beans,
    halved

salt

juice of 1 lime, to taste

2 tbsp chopped fresh
    coriander leaves

1 tbsp shredded fresh
    mint leaves

RECIPE BY
ROOPA GULATI

MANGO AND SNAPPER BROTH

This is a complete meal in a bowl. Raw mangoes add bite to a citrussy broth flecked with fiery red chillies.

1 Combine the soy and fish sauces, sesame oil, mirin, sugar, and lime juice, and spoon over the fish. Refrigerate for 20 minutes. Pound the lemongrass to a paste with a dash of water, using a mortar and pestle. Set aside.

2 Heat the oil in a wok or large pan and fry the chillies, spring onions, ginger, and garlic for 30 seconds over a high heat. Add the mangoes and fry for 1 minute. Stir in the sugar until it begins to caramelize. Add the vinegar, lemongrass, stock, lime leaves, and fish sauce. Bring to the boil.

3 Stir in the noodles, beans, and fish pieces (not the marinating liquid). Simmer for 3–5 minutes, until the noodles are cooked and the fish flakes easily. Season with salt, sharpen with lime juice, and add the herbs.

SERVES **6**
PREP 15 MINS
COOK 1 HR 20 MINS
FREEZE UP TO 2 MONTHS

HAMBURG EEL SOUP

If you enjoy the intense salty-sweetness of eel, you'll love this
German-style soup. Contact your fishmonger in advance to
order a fresh eel, asking for it to be prepared.

750ml (1¼ pints) Riesling wine

2 tbsp white wine vinegar

2 tbsp chopped fresh parsley

1 onion, sliced

2 carrots, diced

1 bay leaf

salt and freshly ground
    black pepper

1 prepared eel (cleaned,
    skinned, and cut into
    5cm (2in) pieces)

30g (1oz) butter

1½ tbsp plain flour

2 litres (3½ pints) hot
    vegetable stock

1 bouquet garni (see p24)

1 Pour the wine and 500ml (16fl oz) of water into a large saucepan with the vinegar, then add the chopped parsley, onion, carrots, and bay leaf, and season with salt and pepper. Bring to the boil and cook for 4–6 minutes. Add the eel pieces and simmer at a low heat for 10 minutes, or until the flesh is tender, then leave to cool.

2 Melt the butter in a saucepan, add the flour, and cook, stirring, until blended. Stir in the stock a little at a time. Add the bouquet garni to the pan, and cook slowly for 1 hour.

3 To serve, remove the eel pieces from the cooking liquid. Stir half the cooking liquid into the vegetable stock, divide the eel pieces among six bowls, and ladle the soup over.

SERVES **4**
PREP **15 MINS**
COOK **25 MINS**
PLUS 5–10 MINS RESTING
FREEZE **NOT SUITABLE**

RECIPE BY
ANGELA NILSEN

WILD SALMON CHOWDER

Chowder makes a hearty lunchtime soup for any time of
the year. Where possible, always buy your wild salmon
from a sustainable source.

2 tbsp olive oil

4 rashers streaky
  bacon, chopped

6 spring onions, cut into
  2.5cm (1in) slices

3 sprigs thyme

2 bay leaves

600g (1lb 5oz) small waxy
  potatoes, such as Desirée or
  Roseval, thickly sliced

25g (scant 1oz) butter

1 tbsp plain flour

700ml (scant 1¼ pints) fish or
  chicken stock

400g (14oz) salmon fillets,
  skinned and cut into chunks

150ml (5fl oz) single cream

2–3 tbsp snipped dill

zest of ½ lemon, finely grated

salt and freshly ground
  black pepper

1 Heat 1 tbsp of the oil in a wide, deep sauté pan. Add the bacon and
fry until crisp. Drain on kitchen paper and set aside. Pour the remaining
oil into the pan, add the spring onions, thyme, and bay leaves and stir-fry
for 1 minute. Add the potatoes and fry for 2–3 minutes.

2 In another saucepan, melt the butter and beat in the flour. Cook
for 1–2 minutes and then gradually add the stock. Bring to the boil and
then simmer gently for 3–4 minutes or until thickened slightly. Add
the thickened stock to the potatoes and bring to the boil. Cook for
10 minutes without stirring, until the potatoes are just tender.

3 Reduce the heat and submerge salmon chunks into the stock. Simmer
very gently for 3–5 minutes, just until the fish is cooked. Do not stir or
the fish will break up.

4 Remove from the heat. Without stirring, pour the cream over, and
scatter with the dill and lemon zest. Let the soup sit for 5–10 minutes
for all the flavours to blend. When ready to serve, warm through gently
and briefly, discard the thyme and bay leaves, and season if needed. Ladle
into bowls and serve scattered with black pepper and the crispy bacon.

SERVES **6**
PREP **15 MINS**
COOK **10 MINS**
FREEZE **UP TO 2 MONTHS**

CREAMY SMOKED TROUT SOUP

This comforting soup is based on a simple roux-based sauce, so
it is vital to use very good stock to make it really sing. It makes
an excellent light lunch.

50g (1¾oz) butter

35g (1¼oz) plain flour

750ml (1¼ pints) hot vegetable
   or fish stock

250ml (8fl oz) whipping cream

4 tbsp white wine

2–3 tsp Worcestershire sauce

salt and freshly ground
   black pepper

squeeze of lemon juice

375g (13oz) hot-smoked trout
   fillets, skinned and flaked

2 tbsp chopped parsley

1 Over a low heat, melt the butter in a pan, stir in the flour, and mix
until smooth. Cook for 2–3 minutes, stirring constantly. Gradually pour
in the hot stock, whisking vigorously to make sure there are no lumps.
Bring to the boil then cook, uncovered, over a low heat for about 3 minutes,
stirring occasionally.

2 Add the cream, white wine, Worcestershire sauce, salt, pepper, and a
little lemon juice, then bring to the boil again. Add the fish pieces and
briefly heat them through. Sprinkle the soup with parsley and serve.

SERVES **4**
PREP **25 MINS**
COOK **15 MINS**
FREEZE **NOT SUITABLE**

RECIPE BY
CAROLYN HUMPHRIES

MISO SOUP WITH TUNA

Make sure you don't boil the soup after adding the miso paste as it spoils the flavour. You'll find wakame (dried seaweed) and miso in large supermarkets.

10cm (4in) piece wakame

2 tbsp dried shiitake mushrooms

2 spring onions, chopped

1 tsp grated fresh root ginger

1 long thin carrot, thinly sliced

450ml (15fl oz) chicken stock

200g (7oz) fresh tuna steak, diced

2 tbsp miso paste

soy sauce, to season

1 tbsp snipped chives

1 Put the wakame and mushrooms in a bowl and cover with cold water. Soak for 15 minutes. Drain, reserving the liquid. Lift out the wakame, remove any hard central ribs, and cut into strips.

2 Put the wakame, mushrooms, spring onions, ginger, and carrot into a saucepan. Make the soaking water up to 750ml (1¼ pints) with the stock and add to the saucepan. Bring to the boil, reduce the heat, cover, and simmer for 10 minutes until the carrot is just tender.

3 Add the tuna and cook for a further 5 minutes. In a small bowl, blend the miso paste with 2 tbsp water and stir into the soup. Season to taste with soy sauce. Heat through but do not boil. Ladle into warm soup cups and sprinkle with snipped chives.

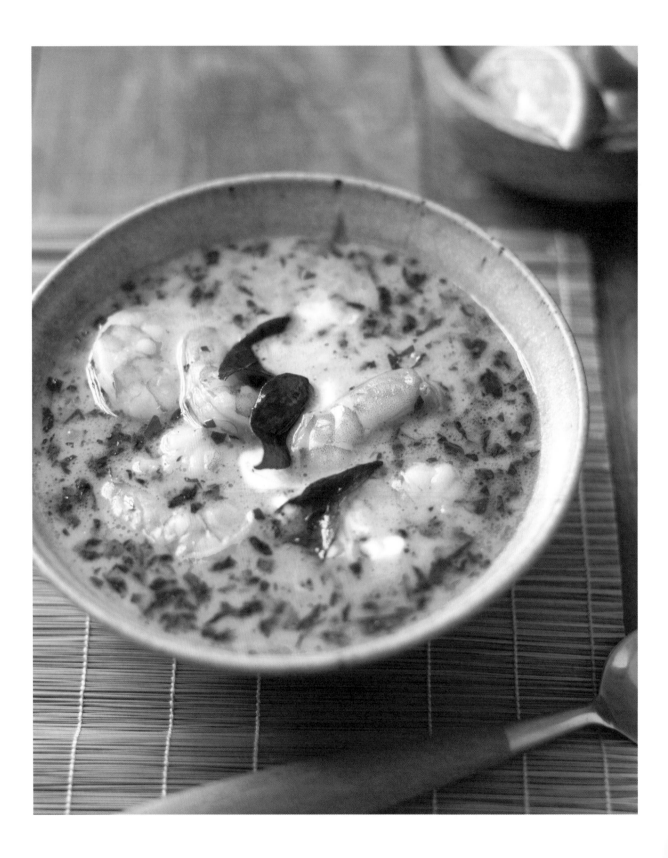

SERVES **4–6**
PREP **20 MINS**
COOK **40 MINS**
FREEZE **NOT SUITABLE**

1 tsp black peppercorns

¾ tsp mustard seeds

2 tsp coriander seeds

½ tsp fenugreek seeds

2–3 large red chillies

4 garlic cloves, chopped

5cm (2in) fresh root
   ginger, chopped

4 tbsp hot water

2–3 tbsp vegetable oil

small handful of fresh
   curry leaves

2 onions, finely chopped

750ml (1¼ pints) fish stock

250ml (8fl oz) coconut milk

250g (9oz) raw king
   prawns, shelled

1 tbsp coconut cream

2 tbsp fresh coriander
   leaves, chopped

juice of 1 lime, to taste

RECIPE BY
ROOPA GULATI

KERALAN PRAWN SOUP

This fragrant soup takes the best ingredients from a cottage garden in the southern Indian state of Kerala. If you are using dried curry leaves, add them with the stock.

1 Heat a sturdy frying pan or small griddle over a low heat. Roast the peppercorns, mustard, coriander, and fenugreek seeds for about 30 seconds, until they give off a spicy aroma and the mustard seeds start to pop. Grind the spices to a powder using a mortar and pestle, and set aside.

2 Roughly chop the chillies – if you like a mild flavour, use just 2 chillies – and remove the seeds. Put the chillies in a small food processor with the garlic and ginger. Pour in the hot water and process to a paste. Set aside.

3 Heat the oil in a wok or saucepan. When hot, toss in the curry leaves and fry for 20 seconds. Be careful – curry leaves spit when added to hot oil. Add the onions, cover, and soften for 10 minutes, stirring occasionally.

4 Stir in the chilli, garlic, and ginger paste and fry for 2–3 minutes, until the water evaporates. Add the ground spice mixture and cook for a further 30 seconds, stirring all the time. Pour in the stock and simmer for 20 minutes or until reduced by one-third. Stir in the coconut milk and reheat before adding the prawns and cooking for a further 4–5 minutes. Add the coconut cream and finish with the coriander leaves and enough lime juice to sharpen.

SERVES **4**
PREP **10 MINS**
COOK **5 MINS**
FREEZE **NOT SUITABLE**

RECIPE BY
SHAUN HILL

PRAWN AND SEA BASS SOUP

This clear seafood soup uses dashi – a Japanese tuna- and seaweed-based fish stock – as its base. For those avoiding gluten in their diet, tamari may be used instead of soy sauce.

100g (3½oz) spinach, blanched

1 litre (1¾ pints) dashi

100g (3½oz) sea bass fillet, cut into 4 pieces

4 large raw prawns, peeled and deveined

1 tsp soy sauce or tamari

½ small red chilli

1 spring onion, chopped

1 tbsp arrowroot

few drops lemon juice

1 Squeeze as much water as possible out of the blanched spinach, then cut into strips and set aside.

2 Bring the dashi to the boil in a saucepan and add the fish and prawns. Cook for a few moments, then add the soy sauce, chilli, and spring onion.

3 Whisk the arrowroot with 1 tbsp cold water in a bowl and stir into the soup. Bring to the boil and then remove the chilli. Add the lemon juice and spinach and serve.

SERVES **4–6**
PREP **10 MINS**
COOK **15 MINS**
FREEZE **NOT SUITABLE**

RECIPE BY
SOPHIE GRIGSON

PRAWN, CHICKEN, COCONUT, AND LEMONGRASS SOUP

This lively soup can be made in a jiffy, if you use tinned coconut milk and have a handy supply of chicken stock. It is filling enough to constitute lunch in itself.

2 cans coconut milk or 800ml (26fl oz) medium coconut milk

300ml (10fl oz) chicken stock

350g (12oz) chicken, cut into slivers

3 stalks lemongrass, heavily bruised (see p25)

1.5cm (½in) piece galangal or root ginger, cut into thin matchsticks

225g (8oz) uncooked prawns, shelled

1 red chilli, deseeded and diced

5 spring onions, sliced

juice of 1–2 limes

3 tbsp roughly chopped coriander

3 tbsp fish sauce

1 Put the coconut milk and stock into a pan. Bring up to the boil. Add the chicken, lemongrass, and galangal or ginger, and lower the heat to a gentle simmer. Cook for 10 minutes, uncovered.

2 Add the prawns and cook for a further 2–3 minutes, then add all the remaining ingredients. Remove the lemongrass and discard. Taste and add more lime juice or fish sauce, if needed, then serve.

SERVES **4**
PREP **45 MINS**
COOK **1 HR 10 MINS**
FREEZE **UP TO 2 MONTHS**
BEFORE CREAM IS ADDED

1 lobster, cooked, about
   1kg (2¼lb) in weight

50g (1¾oz) butter

1 onion, finely chopped

1 carrot, finely chopped

2 celery sticks, finely chopped

1 leek, finely chopped

½ fennel bulb, finely chopped

1 bay leaf

1 sprig of tarragon

2 garlic cloves, crushed

75g (2½oz) tomato purée

4 tomatoes, roughly chopped

120ml (4fl oz) Cognac
   or brandy

100ml (3½fl oz) dry white wine
   or vermouth

1.7 litres (3 pints) fish stock

120ml (4fl oz) cream

salt and freshly ground
   black pepper

pinch of cayenne

juice of ½ lemon

chives, to garnish

LOBSTER BISQUE

The name "bisque" refers to a rich and luxurious shellfish soup with cream and brandy and is thought to have come from the Spanish Biscay region.

1 Split the lobster in half and remove the vein that runs along it. Remove the meat from the body and chop the meat into small pieces. Twist off the claws and legs, break at the joints, and remove the meat, then crack all the shells with the back of a knife. Chop the shells into rough pieces and put the meat into the refrigerator.

2 Melt the butter in a large pan over a medium heat, add the vegetables, herbs, and garlic, and cook for 10 minutes, or until softened, stirring occasionally. Add the lobster shells. Stir in the tomato purée, tomatoes, Cognac, white wine, and fish stock. Bring to the boil and simmer for 1 hour.

3 Leave to cool slightly, then ladle into a food processor. Process in short bursts, until the shell breaks into very small pieces. Strain through a coarse sieve, pushing through as much as you can, then pass it again through a fine sieve before returning to the heat.

4 Bring to the boil, add the reserved lobster meat and the cream, then season to taste, adding the cayenne and lemon. Serve in warm bowls, garnished with chives.

SERVES **4**
PREP **20 MINS**
COOK **1 HR**
FREEZE **UP TO 2 MONTHS**
WITHOUT CREAM OR MANGETOUT

RECIPE BY
CAROLYN HUMPHRIES

BRANDIED LOBSTER CHOWDER

Serve this rich soup with some nutty rye bread and chilled
unsalted butter. If you like, you can use crab for a less expensive
alternative to lobster.

1 small cooked lobster

850ml (scant 1½ pints) water

150ml (5fl oz) dry white wine

1 bay leaf

knob of unsalted butter

2 shallots, finely chopped

4 tbsp brandy

1 large tomato, skinned
and diced

2 tsp anchovy essence

4 large new potatoes, scraped
and diced

8 baby corn, cut in short lengths

salt and freshly ground
black pepper

60g (2oz) mangetout, cut in
short lengths

5 tbsp single cream

4 thick slices lemon

4 sprigs of parsley

1 Twist the legs and claws off the lobster. Cut the body in half lengthways and remove the dark vein that runs along it. Lift out the tail meat, and cut in small pieces. Crack the large claws, remove the meat, and dice. Set all the meat aside. Leave the remaining bits of meat in the shell. Roughly chop it up and put it in a saucepan with the claws and legs. Add the water, wine, and bay leaf. Bring to the boil, reduce the heat, cover, and simmer for 30 minutes. Strain and reserve the stock.

2 Melt the butter in another large saucepan over a low heat. Add the shallots and fry gently, stirring for 1 minute. Add the brandy, ignite, and shake the pan until the flames subside. Add the tomato, anchovy essence, potatoes, and corn. Return the stock to the pan. Season and bring to the boil. Reduce the heat, cover, and simmer gently for 20 minutes until the potatoes are really tender.

3 Meanwhile, blanch the mangetout in a little boiling water for 2 minutes until just tender. Drain, rinse with cold water, and drain again. Then add to the soup along with the cream and lobster meat. Taste and season again. Reheat the soup but do not boil it. Ladle into deep soup cups. Serve with a slice of lemon and a small sprig of parsley in each bowl.

SERVES 6–8
PREP 15 MINS
COOK 45 MINS
FREEZE UP TO 2 MONTHS
WITHOUT THE CRÈME FRAÎCHE

RECIPE BY
SOPHIE GRIGSON

HENNINGSVÆR FISH SOUP

Henningsvær is a picturesque little port right up north
in Norway's Lofoten Islands and this soup is the speciality
of a small restaurant there.

1.5 litres (2¾ pints) good
    fish stock

350g (12oz) cod fillet

60g (2oz) butter

1 onion, finely chopped

1 large carrot, finely chopped

1 large leek, finely chopped

2 tsp caster sugar

2 tbsp white wine vinegar

salt and freshly ground
    black pepper

300ml (10fl oz) crème fraîche

chopped parsley, to serve

1 Bring the stock to the boil. Add the cod, bring gently back to the boil then remove from the heat. When cool enough to handle, lift out the cod and flake, discarding skin and stray bones. Set aside the fish and stock.

2 Melt the butter in a large pan and add the vegetables. Stir to coat in the fat, then cover the pan, reduce the heat to very low and leave to sweat for 20 minutes, stirring once or twice. Add the stock, sugar, and vinegar, season and bring to the boil. Simmer for 10 minutes. Stir in the crème fraîche and flaked fish. Taste and adjust the seasoning, then reheat gently without boiling. Serve immediately, sprinkled with the parsley.

SERVES **4**
PREP **30 MINS**
COOK **40 MINS**
FREEZE **UP TO 2 MONTHS**

1 onion, diced

50g (1¾oz) raw peanuts, skinned

2 tbsp desiccated coconut

3cm (1¼in) piece of root
   ginger, chopped

1 tsp coriander seeds

2 tsp sesame seeds

1 tsp cumin seeds

1 tsp poppy seeds

3 tbsp tamarind pulp

½ tsp turmeric

¾ tsp chilli powder

salt and freshly ground
   black pepper

2 tbsp vegetable oil

1 tsp date palm sugar

400ml (14fl oz) fish stock

200ml (7fl oz) pineapple juice

400ml (14fl oz) coconut milk

200g (8oz) line-caught
   cod, chopped

juice of 1 lime

125g (4½oz) fresh pineapple
   pieces, chopped

2 tbsp mint leaves, roughly torn

2 tbsp raw peanuts, toasted
   and chopped

RECIPE BY
ROOPA GULATI

PINEAPPLE BROTH WITH COD

This combination of South Indian and South East Asian flavours is a marvellous match for any firm-fleshed fish or seafood. Prawns also work well in this soup.

1 Heat a cast-iron frying pan. Add the onion, peanuts, coconut, ginger, and all the seeds. Stir over a low heat until the coconut darkens and spices are aromatic, about 5 minutes. Transfer to a bowl to cool, then place in a food processor and process to a coarse paste. Add the tamarind pulp, turmeric, chilli powder, and seasoning, and process to a smooth paste.

2 Heat the vegetable oil in a large saucepan and fry the paste for about 10 minutes on a low heat. Stir in the sugar and continue cooking until the paste begins to catch on the bottom of the pan. Pour in the stock and pineapple juice and simmer, partially covered, for 20 minutes.

3 Remove the soup from the heat and, using a stick blender or liquidizer, purée until smooth. Stir in the coconut milk and return the pan to the heat. Once it begins to bubble, add the fish and simmer for 3 minutes. Stir in the lime juice, pineapple pieces, and mint leaves. Ladle into bowls and scatter over the peanuts.

SERVES **4**
PREP **20 MINS**
COOK **30 MINS**
FREEZE **NOT SUITABLE**

1 large waxy potato, peeled

1 large carrot, peeled

1 medium-large courgette

400g (14oz) asparagus

300g (10oz) monkfish

1 sole, filleted and skinned

600ml (1 pint) light chicken or
    fish stock

100ml (3½fl oz) dry white wine

3 large spring onions,
    finely chopped

500g (1lb 2oz) mussels, rinsed
    and debearded, scrubbed

100ml (3½fl oz) whipping cream

salt and freshly ground
    black pepper

1 tbsp finely chopped tarragon,
    to serve

RECIPE BY
MARIE-PIERRE MOINE

WATERZOOI

Replace the mussels with shell-on prawns in this Flemish soup if you prefer; peel and add the empty shells to the reduced stock for 3 minutes before straining.

1 Cut the potato and carrot in 1 x 5cm (½ x 2in) batons. Slice the courgette on the diagonal. Cut off the asparagus tips, then chop the spears into 5cm (2in) lengths. Cut the monkfish into 4cm (1½in) chunks and cut each sole fillet crossways in half. Set the vegetables and fish aside separately.

2 Put the stock, wine, and spring onions (reserving a few to serve) in a casserole dish. Bring to the boil over a moderate heat. Add the potato, reduce the heat to a simmer and cook for 5 minutes, then add the carrot and cook for 5 minutes. Add the courgette and asparagus and cook for 1–2 minutes, or until all is al dente. Lift out the vegetables and set aside.

3 Bring the stock to the boil over a high heat and reduce by a third. Reduce the heat to a simmer, add the mussels, cover, and cook for 3–4 minutes. Strain through a muslin-lined sieve into a bowl, leave to cool briefly, then discard any mussels that haven't opened. Shell the rest and set aside. Return the stock to the pan and simmer over a moderate heat, then stir in the cream and season to taste. Add the monkfish, cook for 2–3 minutes, then the sole for 1 minute, then the vegetables and mussels for a final 2 minutes.

4 Using a slotted spoon, distribute the vegetables between the bowls. Place the fish on top, ladle over the broth, and scatter with mussels. Sprinkle with chopped tarragon and the reserved spring onion. Serve hot.

SERVES **4–6**
PREP **10 MINS**
COOK **1 HR**
FREEZE **NOT SUITABLE**

30g (1oz) butter

3 tbsp olive oil

1 large fennel bulb,
    finely chopped

2 garlic cloves, crushed

1 small leek, sliced

4 ripe plum tomatoes, chopped

3 tbsp brandy

¼ tsp saffron threads, infused
    in a little hot water

zest of ½ orange

1 bay leaf

1.7 litres (3 pints) fish stock

300g (10oz) potatoes, diced
    and parboiled for 5 minutes

4 tbsp dry white wine

500g (1lb 2oz) fresh black
    mussels, scrubbed and
    debearded

salt and freshly ground
    black pepper

500g (1lb 2oz) monkfish or
    firm white fish, cut into
    bite-sized pieces

6 raw whole tiger prawns

parsley, chopped, to garnish

FISH SOUP
WITH FENNEL

This rustic, Mediterranean-style fish soup – robustly
flavoured with brandy, orange, and fennel – is simple
to prepare and sure to please.

1 Heat the butter with 2 tbsp of the oil in a large, deep pan. Stir
in the fennel, garlic, and leek, and fry over a moderate heat, stirring
occasionally, for 5 minutes, or until softened and lightly browned.

2 Stir in the tomatoes, add the brandy, and cook rapidly for 2 minutes,
or until the juices are reduced slightly. Stir in the saffron, orange zest, bay
leaf, fish stock, and potatoes. Bring to the boil, then reduce the heat and
skim off any scum from the surface. Cover and simmer for 20 minutes,
or until the potatoes are tender. Remove the bay leaf.

3 Meanwhile, heat the remaining oil with the wine in a large, deep
pan until boiling. Add the mussels, cover, and continue on high heat for
2–3 minutes, shaking the pan often. Discard any mussels that do not
open. Strain, reserving the liquid, and set the mussels aside. Add the liquid
to the soup and season to taste. Bring to the boil, add the monkfish and
prawns, then reduce the heat, cover, and simmer gently for 5 minutes,
or until the fish is just cooked and the prawns are pink. Add the mussels
to the pan and bring almost to the boil. Serve the soup sprinkled with
chopped parsley.

SERVES **6–8**
PREP **15 MINS**
COOK **20 MINS**
FREEZE **NOT SUITABLE**

2 large carrots, chopped

I large potato, such as King Edward or Maris Piper, peeled and diced

I large onion, diced

I litre (1¾ pints) hot vegetable stock

I bay leaf

salt and freshly ground black pepper

500g (1lb 2oz) white fish fillets, such as pollock or haddock, cut into bite-sized pieces

juice of I lemon

200g (7oz) button or chestnut mushrooms, sliced

100g (3½ oz) raw peeled king prawns

120ml (4fl oz) double cream

½ bunch of dill, chopped

BÜSUMER FISH SOUP

A German soup, from the region of Schleswig-Holstein on the North Sea coast. You can use any white fish, so choose whatever is freshest.

I Put the carrots, potato, and onion into a saucepan, add the hot stock and bay leaf, and bring to the boil. Reduce the heat and simmer for 10 minutes.

2 Sprinkle a little salt and pepper, and half the lemon juice, over the fish pieces, then add these to the stock along with the mushrooms and simmer for another 5 minutes at a low heat.

3 Add the prawns to the pan along with the remaining lemon juice, and cook for 3 minutes, or until the prawns turn pink. Remove the bay leaf and season with salt and pepper, to taste. Stir in the cream and half the dill and serve immediately, using the remaining dill to garnish.

SERVES **4**
PREP **20 MINS**
COOK **20 MINS**
FREEZE **NOT SUITABLE**

500g (1lb 2oz) mixed fish fillets
   and shellfish

salt and freshly ground
   black pepper

1 tbsp lemon juice

600ml (1 pint) fish or
   chicken stock

60ml (2fl oz) white wine

2 shallots, chopped

1 egg yolk

1 tbsp double cream

1 tomato, skinned, seeded,
   and chopped

1 tbsp chopped parsley

croûtons, to serve

RECIPE BY
SHAUN HILL

NORTH SEA FISH SOUP

The seafood must be just-cooked, so cut dense fish in small pieces or add it earlier. Try red mullet, bass, haddock, cod, salmon, turbot, raw prawns, or shelled scallops.

1 Skin the fish, if necessary, and cut into 2.5cm (1in) pieces. Season and add the lemon juice. Bring the stock, white wine, and shallots to the boil in a large saucepan.

2 Add the fish in the order it takes to cook: red mullet or bass first, 2 minutes later the turbot, if using, followed by any haddock, cod or salmon and, finally, prawns or scallops. Simmer uncovered until all the fish is just cooked.

3 Stir the egg yolk and cream together in a bowl. Take the soup from the heat, stir in the egg mixture, then add the tomato and parsley. Serve with croûtons.

SERVES **4**
PREP **20 MINS**
COOK **45 MINS**
FREEZE **NOT SUITABLE**

4 tbsp olive oil

1 onion, thinly sliced

2 leeks, thinly sliced

1 small fennel bulb, thinly sliced

2–3 garlic cloves, finely chopped

4 tomatoes, skinned, deseeded, and chopped

1 tbsp tomato purée

250ml (8fl oz) dry white wine

1.5 litres (2¾ pints) fish stock or chicken stock

pinch of saffron threads

strip of orange zest

1 bouquet garni

salt and freshly ground black pepper

2 tbsp Pernod

1.35kg (3lb) mixed white and oily fish and shellfish, such as gurnard, John Dory, monkfish, red mullet, prawns, and mussels, heads and bones removed

8 croûtes, to serve

FOR THE ROUILLE

125g (4¼oz) mayonnaise

1 bird's eye chilli, deseeded and roughly chopped

4 garlic cloves, roughly chopped

1 tbsp tomato purée

½ tsp salt

BOUILLABAISSE

Originally nothing more than a humble fisherman's soup using the remains of the day's catch, bouillabaisse has evolved into one of the great Provençal dishes.

1 Heat the oil in a large pan over a medium heat. Add the onion, leeks, fennel, and garlic and fry, stirring, for 5–8 minutes, or until the vegetables are soft but not coloured. Stir in the tomatoes, tomato purée, and wine.

2 Add the stock, saffron, zest, and bouquet garni. Season with salt and pepper, and bring to the boil. Reduce the heat, partially cover, and simmer for 30 minutes, stirring occasionally. Meanwhile, whizz the rouille ingredients in a blender until smooth. Transfer to a bowl, cover, and chill until required.

3 Just before the liquid finishes simmering, cut the fish into chunks. Remove the zest and bouquet garni and add the firm fish. Reduce the heat to low and simmer for 5 minutes. Add the delicate fish and simmer for 2–3 minutes, or until it is cooked through and flakes easily. Stir in the Pernod and season to taste. To serve, spread the croûtes with rouille and place 2 in the bottom of each bowl. Ladle the soup on top.

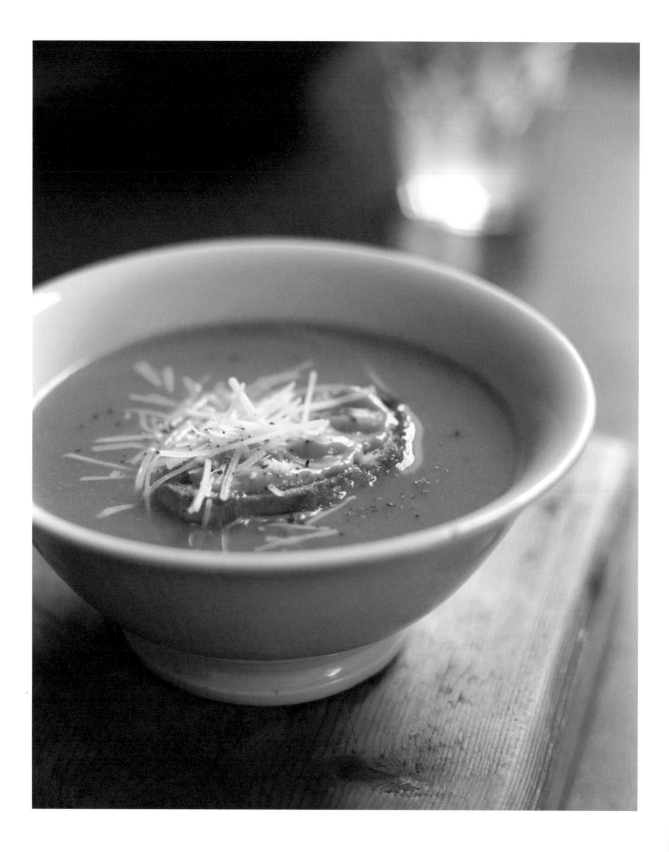

SERVES **6**
PREP **20 MINS**
COOK **1 HR**
FREEZE **UP TO 2 MONTHS**

RECIPE BY
MARIE-PIERRE MOINE

SOUPE DE POISSONS

This flavourful soup needs no accompaniment, but croûtes
rubbed with garlic, spread with rouille (see p84), or topped
with Gruyère cheese are a welcome addition.

5 tbsp olive oil

4 medium onions, chopped

2 leeks, chopped

1.5–2kg (3lb 3oz–4½lb) mixed
    fish and seafood

4 pieces dried fennel stalks,
    5cm (2in) long

4 medium, ripe tomatoes,
    quartered

9 garlic cloves, crushed

5 sprigs of fresh flat-leaf parsley

3 bay leaves

15cm (6in) strip dried
    orange peel

1 tbsp tomato purée

salt and freshly ground
    black pepper

pinch of saffron threads

6 croûtes, to serve

1 Put the oil in a large, heavy saucepan. Add the onions and leeks, and soften over a moderate heat until just golden.

2 Gut the larger fish. Rinse all the fish and seafood. Add to the pan and stir, then add the fennel, tomatoes, garlic, parsley, bay leaves, orange peel, and tomato purée. Stir and cook for 8–10 minutes until the fish is just beginning to flake when pierced with a fork. Pour in 2.5 litres (4 pints) hot water and season lightly with salt and pepper. Reduce the heat and simmer gently for 20 minutes.

3 Remove from the heat. Leave to cool a little, stirring and mashing down the soft fish pieces with the back of a large wooden spoon. Remove the fennel, orange peel, and bay leaves. If you like, whizz the soup to a rough purée in a blender. Push the soup through a chinois or a very fine sieve into a clean saucepan. Return the soup to a simmer over a moderate heat.

4 Soften the saffron in a ladleful of the soup, then stir into the rest of the soup in the pan. Adjust the seasoning. Ladle the soup into bowls. Serve hot, with croûtes.

SERVES **4**
PREP **20 MINS**
COOK **30 MINS**
FREEZE **NOT SUITABLE**

2 large floury potatoes, peeled

2 tbsp groundnut, sunflower,
   or mild olive oil

30g (1oz) butter

2 Spanish onions, coarsely
   chopped

1 litre (1¾ pints) light fish stock

3 sprigs of thyme

3 bay leaves

3 sprigs of flat-leaf parsley

sea salt and freshly ground
   black pepper

800g (1¾lb) mixed fish, skinned,
   cut into large chunks

4 thick slices country bread,
   to serve

FOR THE DRESSING

5–6 tbsp groundnut, sunflower,
   or mild olive oil

½ tsp Dijon mustard

sea salt and freshly ground
   black pepper

1 tbsp white wine or
   cider vinegar

2 tbsp finely chopped parsley

RECIPE BY
MARIE-PIERRE MOINE

COTRIADE

This soup from Brittany was originally a way to use
the leftover catch of the day. Try it with haddock,
smoked haddock, pollock, or cod.

1 Cut the potatoes in half then cut each half into four and set aside.
Put the oil and butter in a large, heavy sauté pan. Add the onions and
soften over a moderate heat until just golden, stirring frequently. Add
the stock then tip in the potatoes and herbs. Season lightly, stir, cover,
and cook for 12–15 minutes or until the potatoes are almost cooked.

2 Place the fish in the pan and season lightly. Gently stir then cook for
10 minutes, or until the fish just starts to flake when pierced with a fork.
Meanwhile, make the dressing. In a cup or small jug, mix together the oil
and mustard and season, then whisk in the vinegar until emulsified. Stir in
the parsley.

3 Remove the soup from the heat and adjust the seasoning. Lift out the
herbs. Put the bread in 4 warm bowls and moisten with a little dressing.
Ladle over the soup and drizzle on the remaining dressing. Serve hot.

SERVES **4**

PREP **12 MINS**
PLUS 90 MINS MARINATING

COOK **40 MINS**

FREEZE **UP TO 2 MONTHS**
BEFORE CUMIN SEEDS ARE ADDED

FOR THE CHICKEN

2 garlic cloves, finely chopped

3cm (1¼in) piece of
    root ginger, peeled
    and finely chopped

¾ tsp garam masala

juice of 2 limes

3 tbsp Greek-style yogurt

salt

2 boneless chicken thighs,
    without skin

drizzle of vegetable oil

FOR THE SOUP

3 tbsp vegetable oil

1 onion, finely chopped

2 green chillies, deseeded and
    finely chopped

1 garlic clove, finely chopped

2 tbsp ground almonds

1 litre (1¾ pints) hot chicken
    stock

3cm (1¼in) piece of root
    ginger, peeled

500g (1lb 2oz) baby spinach
    leaves

large handful coriander leaves,

handful mint leaves

1 tsp sugar

salt and freshly ground
    black pepper

1 tsp roasted and ground cumin
    seeds, to garnish

RECIPE BY
ROOPA GULATI

SPICY CHICKEN AND SPINACH SOUP

Here, the astringent bite of green chillies and root ginger is tempered by the subtlety of herbs and delicate spinach leaves. Add a dollop of cream just before serving.

1 Mix the garlic, ginger, and garam masala with the lime juice, yogurt, and salt. Add the chicken and coat. After 1–2 hours heat some vegetable oil in a griddle pan. Drain any excess yogurt off the chicken, and cook for 5–7 minutes on each side. Cool, then cut into small pieces. Pour any cooking juices over the chicken and set aside.

2 Heat the oil in a large saucepan over a low heat. Add the onions, chillies, and garlic and cover. Cook for about 10 minutes, stirring occasionally. Add the ground almonds and cook for a further minute, stirring. Add the chicken stock and root ginger. Season well and simmer for 10 minutes.

3 Bring to a boil and add the spinach. When it wilts, add the herbs and sugar. Turn the heat off and remove the root ginger. Blend until smooth. Pour the soup into a clean pan. Add the chicken and reheat gently. Check the seasoning and serve sprinkled with roasted ground cumin seeds.

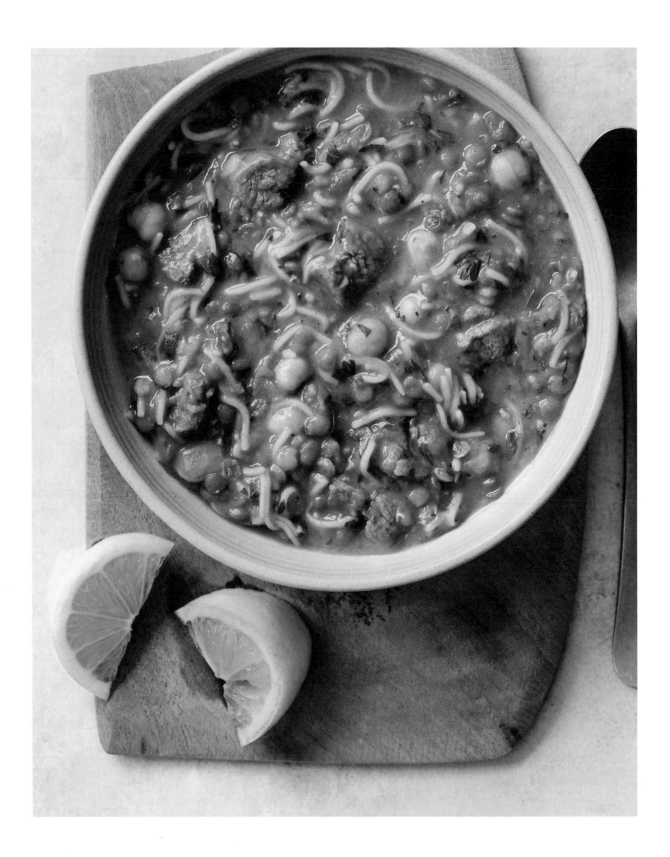

SERVES **6–8**
PREP **15 MINS**
COOK **1 HR 5 MINS**
FREEZE **UP TO 3 MONTHS**

RECIPE BY
SOPHIE GRIGSON

HARIRA

This Moroccan bean and lentil soup is a meal in a bowl,
often served for breakfast during Ramadan to keep people
going right through a day of fasting.

1 large onion, chopped

2 tbsp olive oil

300–500g (10oz–1lb 2oz)
   shoulder of lamb on
   the bone

1 tsp ground ginger

1 tsp ground cinnamon

leaves of 1 small bunch parsley,
   finely chopped

leaves of 1 small bunch
   coriander, finely chopped

150g (5½oz) brown lentils,
   rinsed

400g can chopped tomatoes

2 tbsp tomato purée

salt and freshly ground
   black pepper

100g (3½oz) vermicelli

400g can chickpeas,
   drained, or 400g (14oz)
   cooked chickpeas

30g (1oz) plain flour

lemon wedges, to serve

1 Cook the onion gently in the oil until tender and translucent. While it cooks, cut the meat from the lamb bones in 3cm (1¼in) cubes. Do not throw out the bones.

2 Once the onions are tender, stir in the spices, half the parsley, and half the coriander, then add the meat and bones and turn to coat evenly. Add the lentils, tomatoes, and tomato purée and season. Mix well and simmer for a few minutes, then add 1.7 litres (3 pints) of water. Leave to simmer for 45 minutes. Remove the lamb bones and add the vermicelli and chickpeas.

3 Put the flour in a small bowl with a ladleful of the cooking liquid and stir to make a smooth paste the consistency of thick cream, adding more liquid if needed. Stir this back into the soup and simmer for 3–4 minutes until it has thickened and the vermicelli is cooked.

4 Just before serving, stir in the remaining herbs and adjust the seasoning. Serve with wedges of lemon.

SERVES **4**
PREP **30 MINS**
COOK **2 HRS 30 MINS**
FREEZE **UP TO 3 MONTHS**
WITHOUT THE PASTRY LID

1.5 litres (2¾ pints) chicken stock

350g (12oz) lamb shank

250g (9oz) lamb neck fillet, cut into 4cm (1¾in) pieces

2 onions, roughly chopped

5cm (2in) piece of root ginger, peeled and chopped

5 garlic cloves, halved

1 tsp cumin seeds, dry-roasted (see p25)

½ tsp cloves

2 bay leaves

5cm (2in) cinnamon stick

8 green cardamoms, crushed

1 large brown cardamom, crushed

¼ tsp black peppercorns

1 blade mace

salt

1 tbsp vegetable oil

250g (9oz) chestnut mushrooms, sliced

1 green chilli, deseeded and shredded

375g (13oz) ready-rolled puff pastry

1 egg, beaten

RECIPE BY
ROOPA GULATI

SPICED LAMB BROTH

This broth is served with a puff-pastry lid on each bowl. As you break the lid, the spicy aroma is unleashed. The broth itself is best if you make it the day before.

1 Pour the stock into a large pan with the lamb, onions, ginger, garlic, and spices. Season with salt and bring to the boil. Partly cover, then simmer for 2 hours or until the meat is tender and the broth reduced by one-third. Cool, then remove the lamb with a slotted spoon and cut into small pieces.

2 Strain the broth through a sieve into a clean pan, pressing the ingredients against the sides of the sieve to extract maximum flavour. Bring to a fast boil and season with salt. Meanwhile, heat the oil in a frying pan and cook the mushrooms and chilli for 5 minutes or until just starting to colour. Add to the broth, along with the lamb. If you're working a day ahead, leave to cool, then chill in the fridge. Remove the fat from the surface the next day.

3 Preheat the oven to 220°C (425°F/Gas 7). Almost fill four ovenproof bowls with broth. Cut four circles – about 2.5cm (1in) wider than the bowls – from the pastry. Brush the lip and edge of the bowls with egg and cover with the pastry lids. Each should have an overhang – press this down the sides of the bowl to seal. Brush the top and sides of the lid with egg, make a small hole in the top of each one, and bake for 15–20 minutes or until golden and crisp.

SERVES **4**
PREP **20 MINS**
COOK **I HR 45 MINS**
FREEZE **UP TO 3 MONTHS**

RECIPE BY
MARIE-PIERRE MOINE

TRADITIONAL LAMB BROTH

This light version of Irish stew has a richly aromatic broth.
Middle neck cutlets – good value and meaty, with just enough
flavourful fat – are best for this soup.

6 middle neck lamb cutlets

I celery stalk, including leaves,
   cut into chunks

I parsnip, cut into chunks

I large carrot, cut into chunks

I large floury potato, peeled
   and chopped

3 large spring onions, chopped

3 large sprigs of flat-leaf parsley
   plus 2 tbsp finely chopped
   parsley, to finish

sea salt and freshly ground
   black pepper

I small green cabbage, cored,
   leaves shredded

a few allspice berries

a few black peppercorns

Irish soda bread, heated
   in a low oven, to serve

I Put the lamb in a large saucepan or stockpot. Cover it with cold water to 5cm (2in) above the meat. Add the celery, parsnip, carrot, potato, spring onions, and 3 sprigs of parsley. Season with salt and pepper. Bring to the boil over a medium heat, reduce the heat, part-cover, and simmer gently for about I hour. Skim any foam from the surface with a slotted spoon. Remove from the heat, lift out the meat, and leave until cool enough to handle. Separate the meat from the bones, reserving the meat.

2 Skim any surface fat from the broth. Lift out and discard the parsley stalks. Add the meat, cabbage, allspice berries, and peppercorns. Cover and return to a simmer over a low heat for about 5 minutes. Taste, season if required, and stir in the chopped parsley. Serve very hot with warm Irish soda bread.

SERVES **6**
PREP **20 MINS**
COOK **1 HR 10 MINS**
FREEZE **UP TO 3 MONTHS**
BEFORE CABBAGE IS ADDED

PICHELSTEINER

Thick and hearty, this German meat and vegetable soup is as
filling as a stew. It is versatile enough to work with pork or beef
instead of lamb.

2 tbsp sunflower oil

500g (1lb 2oz) lamb from shoulder or neck, cut into 2cm (¾in) cubes

salt and freshly ground black pepper

2 onions, halved and sliced

pinch of dried marjoram

pinch of dried lovage or thyme

1.5 litres (2¾ pints) vegetable stock

2 medium carrots, diced

1 leek, diced

2 medium potatoes, peeled and diced

½ Savoy cabbage, finely shredded

2 tbsp chopped fresh parsley

1 Heat the oil in a large pan, season the cubed meat with salt and pepper, and add half the meat to the hot oil. Brown the meat lightly, stirring continuously. Remove from the pan and repeat with the rest of the meat. Remove the meat from the pan, add the onions and fry for 2–3 minutes or until softened slightly.

2 Transfer the browned meat back to the pan and add the marjoram, lovage or thyme, and more black pepper. Add the stock, bring to the boil, cover, and cook over a medium heat for about 40 minutes.

3 When the meat is tender, add the carrots, leek, and potatoes. Bring to the boil, season with salt and pepper to taste, cover, and cook for a further 15 minutes. Add the shredded cabbage and cook for 5 minutes, or until just tender. Sprinkle with parsley before serving.

SUMMER

SUMMER
SEASON'S BEST

The warm days of summer are a time of gluts and bounty. Tomatoes, courgettes, fennel, artichokes, and beans are all plentiful in summer, and this chapter is full of recipes to take advantage of the season's generosity. A refreshing delicate gazpacho or cucumber and dill soup makes the most of ingredients that don't even need cooking; fresh sorrel, lovage, or watercress can be whipped into delicious creamy soups; and even fresh fruit comes into play, with tangy chilled melon and ginger soup and an eye-catching cherry soup.

SERVES **4**
PREP **10 MINS**
COOK **10 MINS**
FREEZE **NOT SUITABLE**

500g (1lb 2oz) edamame in the pod
    or 225g (8oz) podded weight

4 tbsp white miso paste

400g (14oz) cooked udon noodles

1 tbsp brown sugar, or to taste

juice of 1 lemon

FOR THE HOT GARLIC OIL

1 small red chilli, snipped

1 clove garlic

½ tsp coarse sea salt

2 tbsp sesame oil

RECIPE BY
CELIA BROOKS BROWN

EDAMAME NOODLE SOUP

Edamame, or fresh soya beans, are widely available fretop frozen. Thaw them slightly before using.

1 Remove the edamame from the pod, if necessary, and set aside. Bring 1 litre (1¾ pints) of water to the boil in a large pan. Meanwhile, make the hot garlic oil. With a mortar and pestle, pound the chilli, garlic, and salt together until smooth, then stir in the sesame oil.

2 Place the miso in a small bowl and mix with a slosh of boiling water from the pan, stirring until you have a pourable paste. Add the edamame, noodles, and sugar to the water in the pan and cook for 3 minutes, or until the edamame are tender but still bright green.

3 Turn off the heat and stir in the diluted miso paste, then add lemon juice to taste. Ladle into warm bowls and drizzle with the hot garlic oil before serving.

SERVES **4–6**
PREP **20 MINS**
COOK **1 HR**
FREEZE **UP TO 3 MONTHS**
WITHOUT THE CROÛTONS

RECIPE BY
MARIE-PIERRE MOINE

BABY BROAD BEAN SOUP

This soup is a perfect summer starter. Try serving it topped with
a splash of extra virgin olive oil and cubes of bread fried in olive oil.

3 slices toasting bread,
  for croûtons

6 tbsp olive oil

3 large mild onions, sliced

1 leek, sliced

1.5kg (3lb 3oz) young broad
  beans, shelled

4 garlic cloves, crushed

a small handful of fresh
  chives, chopped

4 new potatoes, peeled
  and chopped

salt and freshly ground
  black pepper

leaves from a bunch of
  fresh radishes

1 To make the croûtons, cut the bread into 1.5cm (½in) cubes. Heat
3 tbsp oil in a large frying pan over a fairly hot heat. Add the bread cubes
and spread them out. Fry for a minute, then stir and turn them over. Fry
for another minute. Spread the croûtons over a plate lined with kitchen
paper. Pat with more kitchen paper to drain off excess oil. Set aside.

2 In a big stewing pot or flameproof casserole, heat the remaining oil
over a moderate heat. Add the onions and leek. Soften for 10 minutes,
stirring frequently.

3 Add the broad beans to the pot with the garlic, chives, and potatoes.
Stir, then pour in about 3 litres (5¼ pints) water. Season lightly and stir in
the radish leaves. Turn up the heat a little and bring to the boil, then leave
to bubble gently for 15–20 minutes.

4 Allow to cool a little, then work through a food mill. Alternatively, whizz
briefly in a blender, then press through a sieve. (If you prefer, you can omit
the sieving, in which case the soup will serve 6–8 people.) Reheat until
piping hot before serving, topped with the croûtons.

SERVES 4
PREP 30 MINS
COOK 25 MINS
FREEZE UP TO 3 MONTHS
BEFORE YOGURT IS ADDED

RECIPE BY
SOPHIE GRIGSON

BROAD BEAN AND MINT SOUP

This soup is a beautiful cool, pale green, flecked with mint
and bright, skinned beans. Do not reheat once you have
mixed in the yogurt, as it may curdle.

450g (1lb) broad beans
(podded weight), thawed
if frozen

1 onion, chopped

1 stem celery, thinly sliced

30g (1oz) butter

2 tbsp pudding rice

1 generous sprig summer
savory, or thyme

1 litre (1¾ pints) chicken or
vegetable stock

salt and freshly ground black
pepper

110g (4oz) Greek yogurt

handful of fresh mint
leaves, chopped

4 small sprigs of mint

paprika or cayenne pepper,
to serve

1 If the beans are fresh, drop them into a pan of boiling water and simmer for 1 minute. Drain and run under the cold tap. Then, whether using fresh or frozen, skin each bean by slitting the tough outer skin with a small sharp knife or a fingernail and squeezing out the bright green beanlet inside. Take about one eighth of the beans, chop roughly, and set aside.

2 Over a low heat in a covered pan, sweat the onion and celery gently in the butter for 10 minutes, or until very tender. Add the rice and savory or thyme and cook for another minute, uncovered. Now add the unchopped beans, 900ml (1½ pints) of stock, and salt and pepper, then bring to the boil and simmer for 10 minutes, or until the rice is tender. Remove the herbs, then blend in batches, adding more stock if you want a looser consistency.

3 Shortly before serving, reheat thoroughly, then remove from the heat. Stir in a tablespoonful of the yogurt, together with the reserved chopped beans and the mint. Mix in the remaining yogurt, a tablespoon at a time, until it is all added. Taste and adjust seasoning and serve while still warm, floating a sprig of mint and a light dusting of paprika or cayenne on the surface of each bowl.

SERVES **4**
PREP **15 MINS**
COOK **1 HR**
FREEZE **UP TO 3 MONTHS**
BEFORE MADEIRA IS ADDED

RECIPE BY
MARIE-PIERRE MOINE

POTAGE SAINT GERMAIN

If chervil isn't available, you can replace it with a few leaves of
fresh mint to finish. You can also use frozen baby peas if fresh
peas in the pod are out of season.

1 tbsp sunflower, groundnut,
or mild-flavoured olive oil

15g (½oz) butter plus
25g (scant 1oz) chilled
butter, diced

4 large spring onions (white
parts only), chopped

1.5 litres (2¾ pints) hot chicken
or light vegetable stock

150g (5½oz) split green peas,
rinsed and drained

sea salt and freshly ground
black pepper

500g (1lb 2oz) shelled garden
peas (about 800g/1¾lb
unshelled)

1 small head soft lettuce,
leaves snipped

1 large egg yolk

3 tbsp crème fraîche

1–2 tbsp Madeira or port

few sprigs of chervil

1 Put a large sauté pan over a medium heat. Add the oil and 15g (½oz)
butter. Tip in the spring onions. Reduce the heat a little and sweat for
5 minutes, stirring frequently. Pour the hot stock into the pan, and then
add the split peas. Season lightly, and bring back to a simmer. Reduce the
heat a little, cover, and cook for another 20 minutes, stirring occasionally.

2 Add the garden peas and the lettuce, stir, and cook for 5 minutes. Leave
to cool a little, then pour the contents of the pan into a blender or food
processor and whizz until smooth. Push the soup back into the pan through
a fine sieve, mashing the vegetables with the back of a spoon to extract as
much as possible. Pour 100ml (3½fl oz) water through the sieve to thin
down the soup. Reheat gently over a low heat.

3 In a cup or small bowl, combine the egg yolk and the crème fraîche
with 2–3 tablespoons of the hot soup. Whisk this into the pan a little at
a time. Continue cooking until the soup is piping hot. Adjust the seasoning.
Just before serving, stir in the Madeira or port. Whisk in the diced butter
and snip over a little chervil.

SERVES **4–6**
PREP **15 MINS**
COOK **20–25 MINS**
FREEZE **UP TO 2 MONTHS**
BEFORE CRÈME FRAÎCHE IS ADDED

RECIPE BY
ROOPA GULATI

MINTED PEA AND HAM SOUP

Quick to make, this soup transforms everyday ingredients into
a splendid light lunch. Frozen peas, with their natural sweetness,
make a good match for the fresh mint.

2 shallots, finely chopped

40g (1¼oz) butter

1 potato, peeled and chopped

300ml (10fl oz) vegetable
  stock, hot

500g (1lb) frozen peas,
  defrosted

2 handfuls of fresh mint leaves,
  plus 2 tbsp extra for
  garnishing

150g (5oz) cooked ham, diced

salt and freshly ground
  black pepper

150ml (5fl oz) crème fraîche

1 Soften the shallots in the butter in a pan for 2–3 minutes over a
low heat. Add the potato and continue cooking, covered, for another
7–10 minutes or until the potato is tender. Pour over the stock and
simmer for 10–15 minutes.

2 In a separate pan, boil 400ml (14fl oz) water and cook the peas for
2–3 minutes. Add the mint leaves for the last 20 seconds of cooking.
Tip the peas and mint into a sieve placed over a bowl, reserving the
cooking liquid in the bowl. Add the peas and mint to the stock and
whizz the soup using a blender until smooth, pouring in enough cooking
liquid from the peas to loosen the consistency. Stir in the diced ham.

3 For the garnish, stretch a sheet of cling film tightly over a dinner plate.
Brush with olive oil and press the extra mint leaves onto the surface.
Cover with another layer of cling film and cook in the microwave for
2 minutes, until crisp. Reheat the soup, seasoning with salt and pepper
to taste. Serve with a dollop of crème fraîche in the centre, garnished
with the mint leaves.

SERVES **6–8**
PREP **30 MINS**
COOK 1½ **HOURS**
FREEZE **UP TO 3 MONTHS**
WITHOUT THE PISTOU

1 ham hock, or a thick piece
   of smoked bacon, about
   150g (5½oz)

200g (7oz) fresh white haricot
   beans, such as cannellini,
   shelled

100g (3½oz) fresh red haricot
   beans, such as borlotti,
   shelled

250g (9oz) flat green beans,
   sliced

2 medium floury potatoes,
   diced

3 tomatoes, skinned, seeds
   removed, and chopped
   (see p22)

4 medium courgettes, chopped

salt and freshly ground black
   pepper

100g (3½oz) small macaroni

FOR THE PISTOU

3 garlic cloves, smashed
   and peeled

coarse sea salt, to taste

leaves from a large handful
   of fresh basil

2 small tomatoes, skinned,
   seeds removed, and chopped
   (see p22)

freshly ground black pepper

25g (scant 1oz) mimolette
   cheese, grated

3 tbsp olive oil

RECIPE BY
MARIE-PIERRE MOINE

PISTOU SOUP

This rustic soup owes its substance to haricot beans. Buy
fresh beans when they are available in early summer –
they are quicker to cook and easier to digest.

1 To make the pistou, pound the garlic in a mortar with a pestle, then
add a little salt and the basil and pound to a paste. Add the tomatoes and
continue pounding and mixing until you have a thick sauce. Season with
pepper, then add the cheese and oil, mix well, and adjust the seasoning.

2 For the soup, put 2 litres (3½ pints) cold water in a large stewing pot.
Add the ham hock. Bring to a simmer, then partly cover and leave to
bubble gently for 30 minutes, skimming occasionally.

3 Meanwhile, put the haricot beans in a saucepan, cover with plenty of
cold water, and bring to the boil. Simmer for 10 minutes, then drain and
refresh. Add the prepared beans and all the vegetables to the stewing pot.
Season lightly. Return to a simmer, then part-cover and bubble gently for
1 hour, skimming occasionally.

4 Remove the ham hock and shred the meat. Lift half of the ingredients
out of the pan, mash with a fork, then return to the soup with the ham.
Add the macaroni and cook until just tender. Stir in the pistou, and serve.

SERVES **6**
PREP **10 MINS**
COOK **20 MINS**
FREEZE **UP TO 3 MONTHS**

RECIPE BY
SARAH RAVEN

SWISS CHARD AND COCONUT SOUP

Author, gardener, and television presenter Sarah Raven says, "This is a wonderful sweet, earthy soup, which I eat all year round. It is best served warm rather than piping hot."

250g (9oz) Swiss chard (or spinach)

125g (4½oz) Red Giant mustard, kale, or more chard

2 medium onions, finely chopped

1 garlic clove, finely chopped

2 tbsp olive oil

750ml (1¼ pints) vegetable stock

2 x 400ml cans coconut milk

salt and freshly ground black pepper

1 Prepare the chard and Red Giant mustard or kale, stripping the green leaves from the stems and shredding them into ribbons.

2 Sweat the onion and garlic gently in the oil for about 10 minutes, or until soft. Add the shredded greens, stock, and coconut milk and bring to the boil. Simmer for 10 minutes, then blend everything up together with a wand or food processor. Season to taste and serve.

SERVES **4**
PREP **20 MINS**
COOK **20 MINS**
FREEZE **UP TO 3 MONTHS**
BEFORE CREAM IS ADDED

RECIPE BY
MARIE-PIERRE MOINE

GLOBE ARTICHOKE SOUP

Nutmeg and saffron bring out the delicate, nutty taste of the artichoke
in this recipe. Fresh is best, but canned or frozen artichoke hearts can
also be used if need be – just remember to drain or defrost them first.

1 tbsp olive oil

20g (¾oz) butter

½ Spanish onion, finely
  chopped

1 shallot, finely chopped

1 clove garlic, crushed

¼ tsp ground nutmeg

a few saffron strands

800g (1¾lb) artichoke
  hearts, chopped

salt and freshly ground
  black pepper

100ml (3½fl oz) single cream

4 thin rashers smoky streaky
  bacon or pancetta

a large handful of baby spinach
  leaves, chopped

1 Bring a full kettle to the boil. Put a sauté pan over a moderate heat
and add the oil and butter. Tip in the onion, shallot, garlic, nutmeg, and
saffron, and stir for 3 minutes. Add the artichoke hearts and season lightly.
Continue stirring and cooking for 3 minutes. Pour 1 litre (1¾ pints) of hot
water from the kettle into the sauté pan and stir to mix. Bring to a simmer.
Reduce the heat, cover, and simmer for 10 minutes, or until the vegetables
are tender and cooked through. Leave to cool for several minutes.

2 Pour the soup into a blender and process until smooth, then pour back
into the pan. Reheat gently, stirring occasionally. Meanwhile, heat the cream
until simmering in a separate small saucepan over a moderate heat.

3 Place a non-stick frying pan over a moderately high heat. Once the
pan is hot, add the bacon or pancetta. Sizzle for 2 minutes, until crisp and
coloured. Turn over with tongs and cook the other side until crisp. Drain
on a plate lined with kitchen paper. Spread the spinach in the same pan
and stir until wilted. Turn off the heat.

4 Stir the simmering cream into the soup. Taste and adjust the seasoning.
Ladle the soup into bowls and add the spinach, stir lightly, then float a
rasher of bacon or pancetta in the middle of each bowl. Serve immediately.

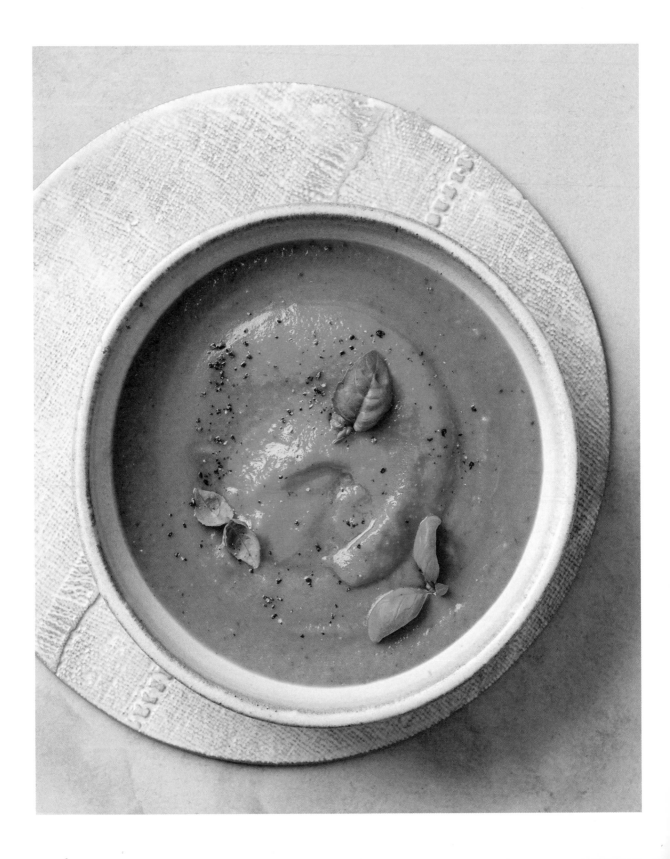

SERVES **6**
PREP **25 MINS**
COOK **40 MINS**
FREEZE **UP TO 3 MONTHS**
SEPARATELY

FOR THE AUBERGINE SOUP

2 tbsp extra virgin olive oil

1 onion, chopped

1 carrot, roughly sliced

2 tbsp chopped parsley

1 tbsp crushed coriander seeds

2 large aubergines, diced

1 tbsp risotto or pudding rice

750ml (1¼ pints) chicken
    or vegetable stock

salt and freshly ground
    black pepper

FOR THE PEPPER SOUP

2 tbsp extra virgin olive oil

2 cloves garlic, chopped

1–2 fresh red chillies, deseeded
    and chopped

2 red peppers, deseeded and
    cut into strips

250g (9oz) tomatoes

1 tbsp tomato purée

1 tbsp caster sugar

salt and freshly ground
    black pepper

600ml (1 pint) chicken
    or vegetable stock

handful of fresh basil leaves

RECIPE BY
SOPHIE GRIGSON

AUBERGINE AND RED PEPPER SOUP

This is a two-in-one soup, a mild and gentle aubergine cream yanked into high gear with a swirl of the sweeter, hotter red pepper.

1 To make the aubergine soup, put the first seven ingredients in a saucepan, cover, and sweat over a low heat for 15 minutes. Add the stock and season. Bring to the boil and simmer for 15 minutes until the carrots and rice are tender. Cool slightly and whizz to a purée in a blender.

2 To make the red pepper soup, place the olive oil, garlic, chilli, and red pepper in a pan, and sauté until the peppers are very tender. Blanch and skin the tomatoes (see p22), then quarter, deseed, and roughly chop, before adding to the pan along with the tomato purée, sugar, salt, and pepper. Cook for a further 5–10 minutes until very thick. Stir in the stock and bring to the boil, then cool slightly and whizz to a purée in a blender.

3 Reheat both soups in separate pans, then taste and adjust seasonings. Divide the aubergine soup between 6 soup bowls and add a ladle of the pepper soup into each bowl, swirling it in lightly. Sprinkle with basil and serve at once.

SERVES **4**
PREP **15 MINS**
PLUS **1 HR CHILLING**
COOK **NONE**
FREEZE **NOT SUITABLE**

3 large or 4 medium ripe
   avocados

juice of 1 lemon

150g (5½oz) wild rocket

750ml (1¼ pints) cold light
   chicken or vegetable stock

¼ tsp harissa

salt and freshly ground
   black pepper

RECIPE BY
MARIE-PIERRE MOINE

AVOCADO AND ROCKET SOUP

Rich, slightly nutty avocado works well with peppery wild
rocket. Hass avocados are particularly good, but always
buy extra in case one turns out to be blemished.

1 Skin the avocados and remove their stones, then chop the flesh and put
it in a blender or food processor with the lemon juice. Coarsely chop the
rocket (save a few sprigs to decorate) and add to the avocados. Pour over
the stock. Add the harissa and season, then blend until smooth. Transfer
to a bowl, cover, and refrigerate for 1 hour.

2 Before serving, taste and adjust the seasoning. Pour into bowls or
glasses, add an ice cube or two to each and decorate with sprigs of
rocket. Serve chilled.

SERVES **4–6**
PREP **5–10 MINS**
COOK **NONE**
FREEZE **NOT SUITABLE**

RECIPE BY
SOPHIE GRIGSON

AVOCADO, CUCUMBER, AND SORREL SOUP

This lovely, cool summer soup is just perfect when it's too hot to cook. Track sorrel down at your local farmer's market; its lemon-spinach flavour is unique.

1 ripe, buttery avocado, stoned and peeled

a generous handful of sorrel leaves (discard any tough stalks)

¼ large cucumber, roughly diced but not skinned

75g (2½oz) Greek yogurt

1–2 cloves of garlic, peeled and chopped

salt and freshly ground black pepper

avocado oil, to serve

1 Put the avocado in a blender with the sorrel, cucumber, yogurt, and garlic, add a good slurp of water, and then blend. As soon as it is smooth, taste and season, adding more sorrel, or salt or pepper, or thinning down with a little more water.

2 Once you are happy, divide between 6 serving bowls or cups and drizzle a thin thread of avocado oil on the surface. Serve at once, or at least within the next hour while it is fresh and vivid.

SERVES **4**
PREP **10 MINS**
COOK **30 MINS**
FREEZE **UP TO 3 MONTHS**

RECIPE BY
CELIA BROOKS BROWN

FENNEL AND APPLE SOUP

Fennel will store better in the fridge if you remove the feathery
fronds, but be sure to save a good handful of those for this
soup as a garnish.

2 tbsp virgin rapeseed oil
or olive oil

4 spring onions, sliced

2 cloves garlic, chopped

600g (1lb 5oz) fennel (trimmed
weight), roughly chopped

1 celery heart with leaves, or
3 celery stalks, chopped

1 cooking apple, peeled, cored,
and roughly chopped

sea salt

750ml (1¼ pints) vegetable
stock

fennel fronds, to serve

1 Heat the oil in a large pan over a medium heat and add the spring
onions. Soften for 3 minutes, then add the garlic. Cook for 1–2 minutes
until fragrant, then add the fennel, celery, and apple with a little salt. Stir,
cover, and sweat for 10 minutes, stirring frequently.

2 Pour in the stock and bring to the boil. Simmer for 15 minutes, until
the fennel is tender. Cool briefly, then purée with a hand blender. Taste
and adjust the seasoning. Serve hot, or allow the soup to cool, then
chill for several hours before serving cold. Garnish each bowl with torn
fennel fronds.

SERVES 4
PREP 15 MINS
PLUS SOAKING OVERNIGHT
COOK 1 HOUR
FREEZE UP TO 3 MONTHS
WITHOUT CHORIZO

RECIPE BY
MARIE-PIERRE MOINE

FENNEL SOUP WITH BEANS, THYME, AND CHORIZO

The last-minute addition of paprika-flavoured chorizo
gives spice to this hearty soup. Keep the texture chunky
by processing only briefly.

250g (9oz) dried haricot beans

1 tbsp sunflower, groundnut, or mild olive oil

1 Spanish onion, finely chopped

2 cloves garlic, crushed

1 head fennel, cored and finely chopped

2 tsp dried fennel seeds

1 tbsp finely chopped fresh parsley

2 tsp thyme leaves

salt and freshly ground black pepper

100g (3½oz) chorizo, diced

1 Soak the beans overnight in plenty of cold water, then drain and rinse. Put a heavy pan over a medium heat. Heat the oil, then add the onion and stir for 2 minutes. Add the garlic, fennel and fennel seeds, parsley, and half the thyme and cook for 3–5 minutes until slightly softened. Tip in the beans. Stir, pour in 2 litres (3½ pints) water, and season lightly.

2 Bring to a simmer and cook for 40 minutes, or until the beans are tender, skimming from time to time. Remove from the heat and leave to cool a little. Transfer to a food processor or blender and whizz briefly until partly puréed. Return to the pan, taste, and adjust the seasoning.

3 Gently reheat the soup. Meanwhile, place a small non-stick pan over a moderately high heat and fry the chorizo for 2–3 minutes until crisp and coloured, stirring frequently. Drain on a plate lined with kitchen paper.

4 Ladle the soup into bowls, add a little chorizo to each, and finish with a scattering of thyme. Serve immediately.

SERVES **4**
PREP **30 MINS**
PLUS 3 HRS CHILLING
COOK **NONE**
FREEZE **NOT SUITABLE**

RECIPE BY
MARIE-PIERRE MOINE

CUCUMBER AND DILL SOUP

This refreshing soup can be prepared ahead and makes an elegant starter for a summer meal. For a lunch or dinner party, try serving it with smoked salmon.

2 medium cucumbers

salt and freshly ground black pepper

1 litre (1¾ pints) whole or semi-skimmed milk

small bunch of fresh dill

150ml (5fl oz) bio natural yogurt

1 Peel the cucumbers, leaving one or two strips of skin on for colour. Slice, put into a colander, and sprinkle with a teaspoon of salt. Toss and stand it over a bowl for one hour. Meanwhile, put the milk in another bowl, add a few whole dill fronds, stir, and refrigerate for an hour to allow the flavours to infuse slightly.

2 Rinse the cucumber under the cold water tap, pressing down to extract as much moisture as possible. Remove the dill fronds from the milk. Put the milk and cucumber in a blender or food processor. Add a few more fronds of dill and some pepper and blend well. Pour into a bowl and refrigerate for 3 hours.

3 Place a sieve over a second bowl, pour in the chilled soup and push through with the back of a wooden spoon, adding 100–150ml (3½–5fl oz) of chilled water, and return to the refrigerator until ready to serve.

4 Stir in the yogurt, taste, and adjust the seasoning if necessary. Whisk until frothy with a handheld or balloon whisk, then pour into cups, bowls, or glasses. Decorate with a little more dill and serve immediately.

SERVES **4–6**
PREP **10–15 MINS**
PLUS 30 MINS CHILLING
COOK **NONE**
FREEZE **NOT SUITABLE**

RECIPE BY
CELIA BROOKS BROWN

CUCUMBER AND WALNUT SOUP

This recipe is delicious in late summer, when it will use up any particularly mature cucumbers, although you may need to remove any hard seeds and bitter skin.

2 medium cucumbers, about 700g (1lb 9oz) in total

500g (1lb 2oz) Greek or thick and creamy yogurt

1 clove garlic

coarse sea salt

50g (1¾oz) walnuts, plus more chopped walnuts for garnish

handful of fresh mint leaves, finely chopped

2 tbsp fresh lemon juice

freshly ground black pepper

extra virgin olive oil, to serve

1 Peel, deseed, and finely dice the cucumbers. Be punctilious about this to ensure your soup is delicately flavoured without any bitterness.

2 In a medium bowl, or large measuring jug, mix together the yogurt and 250ml (8fl oz) cold water until combined. Pound the garlic with a large pinch of coarse sea salt in a mortar until smooth. Scrape it into the yogurt. Pound the walnuts in the garlicky mortar to a coarse paste; do not crush them too fine. Add to the yogurt mixture with the cucumber, mint, lemon juice, and a good grinding of pepper and stir well. Taste for seasoning.

3 Cover and chill for 30 minutes or more. Pour into bowls and garnish with a drizzle of olive oil and a few chopped walnuts.

SERVES **4**
PREP **15 MINS**
COOK **20 MINS**
FREEZE **NOT SUITABLE**

RECIPE BY
MARIE-PIERRE MOINE

HOT CUCUMBER AND TARRAGON SOUP

Cooked cucumber has a subtle flavour which combines particularly well with the more assertive but still delicate tarragon.

2 medium-large or
   3 small cucumbers

1 tbsp sunflower or
   rapeseed oil

50g (1¾oz) chilled butter, diced

2 tbsp chopped fresh tarragon

800ml (1¾ pints) light vegetable
   or chicken stock

salt and freshly ground
   black pepper

2 tbsp cornflour

4 heaped tsp cream cheese
   (optional)

1 Peel, deseed, and roughly chop the cucumbers.

2 Place a sauté pan over a moderate heat. Add the oil and 15g (½oz) of the butter. Once the butter has melted, add the cucumber and half the tarragon. Stir for 2 minutes, then pour in the stock and season lightly.

3 Bring to a simmer, reduce the heat a little, then cover and simmer gently for 10–15 minutes. Stir in the cornflour. Cook for 2 minutes. Take off the heat and leave to cool a little.

4 Transfer to a blender or food processor and blend until smooth. Return to the pan and whisk in the remaining butter. Taste and adjust the seasoning, stir in the rest of the tarragon, and serve hot. If you like, add a dollop of cream cheese to each serving at the last minute.

SERVES **4**
PREP **15 MINS**
COOK **20 MINS**
FREEZE **UP TO 3 MONTHS**

RECIPE BY
MARIE-PIERRE MOINE

MEXICAN SWEETCORN SOUP

If you don't have chilli-flavoured olive oil, stir a very little piquante pimenton, harissa, or smoked paprika into fruity olive oil instead.

3 tbsp olive oil

1 Spanish onion, finely chopped

1 red pepper, halved, cored, deseeded, and finely chopped

1 clove garlic, crushed

1 tsp fennel seeds

1 tsp fresh thyme leaves

400g (14oz) sweetcorn kernels (drained and rinsed, if canned)

salt and freshly ground black pepper

100ml (3½fl oz) single cream

1½ tbsp chilli-flavoured olive oil, to serve

1 Heat the oil in a large sauté pan over a moderate heat, add the onion, pepper (reserving a scant tablespoon to finish), garlic, fennel seeds, and thyme, and stir-fry for 3 minutes. Add the sweetcorn and season lightly. Continue stirring and cooking for 2 minutes, then pour in 500ml (16fl oz) hot water, stir, and bring to a simmer. Lower the heat, cover, and simmer for 15 minutes or until the vegetables are tender and cooked through. Stir in the cream and leave to cool for a few minutes.

2 Process the soup until smooth in a blender (you may need to do this in batches). Return to the pan and reheat gently, stirring occasionally. Taste and adjust the seasoning. Ladle into bowls and add the reserved red pepper. Drizzle over a little chilli-flavoured olive oil and serve immediately.

SERVES 4–6
PREP 10 MINS
COOK 30 MINS
FREEZE UP TO 1 MONTH
WITHOUT MILK OR CREAM CHEESE

4 fresh corn on the cob

salt and freshly ground
    black pepper

2 bay leaves

2 tbsp olive oil

1 large onion, chopped

4 fresh sage leaves, chopped,
    or ½ tsp dried sage, crushed

1 tsp fresh thyme leaves, or
    ½ tsp dried thyme

1 medium carrot, chopped

2 celery sticks, chopped

1 large potato, chopped

200g (7oz) cream cheese

120ml (4fl oz) milk

single cream, to serve

dusting of paprika, to serve

RECIPE BY
CELIA BROOKS BROWN

SWEETCORN CHOWDER

If you have grown your own sweetcorn, wait until the very last minute to harvest it – the quicker you get it from the plot to the pan, the sweeter it will be.

1 Stand each corn cob upright in a large bowl and strip the kernels by cutting downward with a sharp knife. Set the kernels aside. Place the cobs in a large saucepan and add 500ml (16fl oz) water, a generous pinch of salt and the bay leaves. Bring to the boil and simmer, covered, for 15 minutes. Remove and discard the cobs and bay leaves.

2 Heat the oil in a saucepan and cook the onions until translucent. Add the herbs and remaining vegetables except the corn kernels. Cook for about 5 minutes, until softened. Add the corn cob stock and simmer until the potato is collapsing. Meanwhile, place the sweetcorn kernels in a saucepan and barely cover with cold water. Bring to the boil and cook for 2 minutes. Set aside.

3 Add the cream cheese and milk to the soup mixture, then purée until smooth. Stir in the corn kernels with their cooking liquid. Give the chowder one more whizz if desired, to break up the corn kernels slightly. Reheat and adjust the seasoning. Ladle into warm bowls. Drizzle with streaks of single cream and dust with paprika.

SERVES **4**
PREP **10 MINS**
COOK **15 MINS**
FREEZE **UP TO 3 MONTHS**

2 large potatoes, peeled
   and diced

500ml (16fl oz) hot chicken
   stock

1 tsp salt

1 tbsp olive oil

3 medium courgettes, peeled,
   finely diced or grated

1 onion, peeled, finely diced
   or grated

white pepper

100ml (3½fl oz) double cream

300ml (10fl oz) milk

small bunch of fresh dill,
   chopped

COURGETTE AND POTATO SOUP

A very simple soup, easy to make and with very few ingredients, this is lifted out of the ordinary by the gentle aniseed tang of dill.

1 Place the potatoes into a large pan with the hot stock and salt, bring to the boil, and simmer for about 5 minutes, or until tender. Blend with a stick blender until smooth and return to the saucepan.

2 In another saucepan, heat the olive oil, add the courgettes and onion, and fry over a gentle heat for 2–3 minutes or until slightly softened but not coloured. Stir in a dash of the pepper, along with the cream, milk, and puréed potato broth and simmer gently for 5 minutes, or until the courgettes have softened. Add dill and season to taste. Serve hot.

SERVES **4**
PREP **30 MINS**
PLUS 20 MINS STANDING
COOK **25 MINS**
FREEZE **NOT SUITABLE**

3 tbsp vegetable oil

2 dried red chillies

I tsp mustard seeds

¼ tsp fenugreek seeds

I tsp cumin seeds

12 curry leaves

3 tbsp gram flour

½ tsp turmeric

400ml (14fl oz) Greek yogurt

400ml (14fl oz) cold water

2 tbsp tamarind pulp

2 tbsp chopped coriander
leaves, to garnish

FOR THE SAUTÉED
COURGETTE TOPPING

2 tbsp vegetable oil

I small red onion, diced

I courgette, finely diced

I green chilli, deseeded and
finely chopped

salt flakes, to season

RECIPE BY
ROOPA GULATI

WHIPPED YOGURT SOUP WITH SAUTÉED COURGETTE

This spin on a popular Indian curry makes an innovative first course. The crackling curry leaves, toasted spices, and tangy tamarind work well with the yogurt base.

I Heat the oil in a wok over a medium heat. Toss in the chillies and mustard seeds and swirl around for a few seconds before adding the fenugreek, cumin, and curry leaves. Lower the heat and stir-fry for a few seconds. Sprinkle in half the flour and stir-fry for 2–3 minutes or until lightly toasted. Remove from the heat, add the turmeric, and leave to cool slightly.

2 Whisk the remaining flour with the yogurt and water and add to the wok. Return to the heat and, whisking all the time, bring to a simmer and cook for 3–4 minutes. Add more water, if needed, to loosen the consistency. I like to leave the whole spices in, but you can sieve the soup at this stage. Season with salt and enough tamarind to sharpen.

3 For the sautéed courgette topping, heat the oil in a frying pan and soften the onion for 3–4 minutes over a low heat. Turn the heat up, add the courgette and green chilli and continue cooking for a further minute. Season with salt and add to the hot soup. Finish with the chopped coriander.

SERVES **4**
PREP **20 MINS**
COOK **NONE**
FREEZE **NOT SUITABLE**

85g (3oz) white bread (crusts removed), cut into cubes

500ml (16fl oz) iced water

250g (9oz) whole blanched almonds

6 garlic cloves, roughly chopped

3 tbsp olive oil

3 tbsp sherry vinegar or white balsamic vinegar

salt and freshly ground black pepper

150g (5½oz) seedless white grapes

RECIPE BY
JOSEPHINE FAIRLEY

WHITE GAZPACHO

Josephine Fairley, co-founder of Green & Blacks Chocolate, now runs Judges Bakery, an organic bakery in Hastings, East Sussex. "This Spanish soup is heavenly in summer."

1 Soak the bread in all but 3 tbsp of the iced water for 10 minutes. Meanwhile, place the almonds in a food processor and whizz until ground as finely as possible. Add the remaining 3 tbsp iced water and blend to a paste. Remove the bread from the water (reserving the water) and add to the processor, along with the garlic, and blend again.

2 With the motor running, gradually add the water the bread soaked in, followed by the oil. Keep pulsing until the mixture is absolutely smooth. Add the vinegar and season to taste with salt and pepper. To serve, place a handful of grapes in the bottom of each bowl, ladle the soup on top, then drizzle with a little olive oil, if desired.

SERVES **4**
PREP **20 MINS**
COOK **55 MINS**
FREEZE **UP TO 3 MONTHS**

CLASSIC TOMATO SOUP

Easy to make from kitchen cupboard ingredients, using canned tomatoes, this delicious soup will brighten the dullest day.

1 tbsp olive oil

1 onion, chopped

1 garlic clove, sliced

2 celery sticks, sliced

1 carrot, sliced

1 potato, chopped

2 x 400g cans tomatoes

750ml (1¼ pints) vegetable
   or chicken stock

1 bay leaf

1 tsp sugar

salt and freshly ground
   black pepper

1 Heat the oil in a large saucepan over a medium-low heat, add the onion, garlic, and celery and fry, stirring frequently, until softened but not coloured.

2 Add the carrot and potato and stir for 1 minute, then add the tomatoes with their juices, the stock, bay leaf, and sugar. Season to taste, bring to the boil, then reduce the heat, cover, and simmer for 45 minutes, or until the vegetables are very soft.

3 Remove from the heat and allow to cool slightly, then process in a blender or food processor until smooth, working in batches if necessary. Taste and adjust the seasoning, then reheat and serve.

SERVES **4**
PREP **10 MINS**
COOK **30 MINS**
FREEZE **UP TO 3 MONTHS**

RECIPE BY
SOFIA LARRINUA-CRAXTON

ROAST TOMATO SOUP

For home-made food in a jiffy, roast the vegetables up to three days in advance and keep them in the fridge. This soup then takes just minutes to prepare.

8 plum tomatoes, about 675g (1½lb) in total, quartered

1 red onion, cut into 8 wedges

2 garlic cloves, unpeeled

3 tbsp olive oil

sea salt and freshly ground black pepper

1 litre (1¾ pints) hot vegetable stock

3 tbsp sun-dried tomato paste

1 Preheat the oven to 180°C (350°F/Gas 4). Put the tomatoes, onion, and garlic on baking trays covered with greaseproof paper. Drizzle with the oil, and season well with salt and pepper. Roast until they are soft, caramelized, and slightly browned – allow 10–15 minutes for the garlic, 15–20 minutes for the onion, and 25 minutes for the tomatoes. Squeeze the garlic from their skins once they have cooled slightly.

2 Transfer to a blender, add the stock and tomato paste, then whizz until smooth but still slightly chunky. Season again to taste, reheat gently, and serve hot.

SERVES **4–6**
PREP **30 MINS**
COOK **40 MINS**
FREEZE **UP TO 3 MONTHS**
BEFORE CREAM IS ADDED

RECIPE BY
SOFIA LARRINUA-CRAXTON

CREAM OF TOMATO SOUP

This extra-special version of the old standard – using fresh, sun-dried, and roasted tomatoes, takes the humble tomato to new heights.

50g (1¾oz) butter

1 tbsp olive oil

2 onions, finely chopped

2 celery sticks, finely chopped

2 carrots, finely diced

2 garlic cloves, minced

12 plum tomatoes, about 1kg (2¼lb), quartered, roasted, and roughly chopped

8 plum tomatoes, about 600–720g (1¼–1½lb), skinned and finely chopped

6 sun-dried tomatoes, finely chopped

1 litre (1¾ pints) hot vegetable stock

2–3 tbsp double cream

salt and freshly ground black pepper

1 Heat the butter and olive oil in a heavy saucepan over a medium heat. Add the onions and sauté for 8–10 minutes, stirring frequently, until very soft but not coloured. Next, add the celery and carrots, and continue cooking gently without burning for another 10 minutes, stirring from time to time. Add the garlic and sauté for another 2 minutes, stirring.

2 Mix together the roasted plum tomatoes, fresh tomatoes, and sun-dried tomatoes. Tip into the pan with any juices, and cook, stirring, for 5 minutes to allow the flavours to combine; if the sauce looks too thick or starts catching on the bottom of the pan, add a little of the hot vegetable stock. Pour in the remaining vegetable stock, and simmer the soup for 15–20 minutes.

3 Blend the soup to a smooth purée using a food processor or hand-held blender. Pass through a sieve or mouli into a clean pan, unless you prefer to make a chunky soup. Add the double cream a tablespoon at a time until you are happy with the taste and texture. Season with salt and pepper, reheat very gently if needed, and serve.

SERVES **4**
PREP **25 MINS**
COOK **25 MINS**
FREEZE **UP TO 3 MONTHS**

RECIPE BY
SOFIA LARINUA-CRAXTON

TOMATO BORSCHT

In Russia and the Ukraine, borscht often includes tomatoes as well as beetroot. This version may seem unusual, but you will love its rich colour and fantastic taste.

2 tbsp olive oil

I small onion, finely chopped

I garlic clove, chopped

225g (8oz) raw beetroot, peeled and finely grated

I tsp freshly ground toasted cumin seeds

¼ tsp ground cinnamon

225g (8oz) ripe fresh tomatoes, skinned and roughly chopped

I tbsp sun-dried tomatoes, very finely chopped

250ml (8fl oz) tomato juice

600ml (I pint) vegetable stock

I tbsp light soy sauce

salt and freshly ground black pepper

toasted cumin seeds, to serve

soured cream or crème fraîche, to serve

I Heat the oil in a heavy pan over a low heat. Gently cook the onion and garlic for about 5 minutes, then add the beetroot. Sweat gently for a further 10 minutes, stirring from time to time, until softened but not browned.

2 Add the ground spices, fresh and sun-dried tomatoes, and tomato juice, then pour in the stock. Bring to the boil. Reduce the heat slightly, cover, and simmer very gently for 15 minutes or until all the vegetables are soft. Remove from the heat. Blend or process until velvety smooth. Check the seasoning, adding the soy sauce, salt, and pepper to taste.

3 Serve chilled, at room temperature, or slightly warm. If you do reheat the soup, do so gently over a low heat. To serve, spoon into serving bowls, and garnish with toasted cumin seeds and a spoonful of soured cream or crème fraîche.

SERVES **6–8**
PREP **30 MINS**
COOK **NONE**
FREEZE **UP TO 3 MONTHS**

1 red pepper, deseeded
  and chopped

10 spring onions, trimmed and
  chopped, or 1 red onion,
  finely chopped

5 garlic cloves, chopped

1 cucumber, finely chopped

1kg (2¼lb) ripe tomatoes,
  finely chopped

1 tbsp fresh thyme, marjoram,
  parsley, mint, or basil,
  chopped

100g (3½oz) stale bread

1 fresh chilli, deseeded and
  finely chopped, or ½ tsp
  cayenne pepper (optional)

2 tbsp red wine vinegar

3 tbsp olive oil, plus extra
  to serve

100ml (3½fl oz) chilled water

salt and freshly ground black
  pepper

RECIPE BY
GEETIE SINGH

GAZPACHO

Geetie Singh, who is behind Britain's first organic pub,
The Duke of Cambridge, writes, "A wonderfully refreshing
summer lunch, this soup is fantastically quick to make."

1 Place a serving bowl in the fridge. Put the pepper, spring onions or onion,
garlic, cucumber, and tomatoes in a mixing bowl, then add the herbs.

2 Whizz the bread in a blender to make breadcrumbs, then add to the
mixing bowl along with the chilli, if using, the vinegar and oil. Gradually add
the water – 100ml (3½fl oz) will give a nice thick consistency, but you can
use more if you prefer.

3 Transfer to the blender and whizz briefly – I like there to be still the odd
chunk of cucumber, but you can blend the soup until smooth, if you prefer.
Season generously with salt and pepper. Transfer to the serving bowl, add
a few ice cubes, and drizzle with olive oil.

SERVES **4**
PREP **15 MINS**
COOK **30 MINS**
FREEZE **UP TO 3 MONTHS**

10 large plum tomatoes, about
   1.1kg (2½lb) total in weight,
   2 halved and deseeded,
   8 coarsely chopped

60ml (2fl oz) extra virgin
   olive oil

1 large onion, finely chopped

1 large leek, cut in half
   lengthways and then
   thinly sliced crossways

1½ tsp coriander seeds

2 garlic cloves, crushed

2 bay leaves

1 tsp finely grated fresh
   horseradish or drained
   bottled horseradish

250ml (8fl oz) hot chicken stock

pinch of sugar

60g (2oz) unsalted butter,
   softened

salt and freshly ground
   black pepper

basil leaves, to garnish

RECIPE BY
DAN BARBER

SMOKED TOMATO SOUP

Dan Barber, the top US chef with a Blue Hill restaurant
in Manhattan and another on a farm outside New York,
teaches all his staff the principles of good farming.

1 Scatter a handful of apple, pecan, or hickory wood barbecue chips in
a medium-sized, cast-iron frying pan or wok, cover tightly with a lid, and
place over a medium heat. When the chips start to smoke, put the 4 tomato
halves on a rack, and set the rack in the pan. Replace the lid and smoke
the tomatoes for 2–3 minutes or until barely softened. Transfer to a plate
and allow to cool slightly, then skin.

2 Heat the oil in a large pan, add the onion and leek, and cook over a
medium heat, stirring frequently, for 10 minutes or until softened but not
browned. Add the coriander, garlic, bay leaves, and horseradish and cook
for 2 minutes or until fragrant. Add the chopped tomatoes, stock, and
sugar, cover with a lid, and cook over a medium heat for 10 minutes
or until the tomatoes are soft. Pick out and discard the bay leaves.

3 Transfer to a blender, add the butter and smoked tomatoes, and whizz
until smooth. You may need to do this in batches. Strain through a sieve
into a clean pan and season with salt and pepper. Serve garnished
with basil leaves.

SERVES **4**
PREP **15 MINS**
COOK **50 MINS**
FREEZE **UP TO 3 MONTHS**
AT THE END OF STEP 3

SOPA DE TORTILLA

Fresh lime juice, coriander, and dried poblano chillies –
not to mention the corn tortillas – give a Mexican flavour
to this spicy tomato soup.

5 tbsp sunflower oil

½ onion, finely chopped

2 large garlic cloves, finely
chopped

450g (1lb) tomatoes, skinned

1.5 litres (2¾ pints) chicken
stock or vegetable stock

1 or 2 dried poblano chillies,
deseeded

2 soft corn tortillas, cut
into strips

3 tbsp chopped fresh coriander

2 tbsp fresh lime juice

salt and freshly ground
black pepper

85g (3oz) Gruyère cheese,
grated

2 limes, cut into wedges,
to serve

1 Heat 1 tbsp of the oil in a large saucepan over a medium heat. Add the onion and fry, stirring, for 5 minutes, or until softened. Add the garlic and stir for 30 seconds. Using a blender, whizz with the tomatoes until smooth.

2 Tip the tomato-onion purée into the pan and simmer for 8–10 minutes, stirring constantly. Stir in the stock and bring to the boil. Reduce the heat, partially cover the pan, and simmer for 15 minutes, or until thickened.

3 Place a non-stick frying pan over a medium heat. Add the chillies and press them against the pan with a spatula until they blister. Turn them over and repeat. Remove from the pan, cut into small pieces, and set aside.

4 Heat the remaining oil in the frying pan until sizzling hot. Add the tortilla strips in batches and fry until just crisp. Remove with a slotted spoon and drain on kitchen paper.

5 When ready to serve, add the chillies to the soup, bring to the boil and simmer for 3 minutes, or until the chillies are soft. Stir in the coriander and lime juice, and season with salt and pepper to taste. Divide the toasted tortilla strips between four soup bowls. Ladle in the soup and top with a sprinkling of cheese. Serve with wedges of lime.

SERVES **4**
PREP **10 MINS**
COOK **15 MINS**
FREEZE **3 MONTHS**

25g (scant 1oz) butter

1 onion, finely chopped

175g (6oz) watercress

3 ripe pears, cored and
   roughly chopped

1 litre (1¾ pints) vegetable
   stock

salt and freshly ground black
   pepper

200ml (7fl oz) double cream

juice of ½ lemon

Parmesan cheese, shaved,
   to serve

olive oil, to drizzle

WATERCRESS SOUP

Serve this velvety smooth soup hot, topped with shavings
of Parmesan cheese, or chilled with an extra swirl of
cream or crème fraîche.

1 Melt the butter in a saucepan and cook the onion for 10 minutes, or until
soft, stirring occasionally to prevent burning. Meanwhile, trim the watercress
and pick off the leaves. Add the watercress stalks to the onion with the
pears and stock, and season with salt and pepper.

2 Bring to the boil, cover, and simmer gently for 15 minutes. Remove from
the heat and pour into a blender along with the watercress leaves. Process
until the soup has a very smooth texture.

3 Stir in the cream and lemon juice, then adjust the seasoning. This soup
can be served hot (garnished with Parmesan shavings and drizzled with
a little olive oil), or refrigerated for up to 4 hours and served chilled
(topped with crushed ice and drizzled with a little olive oil).

SERVES **4–6**
PREP **20 MINS**
COOK **30 MINS**
FREEZE **UP TO 1 MONTH**
AT THE END OF STEP 2

2 tbsp olive oil

1 onion, chopped

2 medium potatoes, chopped

1 litre (1¾ pints) hot vegetable
   stock

250g (9oz) watercress

2 tbsp crème fraîche

salt and freshly ground
   black pepper

FOR THE CURRY LEAF OIL

3 tbsp fresh curry leaves

150ml (5fl oz) olive oil

FOR THE GARNISH

1 conference pear, peeled
   and finely diced

2 tbsp icing sugar

pinch of coarsely ground
   black peppercorns

1 tbsp crème fraîche

RECIPE BY
ROOPA GULATI

SPICY WATERCRESS SOUP

Peppery watercress, curry leaf oil, and caramelized pear
make a marvellous melange of flavours. The oil can be
made a few days before and kept refrigerated.

1 First make the curry leaf oil. Drop the leaves into a pan of boiling water
and cook for about 30 seconds. Remove and refresh with cold water.
Pat dry with kitchen paper and transfer to a blender. Warm the oil and
gradually pour into the blender as the leaves are being processed. Blend
to a smooth paste. Line a sieve with kitchen paper and pour the curry
leaf mixture into it – the oil will slowly drip through.

2 For the soup, heat the oil in a large pan and add the onion and potato.
Cover and fry over a gentle heat, stirring frequently, until softened but not
coloured. Pour in the stock and simmer for 10 minutes, until the potatoes
are cooked. Add the watercress and cook for a further minute. Season,
remove from the heat, and stir in 2–3 tsp of the curry leaf oil. Blend with
a stick blender until smooth and sieve to remove any tough fibres.

3 For the garnish, toss the diced pear in icing sugar seasoned with pepper.
Heat a frying pan over a moderate heat and fry the pear until caramelized.

4 Reheat and re-season the soup and whisk in 2 tbsp of crème fraîche.
Ladle into bowls, and top with an extra dollop of crème fraîche. Scatter
over the pears and finish with a drizzle of curry leaf oil.

SERVES **4–6**
PREP **10 MINS**
COOK **30 MINS**
FREEZE **UP TO 3 MONTHS**
BEFORE CREAM IS ADDED

60g (2oz) butter

1 onion, chopped

250–300g (9–10oz) floury
   potatoes, peeled and diced

1 large carrot, diced

a large handful of fresh lovage
   leaves

1–1.2 litres (1¾–2 pints)
   chicken, light game or
   vegetable stock

salt and freshly ground
   black pepper

90ml (3fl oz) double cream

cayenne pepper, to serve

RECIPE BY
SOPHIE GRIGSON

LOVAGE SOUP

If you don't grow this old-fashioned herb yourself, ask
around among your gardening friends or head down
to the nearest garden centre to see if they sell it.

1 Melt the butter in a large pan and add the onion, potato, carrot, and
lovage. Stir, then cover and sweat over a low heat for 10 minutes.

2 Add the stock and a little salt and pepper. Bring up to the boil and
simmer for 15 minutes until all the vegetables are very tender. Cool
slightly, liquidize, and, if you would like a smoother soup, pass through
a sieve. Taste and adjust the seasoning if necessary. Reheat when needed
and stir in the cream. Serve with a dusting of cayenne pepper.

SERVES **4**
PREP **10 MINS**
COOK **30 MINS**
FREEZE **UP TO 3 MONTHS**
BEFORE MILK IS ADDED

RECIPE BY
CAROLYN HUMPHRIES

SAMPHIRE SOUP WITH POACHED EGGS

For absolute decadence, omit the poached eggs and top each bowl with a little chopped hard-boiled egg and a shucked oyster in its half shell.

200g (7oz) fresh or frozen samphire

good knob of unsalted butter

1 large leek, washed thoroughly and sliced

1 large potato, diced

1 thick slice of lemon

small handful of fresh parsley

900ml (1½ pints) light vegetable or chicken stock

freshly ground black pepper

a little milk

1 tbsp white wine vinegar

4 eggs

1 Wash the samphire, then boil in a little water for 3–5 minutes or until tender. Drain, rinse with cold water, and drain again. If the samphire stalks are stringy, put them on a chopping board and scrape off the green flesh, then discard the remaining central core (you won't need to with young, fresh samphire).

2 Melt the butter in a large saucepan. Add the leek and potato and fry gently, stirring, for 2 minutes or until soft but not browned. Add the lemon, parsley, stock, and pepper – it's unlikely to need salt as samphire is very salty. Bring to the boil, reduce the heat, cover, and simmer gently for 20 minutes, or until the vegetables are really soft. Discard the lemon and whizz in a blender with the samphire flesh. Return to the pan, taste, and add more pepper if necessary. Thin with a little milk, if desired, then reheat gently.

3 Meanwhile, bring a large pan of water to the boil and add the vinegar. Swirl round to make an eddy and break in the eggs one at a time. Poach until cooked to your liking, then remove with a slotted spoon. Ladle into wide, shallow soup plates then rest a poached egg in the centre of each.

SERVES **4**

PREP 10 MINS

COOK 30 MINS

PLUS REHEATING

FREEZE UP TO 3 MONTHS

WITHOUT THE CRÈME FRAÎCHE

large knob of butter

¼ small celeriac, chopped

1 onion, chopped

1 carrot, chopped

1 potato, chopped

750ml (1¼ pints) vegetable
or chicken stock

1 bay leaf

salt and freshly ground
black pepper

small handful of fresh
chive stalks

150ml (5fl oz) milk

115g (4oz) Cheddar cheese,
grated

4 tbsp crème fraîche, plus
extra to serve

RECIPE BY

CAROLYN HUMPHRIES

CHEDDAR AND CHIVE SOUP

Use well-flavoured Cheddar and serve the soup with plenty of warm, crusty bread. Use blue cheese if you prefer, but crumble it rather than try to grate it!

1 Melt the butter in a large saucepan. Add all the prepared root vegetables and fry gently, stirring, for 2 minutes, or until softened but not browned. Add the stock and bay leaf and season. Bring to the boil, reduce the heat, cover, and simmer gently for 30 minutes. Remove the bay leaf, purée the soup in a blender or food processor, then return to the rinsed-out pan.

2 Reserve 4 chive stalks for garnish, then snip the remainder finely. Add to the soup with the milk, cheese, and crème fraîche. Heat through gently, stirring, until the cheese melts and the soup is piping hot. Do not allow to boil.

3 Taste and adjust the seasoning, then ladle into warm, shallow soup bowls, adding a dollop of crème fraîche to each. Break the reserved chive stalks in half and gently lay them, slightly crossed, on top.

SERVES **4–6**
PREP **10–15 MINS**
COOK **30 MINS**
FREEZE **UP TO 3 MONTHS**

1 small bunch of fresh coriander

2 onions, chopped

2 cloves garlic, chopped

3 tbsp olive oil

900g (2lb) potatoes, peeled
    and cubed

1.2 litres (2 pints) chicken stock,
    vegetable stock or water

salt and freshly ground
    black pepper

RECIPE BY
SOPHIE GRIGSON

POTATO AND CORIANDER SOUP

This is a favourite soup in Portugal, where fresh coriander is used enthusiastically. It is essentially a potato and onion soup, liquidized with lots of fresh coriander.

1 Cut the stalks from the coriander and tie them in a bundle with string. Chop the leaves finely and reserve.

2 Fry the onion and garlic gently in the oil until tender without browning. Add the potatoes and coriander stalks, stir, then cover and sweat over a low heat for 5 minutes.

3 Now add the stock, season, and bring to the boil. Simmer until the potatoes are very tender. Remove the bundle of coriander stalks. Liquidize, adding a little more stock or water if the soup is too thick. Stir in the coriander leaves and reheat gently without boiling. Taste and adjust the seasoning. Serve immediately.

SERVES **6**
PREP 15 MINS
COOK 30–35 MINS
FREEZE **UP TO 3 MONTHS**
WITHOUT CREAM OR YOGURT

3 big handfuls of large-leaved
  sorrel

2 tbsp extra virgin olive oil

1 onion, chopped

400g (14oz) potatoes, peeled
  and diced

1 bay leaf

2 sprigs of parsley

2 sprigs of thyme

1.5 litres (2¾ pints) light
  chicken or vegetable stock

salt and freshly ground
  black pepper

6 tbsp double cream (optional)
  or 3 tbsp Greek yogurt

RECIPE BY
SOPHIE GRIGSON

SORREL SOUP

A real tonic on a summer day, this soup with its bright
sorrel sharpness is always welcome. Later in the summer,
when the temperature rises, serve it chilled.

1 Cut out and discard the larger, tougher stems of the sorrel, then shred
the leaves roughly. Warm the oil in a large saucepan and add the onion,
potatoes, bay leaf, parsley, and thyme, tied together with string to form a
bouquet garni. Stir to coat in the oil, then cover and sweat over a low heat
for around 10 minutes.

2 Pour in the stock, then season with salt and pepper. Bring up to the boil
and simmer for 15 minutes or so until the potato is very tender. Take off
the heat, remove the bouquet garni, then stir in the sorrel. Liquidize in
batches and return to the pan. Reheat when required, stir in the cream if
using, then taste and adjust the seasoning. Serve straight away. Alternatively,
chill the soup down for a few hours in the refrigerator, then serve with a
teaspoonful of Greek yogurt floating in each bowlful.

SERVES **4**
PREP **15 MINS**
COOK **25 MINS**
FREEZE **UP TO 3 MONTHS**

2 tbsp vegetable oil

I star anise

½ tsp chilli flakes

½ tsp nigella seeds

1½ tsp fennel seeds

¼ tsp fenugreek seeds

2 onions, diced

4cm (1½in) piece of root
    ginger, peeled and grated

I orange pepper, diced

I yellow pepper, diced

2 tbsp basmati rice

¾ tsp turmeric

½ tsp garam masala

I litre (1¾ pints) hot
    vegetable stock

I tbsp date palm sugar

grated zest and juice of
    I large lemon

salt and freshly ground black
    pepper

2 tbsp coriander leaves,
    roughly chopped

RECIPE BY
ROOPA GULATI

CURRIED BROTH WITH PEPPERS

This fragrant soup is seasoned with a blend of spices often used to give Indian pickles and preserves their distinctive tang. It is best enjoyed with hot naan.

1 Heat the oil in a large saucepan over a medium heat, add the star anise, chilli, nigella, fennel, and fenugreek, and stir-fry for 30 seconds. Lower the heat, add the onions and ginger, then cover and cook for 5 minutes or until the onions have softened. Stir in the peppers and fry for 2–3 minutes.

2 Add the rice, turmeric, and garam masala, stir well, and cook for I minute. Pour in the stock, then add the sugar and lemon zest. Season with salt and pepper and simmer for 15 minutes or until the soup has thickened slightly and the peppers and rice are tender. Sharpen with the lemon juice and serve garnished with coriander.

SERVES **4–6**

PREP **25 MINS**

COOK **2 HRS**

FREEZE **UP TO 3 MONTHS**

1 large fennel bulb, peeled

1 red onion

2 red peppers, halved and deseeded

500g (1lb) tomatoes

4 garlic cloves, in their skins

1½ tsp sugar

2 tbsp olive oil

1 large sprig of fresh rosemary, leaves only

1–2 tbsp vegetable oil

1½ tsp fennel seeds

½ tsp nigella seeds

400ml (14fl oz) passata

1 litre (2 pints) vegetable stock

1 red chilli, split and deseeded

salt and freshly ground black pepper

handful of fennel leaves

RECIPE BY
ROOPA GULATI

ROASTED RED PEPPER, FENNEL, AND TOMATO SOUP

Make this soup near the end of the summer when tomatoes and peppers are plentiful. It freezes well and is also a cheering stalwart for winter meals.

1 Preheat the oven to 200°C (400°F/Gas 6). Cut the fennel and onion into wedges. Slice a cross into the base of each tomato and squeeze the juice and seeds into a bowl. Strain the juice and set aside.

2 Line a roasting tin with baking parchment and add the fennel, onion, peppers, tomatoes, and garlic cloves. Sprinkle over the sugar, drizzle with the olive oil, and scatter the rosemary on top. Roast the vegetables for about 1 hour, until the tomatoes are soft. Cool the vegetables before peeling the blackened skin from the peppers. Peel the garlic and discard the skins.

3 Heat the vegetable oil in a large pan and toss in the fennel and nigella seeds, swirling them around for a few seconds. Pour over the passata, the stock, and the reserved tomato juice, and bring to the boil. Add the roasted vegetables, pop the chilli into the pan, and season with salt and pepper to taste. Half cover with a lid and simmer for about 45 minutes.

4 Using a blender, whizz the soup until smooth, and press through a sieve. Reheat, re-season, and finish with a sprinkling of fennel leaves.

SERVES **6**
PREP **20 MINS**
PLUS OVERNIGHT SOAKING
COOK **1 HR 20 MINS**
FREEZE **UP TO 3 MONTHS**
WITHOUT THE GREEN BEANS

85g (3oz) dried haricot beans, soaked overnight in water, then drained

2 tbsp olive oil

1 medium leek, finely sliced

1 small turnip, cut into 1cm (½in) dice

2 medium carrots, cut into 1cm (½in) dice

1 large courgette, cut into 1cm (½in) dice

1 celery stalk, cut into 1cm (½in) dice

1 large potato, cut into 1cm (½in) dice

2 tomatoes, skinned and cut into 1cm (½in) dice

2 garlic cloves, finely chopped

2 litres (3½ pints) cold water

salt and freshly ground black pepper

175g (6oz) fine green beans, cut into 2cm (¾in) lengths

RECIPE BY
THANE PRINCE

ALLOTMENT SOUP

Thane Prince's recipe books and teaching promote simple cooking with the best local ingredients. "This French country-style soup is delicious topped with a little pesto."

1 Put the soaked haricot beans in a saucepan with plenty of cold unsalted water. Bring to the boil, cover with a lid, and boil for 15 minutes. Lower the heat, then simmer for 1 hour or until tender and drain.

2 Meanwhile, heat the oil in a large saucepan, add the leek, turnip, carrots, courgette, celery, potato, tomatoes, and garlic, and cook, stirring often, for 10–15 minutes or until they are soft but not brown. Add the water, season with salt and pepper, then bring to the boil, cover with a lid, and simmer for 45 minutes or until all the vegetables are tender.

3 Add the cooked haricot beans to the pan, along with the green beans, and cook for 5 minutes or until tender. Divide the soup among six bowls and serve with some crusty bread.

SERVES **4–6**
PREP **20 MINS**
COOK **10–12 MINS**
FREEZE **UP TO 3 MONTHS**
AT END OF STEP 2

RECIPE BY
RAYMOND BLANC OBE

VEGETABLE AND CHERVIL SOUP

Raymond Blanc OBE, Chef Patron of Le Manoir aux Quat' Saisons, Oxfordshire, writes, "This soup offers a multitude of flavours which can vary according to the seasons."

15g (½oz) unsalted butter

1 onion, finely chopped

1 garlic clove, finely chopped

2 large carrots, finely sliced

3 celery sticks, sliced into ½cm (¼in) pieces

2 medium leeks, sliced into 1cm (¾in) chunks

salt and freshly ground white pepper

1 large courgette, halved lengthways and cut into ½cm (¼in) slices

2 ripe tomatoes, quartered and roughly chopped

15g (½oz) unsalted butter or soured cream

25g (scant 1oz) chervil, finely chopped

crème fraîche, to serve (optional)

1 Melt the butter in a pan and sweat the onion, garlic, carrots, celery, and leeks for 5 minutes (do not allow them to colour). Season with salt and white pepper.

2 Add 1 litre (1¾ pints) boiling water, the courgette, and tomatoes (using boiling water will reduce the cooking time and also keep the lively colours). Fast boil for a further 5 minutes only – it is vital that you do not spoil the fresh, clean flavours of your vegetables by overcooking.

3 Whisk in the butter or sour cream (or both!) and add the chervil. Taste and correct the seasoning if required, and blend the soup if you would like a finer texture. Pour into a large tureen and serve to your guests. A spoon of crème fraîche would always be welcome.

SERVES **6**
PREP **10 MINS**
PLUS 1–2 HRS CHILLING TIME
COOK **NONE**
FREEZE **NOT SUITABLE**

RECIPE BY
SOPHIE GRIGSON

JANE GRIGSON'S MELON AND WINE SOUP

This soup provides an unexpected, beautiful finale to a meal on a summer's day. It comes into its own when a ripe orange charentais or canteloupe is used.

1 melon weighing a generous
   1kg (2¼lb)
150g (5½oz) sugar
250ml (8fl oz) dry white wine
lemon juice
150ml (5fl oz) crème fraîche
almond biscuits or meringues,
   to serve

1 Discard the pips and scoop the flesh from the melon. Ideally you should have 750g (1½lb) weight, but don't worry if you have more or less. The other quantities can be adjusted to your taste and this will depend more on the strength of the melon's flavour than on its bulk.

2 Dissolve the sugar in 600ml (1 pint) of water over a low heat, then simmer for 4–5 minutes. Remove the pan from the heat and allow to cool completely.

3 In a food processor or blender, process the melon with the wine until smooth, then gradually add the cool syrup. Stop when the mixture tastes just a little sweeter than you would ideally like it. Now mix in a few good squeezes of lemon juice and the crème fraîche. Serve chilled, with tiny almond biscuits or meringues.

SERVES **4**
PREP **15 MINS**
FREEZE **UP TO 1 MONTH**
AT THE END OF STEP 3

RECIPE BY
ROOPA GULATI

CHILLED MELON AND GINGER SOUP

This is a soup to make in a hurry. All that's needed to bring out its fruity flavour is a seriously good chill – and a perfectly ripe melon.

1 ripe Galia melon, peeled and deseeded

2.5cm (1in) fresh root ginger

1 tsp fennel seeds

200g (7oz) white seedless grapes

juice and grated zest of 1 lime

1 tsp dried mint

4 tbsp Greek yogurt, beaten

salt and freshly ground black pepper

FOR THE GARNISH

2 tbsp fresh mint leaves

pinch of sugar

25g (1oz) crystallized ginger, finely chopped

1 Roughly chop three quarters of the melon flesh into bite-sized chunks. Finely chop the remainder and set aside. Coarsely grate the root ginger and squeeze any juice over the melon chunks. Discard the leftover ginger.

2 Heat a sturdy frying pan or griddle over a gentle heat and lightly toast the fennel seeds for about 30 seconds, until you smell an aniseed-like aroma. Grind the seeds to a coarse powder using a mortar and pestle.

3 Put the ground fennel seeds into a blender with the roughly chopped melon and ginger juice. Add the grapes, lime juice and zest, and dried mint. Whizz until smooth and push through a sieve to remove the skins.

4 Stir in the yogurt, season, and chill thoroughly – it's best to half-freeze this soup, then give it a good whisk just before serving. Spoon into bowls, adding a small pile of the reserved melon to each one. Shred the fresh mint with the sugar, mix with the crystallized ginger, and scatter over the soup, then serve immediately.

SERVES **4**
PREP **5 MINS**
COOK **15 MINS**
FREEZE **UP TO 6 MONTHS**

300g (10oz) morello cherries,
   fresh or canned
500ml (16fl oz) white wine
55g (scant 2oz) sugar
1 lemon, zest and juice
300ml (10fl oz) soured cream

RECIPE BY
SHAUN HILL

CHERRY SOUP

This Hungarian soup is meant to taste fresh rather
than sweet. The ratio of lemon to sugar is a guideline
only – it depends on how ripe the cherries are.

1 Stone the cherries and reserve the fruit. Add the stones, stalks, and
any juice to the wine and 200ml (7fl oz) water in a saucepan. Bring to
the boil. Simmer, uncovered, for 10 minutes.

2 Strain the liquid into a clean pan and add the reserved fruit, sugar,
and lemon. Bring to the boil then, away from direct heat, whisk in the
soured cream. Chill well before serving.

SERVES **4**
PREP **30 MINS**
COOK **10 MINS**
PLUS 2 HOURS CHILLING
FREEZE **NOT SUITABLE**

500g (1lb 2oz) clams or
    mussels, cleaned

4 tbsp fruity olive oil

1 banana shallot, finely chopped

2 large spring onions, finely
    chopped

2 garlic cloves, crushed

100ml (3½fl oz) dry sherry

3 sprigs flat leaf parsley, plus
    1 tbsp finely chopped parsley
    to serve

1 tsp fennel seeds, crushed

sea salt and freshly ground
    black pepper

½ tsp piquante pimenton

1kg (2¼lb) ripe tomatoes,
    rinsed and halved

2 eggs, hard-boiled and peeled

1 tbsp sherry vinegar

freshly cooked brown and
    white meat of 1 medium
    prepared crab

8 croûtes, rubbed with garlic

RECIPE BY
MARIE-PIERRE MOINE

CRAB GAZPACHO

Seafood and tomato make a flavourful pair in this delicate
summer chilled soup. You can use the cooked clams or
mussels in another dish, such as potato salad.

1 Put a sauté pan over a moderate heat. Tip in the clams or mussels along
with 1 tbsp oil, the shallot, half the spring onion and garlic, the sherry, and
250ml (9fl oz) water. Add the parsley sprigs, fennel seeds, salt, pepper,
and pimenton. Bring to the boil. Cover and cook for 4–5 minutes, shaking
a few times, until the shells open. Strain the stock through a muslin-lined
sieve into a bowl and leave to cool completely. Discard any unopened
clams or mussels.

2 Put the tomatoes, the cold stock from the mussels, 1 tbsp olive oil, 1
hard-boiled egg yolk, and the remaining spring onion and garlic in a blender
and whizz until very smooth. Push through a sieve into a bowl. Rinse out
the blender or food processor with 250ml (9fl oz) water mixed with the
sherry vinegar. Pour through the sieve into the bowl.

3 Chill the soup for at least 2 hours. Press the remaining egg yolk through
a sieve and finely chop the whites. Mix the brown crab meat with 2 tbsp oil
and the egg yolk and whites. Add a little pepper and spread on the croûtes.

4 Ladle the cold soup into bowls and lightly stir in the white crab meat.
Float a croûte on each helping and scatter over the chopped parsley.

SERVES **4**
PREP **45 MINS**
COOK **1 HR 10 MINS**
FREEZE **UP TO 2 MONTHS**
BEFORE CREAM IS ADDED

1 cooked spider crab or
   velvet crab, about 1kg (2¼lb)
   in weight

50g (1¾oz) butter

olive oil

1 onion, finely chopped

1 carrot, finely chopped

2 celery stalks, finely chopped

1 leek, finely chopped

½ fennel bulb, finely chopped

1 bay leaf

1 sprig of tarragon

2 garlic cloves, crushed

2.5cm (1in) fresh ginger, peeled
   and finely chopped

75g (2½oz) tomato purée

4 tomatoes, roughly chopped

120ml (4fl oz) Cognac or
   brandy

100ml (3½fl oz) dry white wine
   or vermouth

1.7 litres (3 pints) fish stock

120ml (4fl oz) cream

salt and freshly ground black
   pepper

pinch of cayenne pepper

juice of ½ lemon

chopped chives, to garnish

CRAB BISQUE

You can buy your crab ready cooked or, for optimum
freshness, buy it live and cook it yourself. Boiling is the
most common way to cook a live crab, although they
can also be steamed.

1 Remove the crab meat from the shell and chop into small pieces. Chop
the shell up roughly and put shell and meat to one side. Heat the butter
and oil in a large saucepan over a medium heat. Add the vegetables, herbs,
garlic, and ginger. Cook, stirring occasionally, for 10 minutes or until softened.

2 Add the chopped shell, then stir in the tomato purée, tomatoes, Cognac,
wine, and stock. Bring to the boil and simmer for 1 hour. Leave to cool
slightly, then blend till smooth. Strain through a coarse sieve, pushing as
much liquid through as you can with the back of a ladle, and then put
through a fine sieve.

3 Return the soup to the pan and bring to the boil. Add the crab meat
and cream, then season with salt and pepper, and add cayenne and lemon
juice to taste. Garnish with chives and serve in warm bowls.

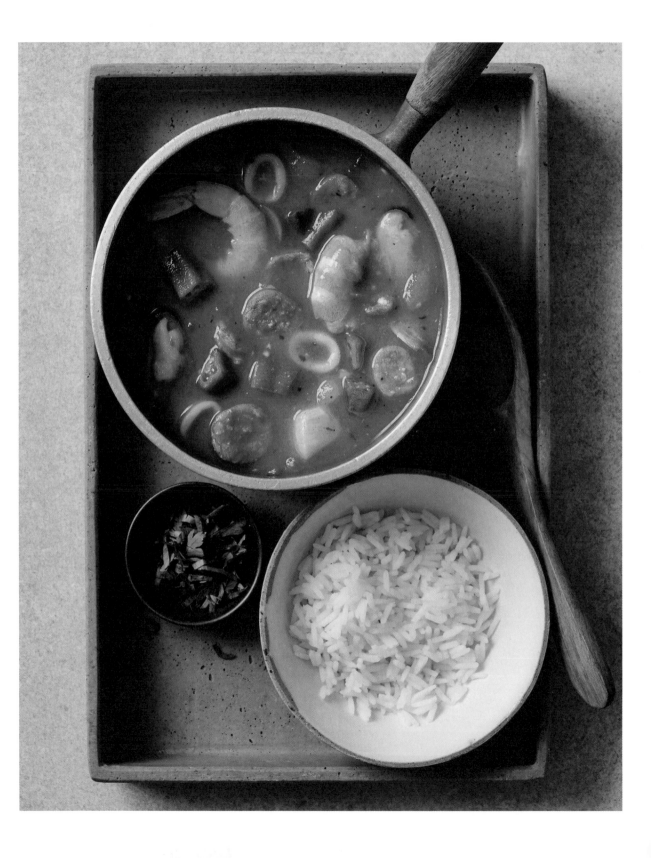

SERVES **6**
PREP **20 MINS**
COOK **50 MINS**
FREEZE **UP TO 2 MONTHS**
AT THE END OF STEP 2

1 tbsp sunflower oil

1 onion, chopped

2 celery sticks, chopped

1 large garlic clove, chopped

115g (4oz) cooking chorizo,
    sliced

2 tbsp plain flour

600ml (1 pint) fish or chicken
    stock

400g can chopped tomatoes

1 green pepper, diced

250g (9oz) okra, trimmed and
    cut in short lengths

¼ tsp cayenne

½ tsp dried oregano

½ tsp caster sugar

salt and freshly ground
    black pepper

200g (7oz) mixed raw seafood
    cocktail

225g (8oz) long-grain rice

chopped parsley, to serve

RECIPE BY
CAROLYN HUMPHRIES

MIXED SEAFOOD GUMBO

A rich main meal soup, naturally thickened with okra,
a classic gumbo ingredient. In its native Louisiana, they
would use sweet ground sassafras leaves.

1 Heat the oil in a large pan. Add the onion and celery and fry gently,
stirring, for about 5 minutes, or until lightly golden. Stir in the garlic and
chorizo and cook for 2 minutes. Stir in the flour and cook for another
minute. Remove from the heat and gradually blend in the stock, then
the tomatoes. Return to the heat and bring to the boil, stirring. Add the
remaining ingredients, except the seafood and rice, bring back to the boil,
reduce the heat, part-cover, and simmer gently for 30 minutes.

2 Add the seafood and simmer for a further 5 minutes, stirring
occasionally. Taste and re-season.

3 Meanwhile, cook the rice in plenty of boiling, lightly salted water for
10 minutes or until just tender. Drain in a colander, rinse with boiling
water, and drain again.

4 Spoon some rice into each of the 6 large soup bowls. Ladle the gumbo
over, sprinkle with a little chopped parsley and serve hot.

SERVES **6**
PREP **20 MINS**
COOK **1 HR**
FREEZE **UP TO 3 MONTHS**

BEEF AND GREEN BEAN SOUP

Choose firm, waxy potatoes that will keep their shape and texture in this deliciously savoury soup. Cooking the beans until just al dente retains maximum taste and colour.

2 tbsp sunflower oil

500g (1lb 2oz) braising beef, e.g. from the shoulder, diced into 2cm (¾in) cubes

salt and freshly ground black pepper

1 onion, chopped

2–3 sprigs of thyme

1 litre (1¾ pints) vegetable stock

1 large potato, peeled and diced

250g (9oz) green beans, trimmed and cut into small pieces

1–2 tbsp chopped fresh parsley (optional)

1 Heat the oil in a pan, season the cubed meat with salt and pepper, and add half the meat to the hot oil. Brown the meat until golden all over. Remove from the pan and repeat with the rest of the meat. Remove the meat from the pan, add the onion, and fry until softened.

2 Transfer the browned meat back to the pan, tie the thyme sprigs together with kitchen string, and add them to the pan with the stock. Bring to the boil, cover, and cook over a medium heat for about 40 minutes.

3 Add the potato, bring back to the boil, cover, and cook for 10–15 minutes, or until just tender. Add the chopped beans and cook for 4–5 minutes, or until the beans are al dente.

4 Remove the thyme. Season to taste with salt and pepper, break up the meat pieces slightly, and sprinkle with parsley, if using, before serving.

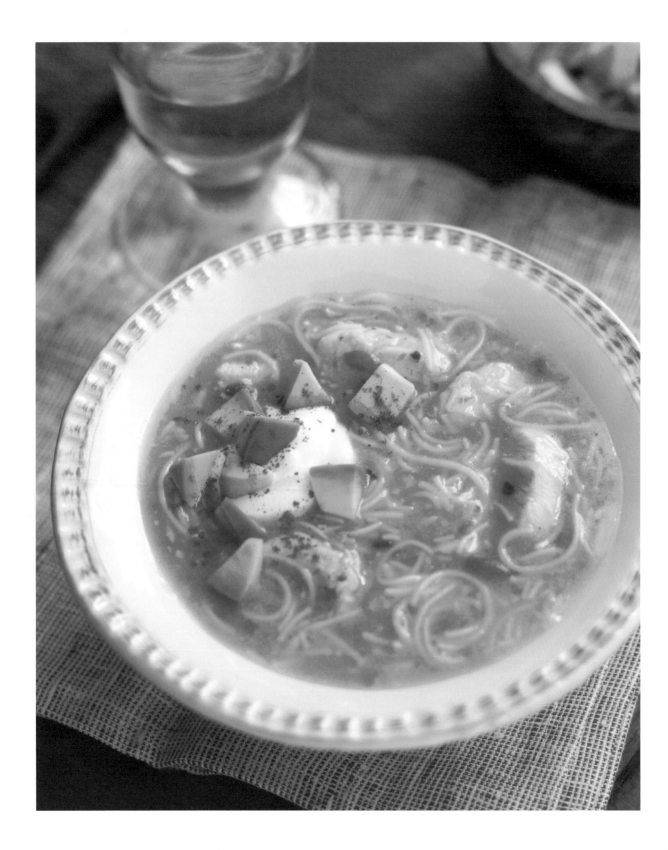

SERVES **4**
PREP **20 MINS**
PLUS 30 MINS SOAKING
COOK **15 MINS**
FREEZE **NOT SUITABLE**

SOPA SECA DE FIDEOS

This Mexican soup is made with thin *fideo* noodles, which are
similar to angel-hair pasta. The avocado and soured cream
offset the spiciness of the broth.

2 dried chipotle chillies

2 large ripe tomatoes, skinned
and deseeded

2 garlic cloves

1 small onion, roughly chopped

900ml (1½ pints) chicken stock

3 tbsp vegetable oil

2 skinless boneless chicken
breasts, diced

225g (8oz) Mexican *fideo*
noodles or dried angel-hair
pasta

4 tbsp soured cream, to serve

1 avocado, stone removed,
chopped, to serve

1 Soak the dried chillies in water for 30 minutes, then drain, discarding
the soaking water. Using a blender, whizz the tomatoes, garlic, onion,
chillies, and 2 tbsp of the stock until smooth. Set aside.

2 Heat 2 tbsp of the oil in a large pan. Add the chicken and stir-fry for
2–3 minutes, or until just cooked. Remove from the pan, drain on kitchen
paper, and set aside.

3 Pour the remaining oil into the pan, add the noodles, and cook over
a low heat, stirring constantly, until the noodles are golden.

4 Pour in the tomato mixture, stir until the noodles are coated, then
add the remaining stock, and return the chicken to the pan. Cook for
2–3 minutes, or until the noodles are just tender. To serve, ladle into
bowls, topping each with soured cream and chopped avocado.

SERVES 4
PREP 5 MINS
COOK 20 MINS
FREEZE NOT SUITABLE

RECIPE BY
SHAUN HILL

AVGOLEMONE

This lemon, chicken, and rice soup is claimed by countries
across the eastern Mediterranean. The stock must be well
flavoured, or it will not withstand the lemon juice.

50g (1¾oz) long-grain rice

1.2 litres (2 pints) well-flavoured
   chicken stock

3 eggs

juice of 1 large lemon

salt and freshly ground
   black pepper

lemon wedges, to serve

1 Bring the rice and stock to the boil in a saucepan. Simmer, uncovered, for 15 minutes, or until the rice is completely cooked.

2 Whisk the eggs and lemon juice in a bowl until the mixture becomes frothy. Add a ladleful of hot stock and continue to whisk.

3 Remove the rice and stock from direct heat. Whisk the egg, lemon, and stock mixture into it. Return to the heat and cook gently and briefly at a temperature below boiling point, whisking until the texture is velvety – do not allow to boil. Season and serve with lemon wedges.

SERVES **4**
PREP **5 MINS**
COOK **20 MINS**
FREEZE **NOT SUITABLE**

RECIPE BY
CAROLYN HUMPHREYS

CHINESE EGG DROP SOUP

This can be a simple chicken broth with just the drizzled egg,
but it's more tasty and filling with the addition of vegetables
and Chinese seasonings.

1 litre (1¾ pints) chicken stock

1 garlic clove, crushed

½ tsp grated fresh root ginger

2 spring onions, chopped

2 tbsp soy sauce

½ tsp Chinese five-spice
   powder

2 corn on the cob or 200g
   can sweetcorn

2 good handfuls of fresh baby
   leaf spinach

2 tbsp cornflour

2 eggs, beaten

1 Put the stock in a pan with the garlic, ginger, spring onions, soy sauce, and five-spice powder. If using fresh corn, place each corn on the cob on its end and slide a sharp knife down the length to remove all the kernels. Add the kernels to the pan, bring to the boil, reduce the heat, cover, and simmer gently for 20 minutes.

2 Add the canned sweetcorn (if using), including any liquid, and the spinach. Bring back to the boil, reduce the heat, and simmer for 1 minute or until the spinach has just wilted. Taste and add more soy sauce if necessary.

3 Blend the cornflour with 4 tbsp water and stir in. Bring back to the boil and simmer, stirring, for 1 minute to thicken slightly. Gradually trickle in the beaten egg, stirring gently, so that it forms thin strands. Serve in warm soup bowls.

SERVES **4–6**
PREP **10 MINS**
COOK **25 MINS**
FREEZE **UP TO 3 MONTHS**
AT THE END OF STEP 1

GERMAN CHICKEN BROTH

Based on a Thuringian vegetable soup, this recipe requires a good-quality, well-flavoured chicken stock, so make your own for best results (see pp18–19).

1.2 litres (2 pints) chicken stock

150g (5oz) green beans, topped, tailed, and strings removed

2 large carrots, peeled and sliced

200g (7oz) kohlrabi, diced

150g (5½oz) mangetout or sugar snap peas, topped and tailed

salt and freshly ground black pepper

single or double cream, to serve

1 bunch chervil, finely chopped

1 Bring the stock to the boil in a medium-sized saucepan, add the green beans and simmer for 5 minutes. Add the carrots and kohlrabi and cook for a further 5 minutes, then add the mangetout or sugar snap peas and cook for a further 5 minutes – be careful not to overcook these or they will lose their delightful crunchiness.

2 Season with salt and pepper and remove the pan from the heat. Ladle into serving bowls, add a swirl of cream to each, and sprinkle with chervil before serving.

SERVES **6**
PREP **20 MINS**
COOK **20 MINS**
FREEZE **UP TO 3 MONTHS**
WITHOUT THE SAUSAGES

PEA AND SAUSAGE SOUP

Try this hearty soup with slices of dark German rye bread
and a glass of white wine or wheat beer. If you can't get
Toulouse sausages, any good-quality pork sausage will do.

30g (1oz) butter

1 large carrot, peeled and diced

1 small leek, diced

2 stalks celery, diced

1 medium potato, peeled
 and diced

½ bunch fresh parsley, chopped

125ml (4fl oz) dry white wine

1.2 litres (2 pints) hot chicken
 stock

3 Toulouse sausages

750g (1lb 10oz) peas (frozen
 or fresh)

salt and freshly ground black
 pepper

1 Preheat the oven to 180°C (350°F/Gas 4). In a large saucepan, melt the butter and add the carrot, leek, celery, and potato and cook, stirring, until softened. Add the parsley, wine, and stock and simmer for 15 minutes.

2 Place the sausages on a baking tray and cook, turning occasionally, for 15–20 minutes, or until cooked through and golden brown on all sides, then slice and set aside.

3 Add the peas to the pot and cook for 3–4 minutes, or until just al dente. Season and process to a purée in a blender. Return to the pot and heat through. Serve in six bowls, garnished with the sliced cooked sausage.

AUTUMN

AUTUMN
SEASON'S BEST

The harvest festival that is autumn celebrates a wide range of produce and offers unusual flavours. Gin, stilton, and beer all make a guest appearance alongside more traditional autumn ingredients such as squash, mushrooms, sweet potato, and beetroot. There are lighter soups for warmer days, such as carrot and lemongrass, or richer offerings for when the temperature drops, such as a hearty pumpkin and apple soup or an earthy beetroot soup with goat's cheese.

SERVES **6**
PREP **10 MINS**
COOK **20 MINS**
FREEZE **UP TO 3 MONTHS**
AT THE END OF STEP 2

1 tbsp olive oil

1 small pumpkin (or part of
a large one), about 750g
(1lb 10oz) in total, skinned
and cubed

2 potatoes, peeled and cubed

600ml (1 pint) vegetable stock

2 tomatoes, chopped

4 fresh sage leaves

sea salt and freshly ground
black pepper

FOR THE GARNISH

olive oil, for frying

18 large fresh sage leaves

RECIPE BY
MONTY DON

PUMPKIN SOUP

Monty Don, presenter of BBC *Gardeners' World* and Soil
Association president from 2008 to 2017, says, "This
creamy soup is an amazing orange colour. If you use a
stock powder or cube, taste before adding extra salt."

1 Heat the oil in a saucepan and sweat the pumpkin and potatoes for
5 minutes. Add the stock, chopped tomatoes, and sage leaves. Cover and
simmer for about 10 minutes, until the vegetables are soft.

2 Using a blender, whizz the soup until smooth, then gently reheat. Season
with salt and pepper to taste.

3 For the garnish, heat a little oil in a frying pan and, once hot, fry the
large sage leaves until crisp. Scatter the crispy leaves over the soup and
serve immediately.

SERVES **6**
PREP **20 MINS**
COOK **40 MINS**
FREEZE **UP TO 3 MONTHS**

RECIPE BY
JEANETTE ORREY

PUMPKIN AND APPLE SOUP

Jeanette Orrey inspired Jamie Oliver's school dinner campaign and
is now Advisor to the Soil Association on improving school dinners.

60g (2oz) unsalted butter

1 medium onion, finely
    chopped

200g (7oz) pumpkin flesh, diced

2 sharp-tasting apples such as
    Granny Smith, diced

150ml (5fl oz) hot water

1.2 litres (2 pints) cold
    vegetable stock or
    chicken stock

salt and freshly ground
    black pepper

30g (1oz) toasted pumpkin
    seeds, to garnish

1 Melt the butter in a large saucepan, add the onion, and cook very gently, stirring often, for 10 minutes or until soft. Do not let it brown. Add the pumpkin and apples and stir to coat well. Pour in the hot water, cover with a lid, and leave on a very, very low heat for 30 minutes, stirring from time to time. If the liquid evaporates, pour in a little more hot water. The vegetables and fruit should be very soft at the end of cooking.

2 Stir in the stock, then blend the soup in batches. As each batch is done, pour it into a sieve set over a clean saucepan. Press the contents through with the back of a ladle, a wooden spoon, or a pestle.

3 When all the soup has been sieved, reheat it very gently, then season to taste with salt and pepper. Serve garnished with the toasted pumpkin seeds.

SERVES **4**
PREP **15 MINS**
COOK **35 MINS**
FREEZE **UP TO 3 MONTHS**

RECIPE BY
ANGELA NILSEN

CARROT SOUP WITH COCONUT AND LEMONGRASS

This spicy carrot soup makes an elegant starter. Serve it with lime wedges so that guests can adjust the flavour to their liking.

2 tbsp vegetable oil or sunflower oil

1 onion, chopped

1 lemongrass stalk, trimmed and tough outer layer discarded

2 garlic cloves, chopped

2 tsp finely grated root ginger

1 tbsp red Thai curry paste

450g (1lb) carrots, sliced

900ml (1½ pints) hot vegetable stock

3 makrut (kaffir) lime leaves

165ml can coconut milk

lime wedges, to serve

salt and freshly ground black pepper

1 Heat the oil in a large saucepan, add the onion, and fry for 3–4 minutes or until it starts to soften. Meanwhile, finely chop the lemongrass, then add to the pan, along with the garlic and ginger, and fry for 2 minutes. Add the curry paste and fry for 1 minute, stirring all the time, then add the carrots and fry for 2 minutes. Pour in the stock, add the lime leaves, and simmer for 20–25 minutes or until the carrots are tender.

2 Remove from the heat and take out and discard the lime leaves. Pour in the coconut milk, then whizz in a blender or food processor until smooth. The soup shouldn't be too thick – dilute with more stock if it is. Season to taste, then serve with lime wedges and a grinding of black pepper.

SERVES **4**
PREP **20 MINS**
COOK **30 MINS**
FREEZE **UP TO 3 MONTHS**
BEFORE CREAM IS ADDED

RECIPE BY
MARIE-PIERRE MOINE

CARROT CREAM WITH ONION AND CUMIN

Pushing this colourful, zingy soup through a sieve may seem fiddly,
but it does wonders for the texture and is worth the effort.

2 tbsp sunflower, groundnut, or
mild olive oil

2 large Spanish onions, peeled
and coarsely chopped

1 tsp cumin seeds

1 tsp ground cumin

1kg (2¼lb) carrots, peeled and
coarsely chopped

sea salt and freshly ground
black pepper

juice and grated zest of 1 small
unwaxed orange

120ml (4fl oz) single cream

1 tbsp finely chopped flat-leaf
parsley

1 Place a large sauté pan over a medium-high heat. Add the oil and
tip in the onion and cumin. Cook for 3–5 minutes, or until softened,
stirring frequently. Add the carrots and 1.5 litres (2¾ pints) water, then
season lightly. Bring to a simmer, reduce the heat, cover, and cook for
20 minutes, or until the carrots are very tender. Turn off the heat and
allow to cool a little.

2 Pour into a blender or food processor and whizz until smooth. Place
a sieve over a saucepan (or the sauté pan if possible). Pour the soup
into the sieve and push it through with the back of a wooden spoon.

3 Taste and adjust the seasoning. Stir in the orange juice and zest. Reheat
until piping hot and stir in the cream, then the parsley. Season with a little
extra pepper. Serve hot.

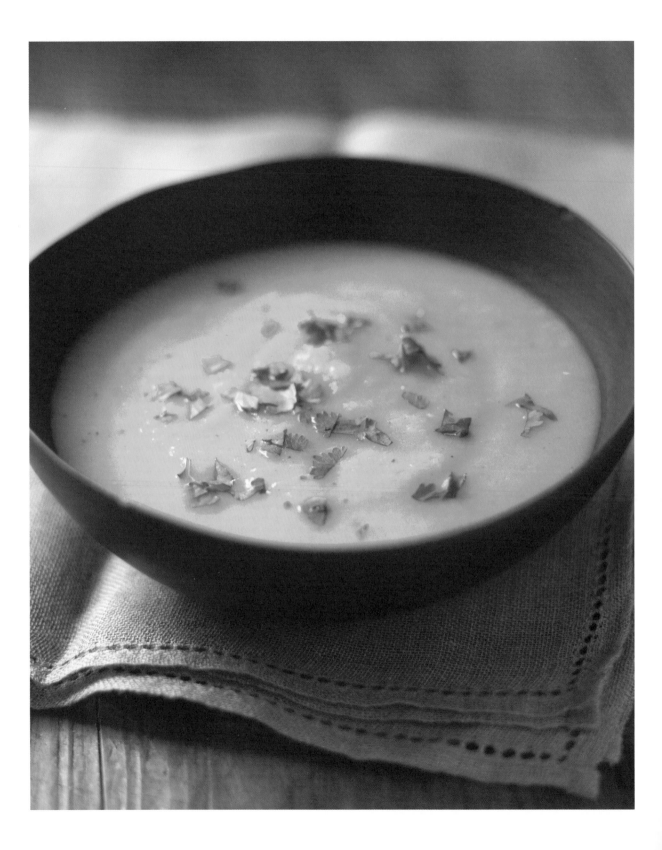

SERVES **4**
PREP **10 MINS**
COOK **40 MINS**
FREEZE **UP TO 3 MONTHS**

CARROT AND ORANGE SOUP

A light, refreshing soup with a hint of spice, this is the perfect
start to an autumn meal. Try adding a swirl of cream or a spoonful
of low-fat plain yogurt before serving.

2 tsp light olive oil or
   sunflower oil

1 leek, sliced

500g (1lb 2oz) carrots, sliced

1 potato, about 115g (4oz),
   chopped

½ tsp ground coriander

pinch of ground cumin

300ml (10fl oz) orange juice

500ml (16fl oz) vegetable or
   chicken stock

1 bay leaf

salt and freshly ground black
   pepper

2 tbsp chopped coriander,
   to garnish

1 Place the oil, leek, and carrots in a large saucepan and cook over a low heat for 5 minutes, stirring frequently, or until the leek has softened. Add the potato, coriander, and cumin, then pour in the orange juice and stock. Add the bay leaf and stir occasionally.

2 Increase the heat, bring the soup to the boil, then lower the heat, cover, and simmer for 40 minutes, or until the vegetables are very tender.

3 Allow the soup to cool slightly, then transfer to a blender or food processor and process until smooth, working in batches if necessary.

4 Return to the saucepan and add a little extra stock or water if the soup is too thick. Bring back to a simmer, season with salt and pepper, then transfer to heated serving bowls and sprinkle with chopped coriander.

SERVES **8**
PREP **20 MINS**
COOK **55–65 MINS**
FREEZE **UP TO 3 MONTHS**

RECIPE BY
SOPHIE GRIGSON

MAPLE-ROASTED CARROT AND GINGER SOUP

The maple syrup helps the carrots to caramelize in the oven, giving this soup its deep, rich flavour. If you cannot find lovage, use chopped chives to finish.

2kg (4½lb) carrots, cut into roughly little-finger-sized pieces

2 onions, cut into eighths

4cm (1¾in) piece of stem ginger, cut into matchsticks

4 garlic cloves, peeled

3 tbsp sunflower oil

4 tbsp maple syrup

1½ litres (2¾ pints) chicken or vegetable stock

salt and freshly ground black pepper

a couple of squeezes of lemon juice (optional)

chopped lovage or chives, to serve

1 Preheat the oven to 220°C (425°F/Gas 7). Place the carrots in a roasting tin with all the rest of the ingredients except the stock, lemon juice, salt and pepper, and the lovage or chives. Mix thoroughly with your hands, then smooth down lightly. Roast for some 45–60 minutes, turning occasionally, until the vegetables are very tender and patched here and there with brown.

2 Cool slightly, then scrape into a liquidizer, including as much as you can scrape off of the brown sticky residues at the bottom of the tin. Add half the stock and whizz until smooth, adding more stock if necessary. You may need to do this in batches.

3 Pour into a saucepan, stir in the last of the stock, adding extra if necessary to thin the soup, then taste and correct the seasoning, adding a couple of squeezes of lemon juice if you find the sweetness too intense. Adequate seasoning will also balance this. Heat up well just before serving, and sprinkle each bowlful with chopped lovage or chives.

SERVES **4**
PREP **15 MINS**
COOK **1 HR**
FREEZE **UP TO 3 MONTHS**

RECIPE BY
ANNA DEL CONTE

MIXED FUNGI SOUP

This simple soup recipe with onion, garlic, and parsley brings
out the flavour of mixed wild mushrooms beautifully. Delicious
served with soured cream.

75g (2½oz) unsalted butter

100g (3½oz) onion, finely
    chopped

1 garlic clove, finely chopped

15g (½oz) flat-leaf parsley,
    chopped

225g (8oz) mixed wild
    mushrooms, diced

4 tbsp milk

salt and freshly ground
    black pepper

grated nutmeg

40g (1½oz) flour

1.2 litres (2 pints) vegetable
    or chicken stock

4 tbsp soured cream

1 Heat half the butter with the onion, garlic, and parsley in a sauté
pan and cook for 3 minutes. Add the mushrooms, and sauté for another
3 minutes. Pour in the milk, and season with salt and nutmeg. Cook for
a few more minutes and set aside.

2 In another saucepan, melt the remaining butter. Remove the pan from
the heat and beat in the flour. Return the pan to a low heat and cook
until the mixture deepens in colour. Remove the pan from the heat once
more, and add the stock gradually by the ladleful. Stir constantly to avoid
lumps forming, and return the pan to a low heat.

3 When all the stock has been combined with the flour, add the mushroom
mixture and the juices. Bring to the boil, and simmer for 15–20 minutes.
Season with salt and pepper to taste. Spoon a tablespoon of soured
cream into each bowl and serve.

SERVES **4**
PREP **10 MINS**
COOK **45 MINS**
FREEZE **UP TO 3 MONTHS**

30g (1oz) butter

1 onion, finely chopped

2 celery sticks, finely chopped

1 garlic clove, crushed

450g (1lb) mixed mushrooms,
roughly chopped

200g (7oz) potatoes, peeled
and cubed

1 litre (1¾ pints) vegetable
stock

2 tbsp finely chopped fresh
parsley

salt and freshly ground black
pepper

horseradish cream, to serve
(optional)

MUSHROOM SOUP

Using a selection of both wild and cultivated mushrooms
produces a soup bursting with flavour. The horseradish
cream provides a welcome kick.

1 Melt the butter in a large saucepan, add the onion, celery, and garlic,
and fry for 3–4 minutes, or until softened.

2 Stir in the mushrooms and continue to fry for a further 5–6 minutes.
Add the potatoes and the stock, and bring to the boil. Reduce the heat
and leave to simmer gently for 30 minutes.

3 Using a blender, whizz the soup until smooth, working in batches if
necessary. Sprinkle over the parsley and season to taste with salt and
pepper. Serve immediately, stirring a little horseradish cream into each
soup bowl, if desired, for an extra kick.

SERVES **4**
PREP **20 MINS**
PLUS 30 MINS STANDING
COOK **1 HR**
FREEZE **UP TO 3 MONTHS**
WITHOUT THE BREAD

PORCINI MUSHROOM SOUP

This hearty Italian country soup has deep, earthy flavours.
Check the mushrooms after soaking, as there may be bits
of dirt or straw that need removing.

30g (1oz) dried porcini
   mushrooms

3 tbsp extra virgin olive oil,
   plus extra to serve

2 onions, finely chopped

2 tsp chopped fresh rosemary
   leaves

1 tsp fresh thyme leaves

2 garlic cloves, finely sliced

115g (4oz) chestnut
   mushrooms, sliced

2 celery sticks with leaves,
   finely chopped

400g can chopped tomatoes

750ml (1¼ pints) vegetable
   stock

salt and freshly ground black
   pepper

½ stale ciabatta or small crusty
   white loaf, torn into chunks

1 Put the dried porcini mushrooms in a heatproof bowl, pour over 300ml (10fl oz) boiling water, and leave to stand for 30 minutes. Drain, reserving the soaking liquid, then chop any large pieces of porcini.

2 Heat the oil in a saucepan, add the onions, cover, and leave to cook for 10 minutes, or until soft. Add the rosemary, thyme, garlic, chestnut mushrooms, and celery, and continue cooking, uncovered, until the celery has softened.

3 Add the tomatoes, porcini, and the stock. Strain the soaking liquid through a piece of muslin or a fine sieve into the pan. Bring the soup to the boil, then lower the heat and simmer gently for 45 minutes.

4 Season to taste with salt and pepper, and add the chunks of bread. Remove the pan from the heat. Cover and leave to stand for 10 minutes before serving. Spoon into deep bowls and drizzle each serving with a little olive oil.

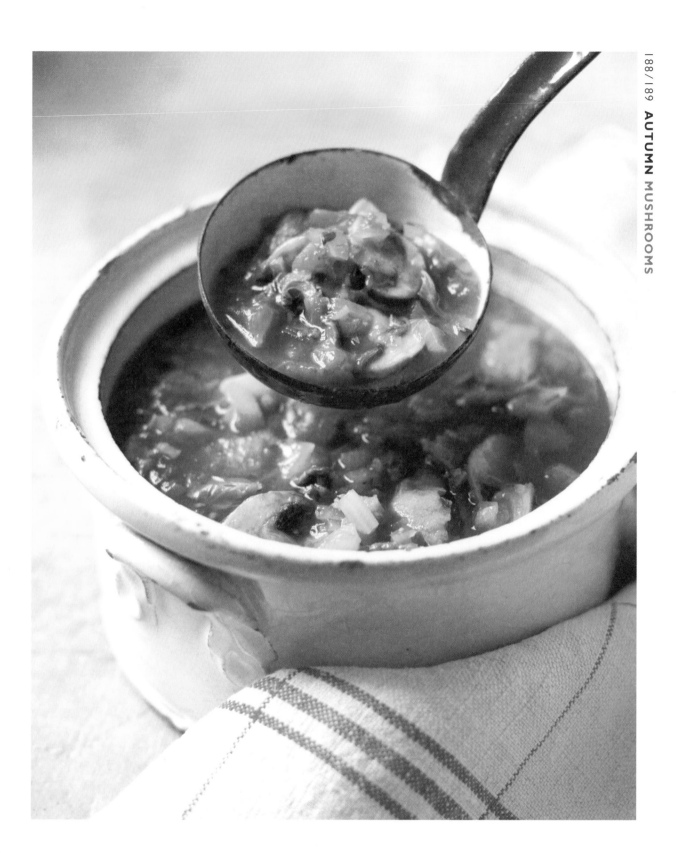

SERVES **6**
PREP **5 MINS**
COOK **15 MINS**
FREEZE **UP TO 3 MONTHS**

KOHLRABI SOUP WITH PESTO

If you are a fan of smooth soups, you can whizz this in a blender
at the end of step 1 and then swirl the pesto through the resulting
delicate light green purée.

25g (scant 1oz) butter

3–4 kohlrabi, cut into
  bite-sized dice

1 litre (1¾ pints) hot
  vegetable stock

2 tbsp crème fraîche

salt and freshly ground
  black pepper

6 tsp pesto, to garnish

1 Melt the butter in a frying pan, add the kohlrabi, and fry for 5 minutes
or until light golden brown. Pour in the stock and bring to the boil.
Add the crème fraîche and season with salt and pepper. Cook for
8–10 minutes or until the kohlrabi is tender but not mushy.

2 Taste and adjust the seasoning, then ladle the soup into warm bowls
and garnish each with a teaspoon of pesto.

SERVES **4–6**
PREP **10 MINS**
COOK **40 MINS**
FREEZE **UP TO 3 MONTHS**
WITHOUT THE CREAM

RECIPE BY
JEFF COX

BROCCOLI SOUP

Jeff Cox was an editor on one of America's first organic gardening magazines, and now writes on cooking and gardening from his home in Sonoma, California.

1 tbsp lemon juice

675g (1½ lb) broccoli florets

45g (1½oz) butter

60g (2oz) celery, finely chopped

125g (4½oz) leeks, white parts only, chopped

4 tbsp plain flour

1.5 litres (2¾ pints) hot chicken stock

salt and freshly ground black pepper

125ml (4fl oz) double cream

2 tbsp snipped chives, to serve

1 Bring a large pot of salted water to the boil and add ½ tbsp of the lemon juice. Add half the florets and cook for 3 minutes, or until just tender. Remove to a colander and run cold water over them to stop the cooking. Let them drain and set aside.

2 In a large saucepan, melt the butter over a medium-low heat. Add the celery and leeks and cook, stirring, for 5–7 minutes or until the vegetables are tender. Add the flour and stir it in thoroughly, then whisk in the stock until the flour is entirely absorbed. Turn the heat to high and bring to a vigorous boil, then reduce the heat to low and simmer for 5 minutes.

3 Chop the uncooked broccoli into small pieces and add to the soup. Simmer for 15 minutes, or until very tender. Process in a blender until almost smooth – you want to retain a slightly grainy texture. Return the purée to the saucepan, season to taste with salt and pepper and the rest of the lemon juice, then add the cream and the reserved broccoli. Reheat and serve, sprinkled with chives.

SERVES **4**
PREP **15 MINS**
COOK **20 MINS**
FREEZE **NOT SUITABLE**

RECIPE BY
SOPHIE GRIGSON

GARLIC BROTH

In Provence, they say "*aïgo boulido sauvo la vido*" – "garlic broth saves your life". Ten cloves of garlic go into this dish, yet it is not terrifyingly garlicky.

10 garlic cloves, crushed

6 sage leaves

1 bay leaf

1 large sprig of thyme

2 tbsp extra virgin olive oil, plus extra to drizzle

1 litre (1¾ pints) water or light chicken stock

salt and freshly ground black pepper

8 croûtes (see p39)

1 garlic clove, halved (optional)

3 egg yolks

grated Gruyère, to serve

1 Put the garlic into a saucepan with the sage, bay leaf, thyme, oil, water or stock, and some salt and pepper. Bring to the boil, then simmer gently for 15 minutes. Meanwhile, rub one side of each croûte with the cut clove of garlic, if using, and place two in each bowl. Drizzle a little oil over each one.

2 Turn off the heat and pick out and discard the bay leaf and thyme (but not the sage). Whisk 3 tbsp of the hot soup into the egg yolks, then pour the whole lot back into the pan and stir. Taste and adjust the seasoning, then transfer the soup to a hot tureen. At the table, ladle the soup into the bowls, set before the diners, and pass round the Gruyère.

SERVES **4**
PREP **20 MINS**
COOK **40 MINS**
FREEZE **NOT SUITABLE**

RECIPE BY
MARIE-PIERRE MOINE

ONION AND GARLIC SOUP

This is excellent with croûtes (see p39). Top them with grated
Gruyère or Cheddar and some freshly ground black pepper,
then flash them under the grill until bubbling.

1 tbsp light olive oil

15g (½oz) butter

1 Spanish onion, finely chopped

1 banana shallot, very finely
chopped

sea salt and freshly ground
black pepper

100ml (3½fl oz) hot water

1 small head of garlic, broken
up into individual cloves but
left unpeeled

150ml (5fl oz) dry white wine

600ml (1 pint) hot vegetable
stock or chicken stock

100ml (3½fl oz) full-fat or
semi-skimmed milk

2 egg yolks

4 heaped tbsp double cream

1 heaped tsp Dijon mustard

1 Heat the oil and butter in a large sauté pan or other heavy-based
pan over a moderate heat. Add the onion and shallot, season lightly
with salt and pepper, and cook for 3 minutes, stirring all the time.
Lower the heat, add the hot water, and cook gently, stirring frequently,
for 20 minutes or until the water has evaporated and the onion
mixture is very soft.

2 Meanwhile, bring some lightly salted water to the boil in a small
pan. Add the garlic and bring back to the boil, then lower the heat
and simmer for 10–15 minutes or until very soft. Drain, then refresh
under cold running water. Pour the wine, stock, and milk into the
onion mixture and bring to a simmer over a moderate heat,
stirring occasionally.

3 Working over a bowl, squeeze each garlic clove between your thumb
and forefinger until the flesh pops out. Add the egg yolks, then mash
the garlic, stirring to make a smooth mix. Gradually whisk in the cream.
Pour in 3 tbsp of the simmering soup and whisk well. Season lightly
with salt and pepper. Whisking vigorously, pour or spoon the garlic
mixture into the soup, keeping the pan over a low heat. Stir in the
mustard, adjust the seasoning, and serve.

SERVES 4
PREP 10 MINS
COOK 1 HR 20 MINS
FREEZE UP TO 1 MONTH
WITHOUT THE CROÛTES AND CHEESE

FRENCH ONION SOUP

This Parisian classic is given extra punch with a spoonful
of brandy in every bowl. Serve it the moment you've made
it – French onion soup must be piping hot.

30g (1oz) butter

1 tbsp sunflower oil

675g (1½lb) onions,
  thinly sliced

1 tsp sugar

salt and freshly ground black
  pepper

120ml (4fl oz) red wine

2 tbsp plain flour

1.5 litres (2¾ pints) hot
  beef stock

4 tbsp brandy

8 croûtes (see p39)

1 garlic clove, cut in half

115g (4oz) Gruyère or
  Emmental, grated

1 Melt the butter with the oil in a large, heavy pan over a low heat.
Add the onions and sugar and turn to coat well. Season with salt and
pepper, then press a piece of damp greaseproof paper on top of the
onions. Cook, uncovered, stirring occasionally, for 40 minutes or until they
are a rich dark brown colour. Take care not to let them stick and burn.

2 Remove the greaseproof paper and stir in the wine. Increase the
heat to medium and stir for 5 minutes while the onions glaze. Sprinkle
in the flour and stir for 2 minutes, then pour in the stock and bring to
the boil. Reduce the heat to low, cover with a lid, and leave to simmer
for 30 minutes. Taste and season with salt and pepper, if necessary.

3 Preheat the grill to its highest setting. Divide the soup among flameproof
bowls and stir 1 tbsp of the brandy into each. Rub the croûtes with the
cut garlic and place one in each bowl. Sprinkle with the cheese and grill
for 2–3 minutes or until the cheese is bubbling and golden. Serve at once.

SERVES **4**
PREP **20 MINS**
PLUS 2 HOURS SALTING
COOK **1 HR**
FREEZE **UP TO 2 MONTHS**
BEFORE CREAM IS ADDED

RECIPE BY
ROOPA GULATI

ONION AND ALMOND SOUP

Meltingly soft onions make a flavoursome base for this
lightly spiced soup enriched with almonds and sweetened
with a hint of caramel.

1 onion, very finely sliced

½ tsp sea salt flakes

vegetable oil, to deep-fry

100g (3½oz) almonds (with
skins on)

750ml (1¼ pints) hot
chicken stock

60g (2oz) butter

¼ tsp nigella seeds

4 large onions, diced

1 red chilli, chopped

1 tsp muscovado sugar

2 tbsp balsamic vinegar

120ml (4fl oz) single cream

salt and freshly ground
black pepper

1 For a fried onion garnish, put the onion slices in a shallow dish, sprinkle with the sea salt, then set to one side for at least 2 hours. Using your hands, squeeze out the liquid, then pat dry with kitchen paper. Deep-fry in hot oil for 1–2 minutes or until golden, then drain on kitchen paper.

2 Bring a small pan of water to the boil, add the almonds, turn off the heat, and cover with a lid. Leave to soak for 15 minutes, then drain and slip off the skins once the nuts are cool enough to handle. Transfer to a food processor with 100ml (3½fl oz) of the stock, then whizz to a paste and set aside.

3 Meanwhile, melt the butter in a large pan, add the nigella seeds, and fry over a gentle heat for 1 minute. Stir in the diced onions and chilli, cover, and cook over a very low heat for 20–30 minutes or until soft but not brown, then turn up the heat and remove the lid. When the onions begin to turn a golden colour, stir in the sugar, and cook until it starts catching on the bottom of the pan. Add the vinegar and continue cooking until sticky.

4 Add the rest of the stock and the almond paste and simmer for 20 minutes. Whizz the soup until smooth in a blender, then return to the pan, stir in the cream, and season with salt and pepper. Reheat gently and serve garnished with the fried onions.

SERVES 6
PREP 20 MINS
PLUS 3 HRS CHILLING
COOK 55 MINS
FREEZE UP TO 3 MONTHS
AT THE END OF STEP 2

½ head new-season garlic,
  roughly chopped

1 large onion, roughly chopped

4 celery stalks, roughly chopped

1 bulb fennel, roughly chopped

90ml (3fl oz) olive oil, plus extra
  to garnish

500g (1lb 2oz) very ripe plum
  tomatoes, roughly chopped

500g (1lb 2oz) very ripe
  beefsteak tomatoes, roughly
  chopped

250g (9oz) cooked beetroot,
  roughly chopped

2 tbsp freshly chopped basil
  (stalks reserved), plus
  6 sprigs, to garnish

salt and freshly ground
  black pepper

50g (1¾oz) red, yellow, or pink
  baby beetroot, to garnish

1 tbsp chives, with blossoms
  if available, to garnish

115g (4oz) red, yellow, or orange
  cherry tomatoes, to garnish

crème fraîche, to garnish
  (optional)

RECIPE BY
SALLY CLARKE

BEETROOT AND TOMATO SOUP

Sally Clarke was one of the first British chefs to champion seasonal, organic food at her London restaurant, Clarkes. "This chilled, fresh-tasting soup is perfect in early autumn."

1 Preheat the oven to 200°C (400°F/Gas 6). In a casserole pan over a low heat, cook the garlic, onion, celery, and fennel in the oil, stirring, for 6–8 minutes. Add the tomatoes, beetroot, and basil stalks. Season. Barely cover with water, bring to the boil, then place, uncovered, in the oven for 40 minutes.

2 Transfer to a blender and whizz until smooth, adding a little water if necessary. Pass through a sieve, pushing as much as you can through with the back of the ladle. Season, then chill in the fridge for at least 3 hours.

3 Cook the baby beetroot in boiling salted water for 20–25 minutes or until tender, then drain, cool, and peel. Top, tail, and halve or quarter, depending on size. Season and stir in the chopped basil, half the chives, and a drizzle of oil. Halve and season the cherry tomatoes.

4 Stir the soup well, check the seasoning, and half-fill six chilled bowls. Spoon the baby beetroots and cherry tomatoes into the centre of each bowl, then garnish with a drizzle of olive oil or a generous scoop of crème fraîche, the basil sprigs, and the rest of the chives, snipped.

SERVES **4**
PREP **15 MINS**
COOK **1½ HRS**
FREEZE **UP TO 3 MONTHS**

45g (1½oz) butter or goose fat

2 large beetroot, roughly grated

1 onion, roughly grated

1 carrot, roughly grated

1 celery stalk, roughly grated

400g can chopped tomatoes

1 garlic clove, crushed (optional)

1.7 litres (3 pints) hot vegetable stock

2 bay leaves

4 cloves

2 tbsp lemon juice

salt and freshly ground black pepper

200ml (7fl oz) soured cream

BORSCHT

This thickly textured, satisfying soup is a Russian classic to enjoy at any time of year and on any occasion. Try it with grated carrot piled on top and hunks of dark rye bread.

1 Melt the butter in a large saucepan over a medium heat. Add the beetroot, onion, carrot, and celery, and cook, stirring, for 5 minutes or until just softened. Add the tomatoes and garlic, if using, and cook for 2–3 minutes, stirring frequently, then stir in the stock.

2 Tie the bay leaves and cloves in a small piece of muslin and add to the pan. Bring the soup to the boil, then lower the heat, cover, and simmer for 1 hour 20 minutes. Discard the muslin bag, stir in the lemon juice, and season to taste with salt and pepper. Ladle the soup into warm bowls and add a swirl of soured cream to each one.

SERVES **4–6**
PREP **10 MINS**
COOK **50 MINS**
FREEZE **UP TO 3 MONTHS**
BEFORE GIN IS ADDED

2 stems of fresh parsley

1 bay leaf

2 large sprigs of fresh dill
    or fennel

2 tbsp sunflower oil

1 onion, chopped

½ tbsp caraway seeds

3 tbsp risotto rice (e.g. arborio)

650g (1½lb) beetroot, peeled
    and grated

1 tbsp lemon juice

1 litre (1¾ pints) beef stock,
    chicken stock, or vegetable
    stock

salt and freshly ground black
    pepper

2 tbsp gin or vodka

soured cream or crème fraîche,
    to serve

chopped fresh dill or chives,
    to serve

RECIPE BY
SOPHIE GRIGSON

BEETROOT AND GIN SOUP

For adults only, with a finishing kick of gin, this dramatic-
looking dark pink dish carries distinct eastern European
flavours of dill, caraway, and soured cream.

1 Make a bouquet garni (see p24) using the parsley, bay leaf, and sprigs
of dill or fennel. Heat the oil in a saucepan and sweat the onion, caraway
seeds, and bouquet garni over a low heat, covered, for 10 minutes.

2 Add the rice to the pan, and stir for about 1 minute to coat it in
the juices. Add the beetroot and lemon juice (to set the colour),
and continue cooking, stirring constantly, for a further 2–3 minutes.

3 Pour in the stock, season with salt and pepper, and bring to the boil.
Simmer for 25–30 minutes, until both the beetroot and rice are tender.
Remove and discard the bouquet garni. Add a splash of water – about
120ml (4fl oz) – to the pan.

4 Whizz the soup in a blender until smooth, in batches if needed. Return
to the pan, adjust the seasoning, and stir in the gin. Reheat thoroughly,
without letting the soup boil. Serve steaming hot, with a generous swirl
of soured cream in each bowl and a sprinkling of dill or chives.

SERVES **4**
PREP **15 MINS**
COOK **45 MINS**
FREEZE **UP TO 3 MONTHS**
WITHOUT THE GOAT'S CHEESE

500–600g (1lb 2oz–1lb 5oz)
  beetroot

500g (1lb 2oz) ripe tomatoes,
  halved

250g (9oz) apples, diced

2 tbsp olive or sunflower oil

1 medium onion, peeled and
  finely chopped

500ml (16fl oz) good strong
  beef stock

salt and freshly ground black
  pepper

125g (4½oz) hard goat's cheese

RECIPE BY
REBECCA SULLIVAN

BEETROOT SOUP WITH GOAT'S CHEESE

Rebecca Sullivan founded Dirty Girl Kitchen and Reap and Sow. "This is a fantastic way to cook beetroot. The cheese complements the round sweetness of the beets."

1 Preheat the oven to 190°C (375°F/Gas 5). Wearing gloves to prevent staining your hands, peel and coarsely grate the beetroot and set aside, then place the tomatoes and apples in an ovenproof dish and drizzle with half the oil. Roast for 25–30 minutes, or until soft and pulpy, then rub them through a sieve to remove the skin and pips.

2 Heat the remaining oil in a pan and sweat the onion for a few minutes until soft. Add the beetroot and stock and bring to the boil, then season to taste and simmer gently for 10 minutes, or until the beetroot is tender. Stir in the tomato and apple purée, transfer to a blender, and process until completely smooth. Taste and adjust the seasoning.

3 To serve cold, chill in the fridge then divide between four bowls. To serve hot, reheat until piping hot but not boiling. In either case, crumble the cheese over each bowl. Serve with crusty bread and butter.

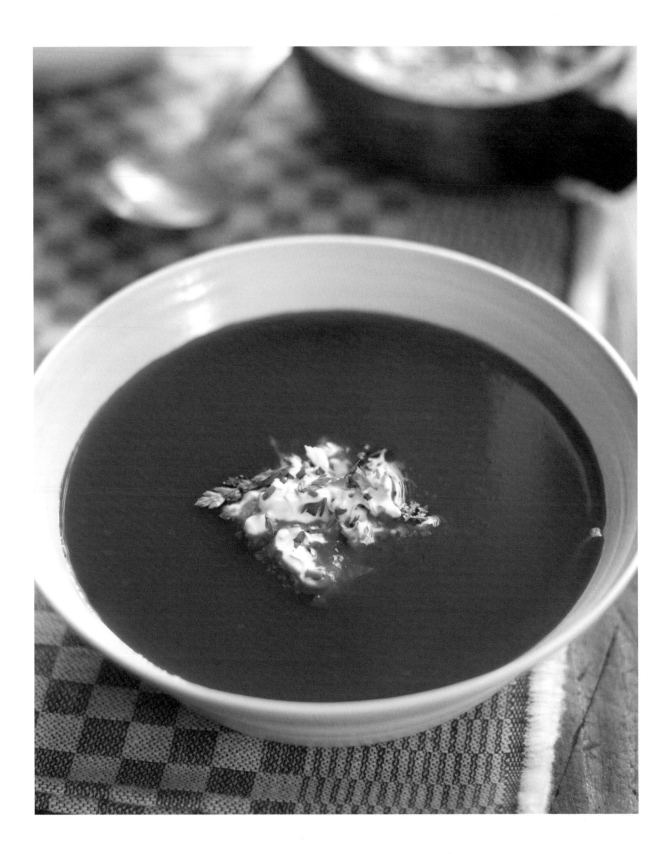

SERVES **6–8**
PREP **20 MINS**
COOK **1 HR**
FREEZE **UP TO 3 MONTHS**
WITHOUT THE HERB CREAM

RECIPE BY
JULIET KINDERSLEY

BEETROOT AND APPLE SOUP

Juliet Kindersley and her husband Peter rear and produce organic meat from Sheepdrove Organic Farm in Berkshire. "We like this soup with plenty of lemon, sugar, salt, and pepper."

1 onion, halved

2 garlic cloves

3 tbsp olive oil

salt and freshly ground black pepper

350g (12oz) raw beetroot, peeled and halved

1 potato, halved

4 eating apples, peeled and cored

1.5 litres (2¾ pints) hot vegetable stock or chicken stock

1–2 tbsp dark brown sugar

juice of 1 lemon

2 tbsp finely chopped parsley, chives, dill, or coriander, or a mixture

200g (7oz) crème fraîche, soured cream, or thick creamy yogurt

1 Grate the onion and garlic in a food processor. Heat the oil in a large pan over a low heat, add the onion, garlic, and a pinch of salt, and cook gently, stirring once or twice, for 5 minutes or until soft. Meanwhile, grate the beetroot, potato, and apples in the food processor.

2 Add the beetroot, potato, and apples to the pan and stew gently for 10 minutes, stirring occasionally. Pour in the stock, bring to the boil, then cover with a lid and simmer gently for 45 minutes or until the beetroot is cooked through.

3 Transfer the mixture to a blender and whizz till smooth. You may need to do this in batches. Season with the sugar, lemon juice, and some salt and pepper.

4 Stir the chopped herbs into the cream or yogurt, then ladle the soup into warm bowls and drop a big spoonful of green-speckled cream into the middle of the deep pink soup.

SERVES **4**
PREP **10 MINS**
COOK **25 MINS**
FREEZE **UP TO 3 MONTHS**
WITHOUT THE CREAM

20g (¾oz) butter

500g (1lb 2oz) butternut squash, deseeded and chopped into 2.5cm (1in) pieces

1 medium onion, chopped

1 garlic clove, crushed

a generous grating of nutmeg

500ml (16fl oz) hot chicken stock

100ml (3½fl oz) single or double cream

salt and freshly ground black pepper

RECIPE BY
CLODAGH MCKENNA

BUTTERNUT SQUASH SOUP

Clodagh McKenna, chef, journalist, and television presenter, has been a driving force behind the Slow Food movement in Ireland and the country's farmers' markets.

1 Melt the butter in a heavy-bottomed saucepan. Add the squash, onion, and garlic, cover with a lid, and cook for 15 minutes, stirring occasionally. Grate in the nutmeg and sweat with the lid on for a further 5 minutes.

2 Stir in the stock and bring to the boil. When the squash is tender, add the cream, and simmer for 1 minute. Transfer the soup to a blender and whizz until smooth. You may need to do this in batches. Season with salt and pepper and serve.

SERVES **4**
PREP **20 MINS**
COOK **50 MINS**
FREEZE **UP TO 3 MONTHS**
BEFORE THE YOGURT IS ADDED

675g (1½lb) sweet potatoes,
cut into big chunks

6 large shallots, quartered

3 plump garlic cloves, unpeeled

1 carrot, cut into big chunks

1 tbsp harissa (see p208), plus
extra to serve

2 tbsp olive oil

salt and freshly ground black
pepper

900ml (1½ pints) hot vegetable
stock

1 tsp runny honey

generous squeeze of lemon
juice

natural yogurt, to serve

warm pitta bread, to serve

RECIPE BY
ANGELA NILSEN

MOROCCAN ROASTED SWEET POTATO SOUP

The vegetables for this soup are cooked in the oven, which brings out their naturally sweet flavour. This is delicious served with warm pitta bread.

1 Preheat the oven to 200°C (400°F/Gas 6). Put the sweet potatoes, shallots, garlic, and carrot in a roasting tin. Mix the harissa with the oil, then pour over the vegetables and toss together so they are all well coated. Season with pepper, then roast, turning occasionally, for 40 minutes or until tender and turning golden. Remove from the oven.

2 Squeeze the garlic cloves out of their skins into the roasting tin. Stir in the stock and honey, then scrape up all the bits from the bottom of the tin. Carefully transfer to a blender and whizz until smooth. You may need to do this in batches. Pour into a saucepan and reheat gently.

3 Add a good squeeze of lemon juice and season to taste with salt and pepper. Swirl the yogurt with a little harissa and top each bowl with a spoonful. Serve with warm pitta bread.

SERVES **4**
PREP **20 MINS**
COOK **20–25 MINS**
FREEZE **UP TO 3 MONTHS**

2 tbsp olive oil

1 onion, chopped

2 garlic cloves, finely chopped

2 tsp finely grated root ginger

¼ tsp dried crushed chillies

450g (1lb) sweet potatoes, cut into small chunks

1 red pepper, deseeded and chopped

230g can tomatoes

1 tsp cumin seeds, dry-roasted and crushed (see p25)

1 tsp coriander seeds, dry-roasted and crushed

900ml (1½ pints) hot vegetable stock

2–3 tbsp smooth or crunchy peanut butter

few drops of Tabasco (optional)

chilli oil, to serve

RECIPE BY
ANGELA NILSEN

AFRICAN SWEET POTATO SOUP

This recipe is based on a classic African soup that is hot and spicy and full of flavour. The peanut butter lends a rich, satisfying earthiness.

1 Heat the oil in a large pan, add the onion, and fry for 3 minutes. Stir in the garlic, ginger, and chillies and fry for 1 minute, then stir in the sweet potatoes, pepper, tomatoes, and crushed spices and fry for 2 minutes. Pour in the stock, bring to the boil, then simmer for 12–15 minutes or until the sweet potatoes are tender.

2 Remove from the heat and whizz in a blender until smooth. You may need to do this in batches. Pass the soup through a sieve to remove the pepper skin and then stir in the peanut butter, tasting to decide the amount you like. If you want to add more heat, splash in some Tabasco. Reheat gently, then drizzle a little chilli oil over each bowl to serve.

SERVES **4**
PREP **25 MINS**
COOK **45 MINS**
FREEZE **UP TO 3 MONTHS**

FOR THE HARISSA PASTE

1 red pepper

2 tbsp olive oil

½ tsp coriander seeds

2 tsp cumin seeds

1 tsp caraway seeds

2 tsp tomato purée

3 garlic cloves, roughly chopped

4 red chillies, seeds removed, roughly chopped

1 tsp smoked paprika

juice of 1 lemon

FOR THE SOUP

1 tbsp olive oil

100g (3½oz) smoked pancetta, cubed

2 red onions, diced

1 potato, peeled and diced

3 sticks celery, diced

1 small fennel, thinly sliced

3 tbsp oregano leaves, chopped

400g (14oz) can chopped tomatoes

750ml (1¼ pints) vegetable stock

400g can chickpeas, drained

1 bay leaf

RECIPE BY
ROOPA GULATI

HARISSA AND CHICKPEA SOUP

This chunky vegetable soup owes much of its appeal to the robust nature of homemade harissa, which can be made in advance and stored in the refrigerator.

1 To make the harissa, rub the red pepper with olive oil and cook under a hot grill for 10–15 minutes, turning frequently, until the skin is blackened and charred. Remove to a bowl, cover with cling film, and leave to cool. Peel away the skin, discard the seeds, and roughly chop the flesh.

2 Heat a small frying pan over a low heat and roast the coriander, cumin, and caraway seeds for about a minute, stirring. Using a mortar and pestle, pound the spices to a powder. Transfer to a food processor and add the red pepper along with the tomato purée, garlic, red chillies, paprika, and lemon juice. Process until smooth, gradually adding the remaining olive oil.

3 For the soup, heat the olive oil in a large saucepan and fry the pancetta until golden, then remove. Add the onion, potato, celery, fennel, and oregano to the pan. Cover and soften over a low heat for 10 minutes. Stir in 1–2 tbsp of the harissa paste and the tomatoes and continue cooking for 5 minutes. Add the stock, pancetta, chickpeas, and bay leaf. Season well and simmer in a half-covered pan for 20 minutes. Remove the bay leaf and serve.

SERVES **4**
PREP **30 MINS**
COOK **I HR**
PLUS I HR CHILLING
FREEZE **NOT SUITABLE**

500g (Ilb 2oz) ripe rosehips, rinsed

I vanilla pod, split lengthways

caster sugar, to taste

100ml (3½fl oz) whipping cream

3 tbsp natural yogurt

2 tbsp lemon juice

50g (1¾oz) slivered almonds, toasted and sprinkled with sugar, to serve

Amaretti biscuits, to serve

RECIPE BY
MARIE-PIERRE MOINE

ROSEHIP SOUP

Rosehip soup is very popular in Scandinavia where it is served both chilled and hot. Fresh rosehips are best, but you can also make this soup with pre-soaked dried rosehips.

I Put the rosehips in a large saucepan and pour over boiling water to cover generously. Add the vanilla pod. Simmer over a low heat for about 20–30 minutes until soft. Strain the rosehips through a sieve over a bowl, then set aside the cooking liquid as well as the vanilla pod.

2 Over a clean bowl, press the rosehips through the sieve to extract a purée, and set aside. Tip what's left in the sieve into the saucepan. Add the reserved cooking liquid and the vanilla pod. Return to a simmer, and cook for 20 minutes. Strain enough of the mixture into the reserved purée to produce a smooth soup. Stir in sugar to taste. Chill for one hour or until ready to serve.

3 Just before serving, whisk the cream and yogurt together, and sweeten to taste. Stir the lemon juice into the chilled soup, and pour or spoon into glass coupes or bowls. Add a sprinkling of almonds and a dollop of whisked cream, and serve chilled with the Amaretti biscuits on the side.

SERVES **2–3**
PREP **40 MINS**
COOK **20 MINS**
FREEZE **UP TO 2 MONTHS**
WITHOUT CREAM AND CORIANDER

125g (4½oz) (shelled weight)
  unsalted pistachio nuts

1 green chilli, cut in half and
  deseeded

120ml (4fl oz) hot water

6 green cardamom pods,
  crushed and seeds extracted

1 small blade of mace

½ tsp coriander seeds,
  dry-roasted (see p25)

25g (scant 1oz) butter

2 large garlic cloves, finely
  chopped

small bunch of spring onions
  (white parts only), finely
  chopped

2.5cm (1in) piece of root
  ginger, peeled and finely
  chopped

½ tsp garam masala

450ml (15fl oz) hot vegetable
  stock

100ml (3½fl oz) single cream

1 tbsp chopped coriander
  leaves

salt and freshly ground
  black pepper

RECIPE BY
ROOPA GULATI

CREAMY PISTACHIO SOUP

As delicate as it is delicious, this pretty, pastel-green soup
is scented with citrussy cardamom notes, which make a
marvellous marriage with the pounded pistachios.

1 Bring a pan of water to the boil, add the pistachios, and cook for
2–3 minutes. Drain in a colander and refresh under cold running water.
Pat the nuts dry with kitchen paper, then turn out on to a tea towel.
Give them a vigorous rub with the towel – the skins should slip off easily.
Roughly chop a generous tablespoon of the nuts, then set them aside for
garnish. Put the remaining nuts in a food processor. Add the chilli and hot
water and process to a rough paste, then set aside.

2 Grind the cardamom seeds, mace, and coriander to a powder with
a pestle and mortar. Melt the butter in a saucepan over a medium heat,
add the garlic, spring onions, and ginger, and soften for 2–3 minutes. Stir
in the ground spices and garam masala and cook for a few seconds, then
add the pistachio paste and stock. Simmer, without a lid, for 10–15 minutes,
stirring occasionally.

3 Blend in batches until smooth. Stir in the cream and coriander leaves,
then season with salt and pepper. Serve the soup garnished with the
reserved pistachio nuts.

SERVES **4–6**
PREP **7 MINS**
COOK **40 MINS**
FREEZE **NOT SUITABLE**

RECIPE BY
SOPHIE GRIGSON

WIDOW'S SOUP

A Maltese tale tells of a poor widow who had only home-grown vegetables, eggs from her chickens, and a little soft cheese. She made this simple, delicious soup.

1 tbsp olive oil

1 large onion, chopped

1 large potato, chopped

175g (6oz) cauliflower
   florets, quartered

175g (6oz) carrots, sliced

1 small lettuce, shredded

175g (6oz) shelled fresh peas
   or thawed frozen peas

250g (9oz) tomatoes, skinned
   and roughly chopped, or
   half a 400g (14oz) tin
   chopped tomatoes

1½ tbsp tomato purée

1 tsp sugar

1 tsp red wine vinegar

salt and freshly ground
   black pepper

4–6 eggs

250g (9oz) ricotta cheese or
   firm young goat's cheese

1 Heat the oil in a large pan, and fry the onion until soft, but not coloured. Add the potato, cauliflower, carrots, lettuce, and fresh peas, if using. Stir, then add the tomatoes, tomato purée, sugar, vinegar, salt and pepper, and enough water (or stock) to cover generously. Bring to the boil and simmer until the vegetables are almost tender. If using thawed frozen peas, add them now. Taste and adjust the seasoning.

2 Reduce the heat so that the surface of the soup is barely trembling. Break the eggs one at a time onto a saucer, and slip them into the soup to poach them until the white has just set, about 8–10 minutes.

3 Cut the cheese into 4–6 pieces, according to the number of serving bowls, and place one in each bowl. Carefully place one egg in each bowl, and ladle the soup around the eggs and cheese before serving.

SERVES **4**
PREP **10 MINS**
COOK **20 MINS**
FREEZE **UP TO 3 MONTHS**
AT THE END OF STEP 1

RECIPE BY
SOPHIE GRIGSON

PEAR AND STILTON SOUP

Rich and fragrant, this characterful soup should be served
in small portions. Play around with the quantities of pear and
Stilton to find the right balance for you.

1 onion, chopped

15g (½oz) unsalted butter

4 ripe pears, cored and
  chopped

750ml (1¼ pints) chicken stock

salt and freshly ground black
  pepper

125g (4½oz) Stilton, crumbled

juice of ½–1 lemon, to taste

fresh chives, chopped, to serve

1 In a large pan, cook the onion gently in the butter without browning. Add the pears and the stock and season lightly. Simmer until the pears are very tender. Pass through the fine blade of a mouli-legumes, or process in a blender until smooth. If making this soup in advance, cool it now and continue when you want to serve.

2 Return to the pan and reheat, without boiling. Add the Stilton and stir until melted. Sharpen with lemon juice to taste and adjust the seasoning. Sprinkle the chives over the top and serve.

SERVES **4**
PREP **15 MINS**
COOK **35 MINS**
FREEZE **NOT SUITABLE**

RECIPE BY
ROSEMARY SHRAGER

MUSSEL AND SAFFRON SOUP

Rosemary Shrager is a chef, food writer, and television presenter, and also runs an acclaimed cookery school. "This is a wonderful, unusual, inspired soup."

2kg (4½lb) mussels, scrubbed and debearded

100ml (3½fl oz) dry white wine

500ml (16fl oz) fish or chicken stock

30g (1oz) butter

125g (4½oz) onions, finely chopped

125g (4½oz) carrots, diced

85g (3oz) celeriac, diced

1 thin leek, finely sliced

1 garlic clove, chopped

1 tbsp curry powder

good pinch of saffron threads, soaked in 2 tbsp hot water

250ml (8fl oz) double cream

salt and freshly ground black pepper

2 tbsp parsley, finely chopped

1 Wash the mussels under cold running water. Give any open ones a firm tap against the counter top and discard any that don't close.

2 Bring the wine and stock to a boil in a large sauté pan over a high heat. Add the mussels, cover, and cook. As the mussels open, remove them to a bowl. When all are open, filter the liquid through muslin into another bowl.

3 Clean the sauté pan. Melt the butter over a low heat and add the vegetables and garlic, stirring well. Cook for 10 minutes, then stir in the curry powder and add the mussel liquid and the saffron in its water. Add the cream and cook without boiling for 5 minutes. Return the mussels to the pan, heat through gently, and season well. Sprinkle over the parsley, and serve.

SERVES **4**
PREP **15 MINS**
COOK **45 MINS**
FREEZE **UP TO 1 MONTH**

RECIPE BY
MARIE-PIERRE MOINE

MUSSEL AND FENNEL SOUP

A typical Provence concoction, this mussel and fennel
soup harmoniously combines seafood and vegetables
in a fragrant broth.

1kg (2¼lb) mussels, scrubbed
and debearded

500ml (16fl oz) dry white wine

4 medium, ripe tomatoes

3 tbsp olive oil

1 leek, chopped

2 sprigs of fresh flat-leaf parsley

2 sprigs of thyme

1 bay leaf

¼ small fennel bulb, chopped

5cm (2in) piece dried orange
peel

fine sea salt and freshly ground
black pepper

1 large floury potato, peeled
and chopped

pinch of saffron strands

1 Wash the mussels under cold running water. Give any open ones
a firm tap against the counter top and discard any that don't close.

2 Tip the mussels into a large saucepan and add the wine. Cover the pan,
put over a high heat, and cook for 5–6 minutes, shaking occasionally, until
the mussels open (discard any that remain stubbornly closed). Remove
from the heat. Line a sieve with muslin and place over a bowl. Tip the
mussels into the sieve and leave until cool enough to handle, then remove
and discard the shells. Reserve both the mussels and the cooking liquid.

3 Pierce the tomatoes with a knife, put them in a bowl and pour over
boiling water to cover. Leave for 1 minute, then drain and slip off the skins.
Quarter the tomatoes, remove and discard the seeds, and chop the flesh.
Heat the oil in a large sauté pan over a moderate heat. Add the tomatoes,
leek, herbs, fennel, and orange peel and season. Cook until softened,
stirring frequently.

4 Add the mussel cooking liquid to the pan, then 500ml (16fl oz) of
just-boiled water. Bring to a simmer. Add the potato and cook until soft.
Remove from the heat, leave to cool a little, then remove the herbs and
orange peel. Mash the potato pieces into the soup to thicken.

5 Soften the saffron in a small bowl with a spoonful of soup, then stir
it back in. Taste and adjust the seasoning, add the mussels, reheat gently,
and serve immediately.

SERVES 2–4
PREP 20 MINS
COOK 30–35 MINS
FREEZE NOT SUITABLE

RECIPE BY
ROOPA GULATI

MUSSELS IN A GINGER AND CHILLI BROTH

These succulent mussels in their moat of gingery juices are terrific with a mound of fluffy rice on the side, but crusty bread mops up the broth just as nicely.

1.5kg (3lb) mussels, scrubbed and debearded

100g (4oz) butter

2 onions, finely chopped

2 bird's eye red chillies, finely chopped

5cm (2in) fresh root ginger, finely shredded

5 large garlic cloves, finely chopped

2 stalks lemongrass, split lengthways and lightly bruised

125ml (4fl oz) ginger wine

400ml (14fl oz) fish stock

150ml (5fl oz) coconut milk

3 tbsp coconut cream

salt and freshly ground black pepper

juice of 1–2 limes, to taste

3 tbsp chopped fresh coriander leaves

1 Wash the mussels under cold running water. Give any open ones a firm tap against the counter top and discard any that don't close.

2 Melt the butter in a large pan over a low heat and gently cook the onions, chillies, ginger, garlic, and lemongrass for 10 minutes until soft but not coloured.

3 Turn the heat up high and add the ginger wine followed by the stock. Bring to the boil before tipping in the mussels. Cover the pan and cook for 5–7 minutes, until the mussel shells have opened. Discard the lemongrass along with any mussels that remain closed after cooking.

4 Pour in the coconut milk and cream, and bring to the boil. Season with salt and pepper, sharpen with lime juice, and stir in the coriander leaves before serving.

SERVES 4
PREP 20 MINS
COOK 30 MINS
FREEZE NOT SUITABLE

RECIPE BY
MARIE-PIERRE MOINE

MOUCLADE

This aromatic soup comes from France's Atlantic coast. You can prepare it ahead but take care to reheat the mussels gently or they will become tough and overcooked.

1.5kg (3lb 3oz) small fresh mussels, scrubbed and debearded

45g (1¼oz) butter

1 large banana shallot, finely chopped

350ml (12fl oz) dry white wine

several sprigs of flat-leaf parsley

¼ small fennel bulb, chopped

1 bay leaf

sea salt and freshly ground black pepper

pinch of cayenne

1 large egg yolk

5 tbsp soured cream or crème fraîche

1 large garlic clove, crushed

½ tsp mild paprika or 1 tsp mild curry powder

a few strands of saffron or ¼ tsp ground saffron

chunks of fresh warm bread, to serve

1 Wash the mussels under cold running water. Give any open ones a firm tap against the counter top and discard any that don't close.

2 Put a large sauté pan over a moderate heat. Tip in the mussels with 15g (½oz) of the butter, the shallot, wine, and 350ml (12fl oz) water. Add the parsley, fennel and bay leaf, season lightly, and add the cayenne. Increase the heat and bring to the boil. Cover and cook the mussels for 4–5 minutes, or until they open, shaking the pan a few times.

3 Using a slotted spoon, lift out the mussels and put in a bowl. Discard any that haven't opened and set aside the rest. Strain the liquor through a muslin-lined sieve into a bowl and set aside. In a small bowl, mix the egg yolk with the soured cream until smooth. In a separate bowl, using a fork, mash the remaining butter with the garlic, paprika, and saffron.

4 Shell the mussels, keeping 12 in their shells, and moisten them all with a little of the cooking liquid. Keep warm.

5 Put a large pan over a low heat. Add the butter and, when it bubbles, pour in the mussel liquor, stir and bring to a simmer. Remove 3 tbsp and whisk it into the egg mixture, then whisk this back into the pan and stir until hot and blended. Adjust the seasoning and divide the mussels between four warm bowls. Pour the broth over and serve with the bread.

SERVES **4**
PREP **15 MINS**
COOK **35 MINS**
FREEZE **NOT SUITABLE**

MANHATTAN CLAM CHOWDER

There are several variations on Manhattan clam chowder, using vegetables such as celery and green peppers. Its defining feature is its tomato base.

36 live clams, freshly bought

1 tbsp oil

115g (4oz) thick-cut rindless streaky bacon rashers, diced

1 onion, finely chopped

2 floury potatoes, such as King Edward, peeled and cut into 1cm (½in) cubes

2 tbsp plain white flour

2 x 400g cans of chopped tomatoes with their juice

salt and freshly ground black pepper

fresh thyme, to garnish

1 Discard any clams that are open. Shuck the clams and reserve the juice in a measuring jug, topping up with water to make 600ml (1 pint). Chop the clams.

2 Heat the oil in a large, heavy saucepan and fry the bacon over a medium heat, stirring frequently, for 5 minutes, or until it is crisp. Remove from the pan with a slotted spoon, drain on kitchen paper and set aside.

3 Add the onion and potatoes to the pan and fry for 5 minutes, or until the onion has softened. Add the flour and stir for 2 minutes.

4 Stir in the tomatoes and their juice and season to taste with salt and pepper. Cover the pan, reduce the heat and leave to simmer for 20 minutes or until the potatoes are tender. Add the clams and simmer gently, uncovered, for 5 minutes. Serve the chowder hot, sprinkled with bacon and thyme.

SERVES **4–6**
PREP **25 MINS**
COOK **1 HR 30 MINS**
FREEZE **NOT SUITABLE**

1kg (2¼lb) clams

120ml (4fl oz) dry white wine

2–3 tbsp olive oil

2 celery stalks, finely diced

1 red onion, finely chopped

1 carrot, finely chopped

4 tomatoes, skinned, deseeded, and chopped

2 medium potatoes, finely diced

1 litre (1¾ pints) cold filtered water

1 sprig of rosemary

1 tbsp finely chopped flat-leaf parsley or chervil

salt and freshly ground black pepper

4–6 slices country bread

RECIPE BY
ARTHUR POTTS DAWSON

POTATO AND CLAM SOUP

Arthur Potts Dawson, founder of the eco-friendly restaurant Acorn House in London, writes, "This is a delicious autumn soup for all the family."

1 Wash the clams thoroughly in cold running water, throwing away any with broken shells and any that are open and won't close when gently tapped. Put them in a large frying pan with the wine, cover with a lid, and place on a high heat for 5 minutes or until the shells open. Discard any that remain closed as they will not be edible. Drain, reserving the liquid. Remove the clams from their shells, place in a bowl, cover, and refrigerate until needed. Strain the cooking liquid through a fine sieve.

2 Heat the oil in a large, heavy pan, add the celery, onion, and carrot, and cook on a low heat for 10 minutes or until light brown. Add the tomatoes, potatoes, the reserved cooking liquid, and the filtered water, and bring to the boil. Add the rosemary, then lower the heat, cover with a lid, and simmer for 1 hour.

3 Stir in the clams and the parsley or chervil, then season with salt and pepper. Remove the rosemary, put a slice of bread in the bottom of each bowl, and ladle over the soup.

SERVES **4**
PREP **15 MINS**
COOK **35 MINS**
FREEZE **NOT SUITABLE**

NEW ENGLAND CLAM CHOWDER

Americans often serve this traditional, creamy soup with saltine crackers, though cream crackers are also good. The clams must be cooked on the day of purchase.

36 live clams

1 tbsp oil

115g (4oz) thick-cut rindless streaky bacon rashers, diced

2 floury potatoes, such as King Edward, peeled and cut into 1cm (½in) cubes

1 onion, finely chopped

2 tbsp plain white flour

600ml (1 pint) whole milk

salt and freshly ground black pepper

120ml (4fl oz) single cream

2 tbsp finely chopped flat-leaf parsley

1 Discard any open clams, then shuck the rest, reserving the juices. Add enough water to the juices to make 600ml (1 pint). Chop the clams. Heat the oil in a large, heavy saucepan and fry the bacon over a medium heat for 5 minutes or until crisp. Remove and drain on kitchen paper.

2 Add the potatoes and onion to the pan and fry for 5 minutes or until the onion has softened. Add the flour and stir for 2 minutes. Stir in the clam juice and milk and season to taste. Cover with a lid, lower the heat, and simmer for 20 minutes or until the potatoes are tender. Add the clams and simmer gently, uncovered, for 5 minutes. Stir in the cream and reheat without boiling. Serve sprinkled with the bacon and parsley.

SERVES **6**
PREP **10 MINS**
COOK **30 MINS**
FREEZE **NOT SUITABLE**

25g (scant 1oz) butter

2 onions, finely chopped

1 clove garlic, chopped

45g (1½oz) plain flour

750ml (1¼ pints) chicken stock

150ml (5fl oz) German
  wheat beer

150g (5½oz) Emmental,
  finely grated

150g (5½oz) Gruyère,
  finely grated

freshly ground white pepper

1 tbsp fresh thyme leaves,
  to garnish

EMMENTAL AND BEER SOUP

German-style cheese soups are often flavoured with beer, sometimes using lager or pilsner. This version uses wheat beer, and is thick and rich with a good blend of flavours.

1 Melt the butter over a low heat in a large, heavy pan. Add the onion and garlic and sauté for 10 minutes until soft but not coloured. Gradually stir in the flour, then add the stock a little at a time, stirring constantly until smooth. Bring to the boil, then keep at a gentle bubbling boil for 10 minutes or until the liquid begins to thicken slightly. Stir regularly to ensure the mixture doesn't start to stick to the pan. Add the wheat beer and return to a gentle boil.

2 Remove from the heat and very gradually add the two cheeses, adding a handful at a time and stirring constantly. Season to taste with pepper, pour into warm soup bowls and top with fresh thyme. Serve with German bread and beer.

SERVES **4–6**
PREP **10 MINS**
COOK **20 MINS**
FREEZE **NOT SUITABLE**

1.5 litres (2¾ pints) chicken
   stock

100g (3½oz) soup pasta

4 eggs

½ tsp freshly grated nutmeg

salt and freshly ground black
   pepper

2 tbsp grated Parmesan cheese

1 tbsp chopped parsley

1 tbsp olive oil

STRACCIATELLA WITH PASTA

This recipe depends on the quality of its few ingredients,
so always try to use homemade stock, organic eggs, and
the best Parmesan cheese you can find.

1 Place the stock in a large pan and bring to the boil. Add the pasta and
cook according to packet directions, or until al dente.

2 Break the eggs into a small bowl, add the nutmeg, season to taste with
salt and pepper, and whisk lightly with a fork to break up the egg. Add the
Parmesan and parsley.

3 Add the olive oil to the simmering stock, reduce the heat to low, then
stir the stock lightly to create a gentle "whirlpool". Gradually pour in
the eggs and cook for 1 minute, without boiling, so they set into fine
strands. Leave to stand for 1 minute before serving.

SERVES 4
PREP 10 MINS
PLUS 30 MINS SOAKING
COOK 15 MINS
FREEZE NOT SUITABLE

45g (1½oz) dried shiitake
 mushrooms

600ml (1 pint) chicken stock

2 skinless boneless chicken breasts

175g (6oz) dried rice vermicelli

100g (3½oz) sweetcorn kernels

SHIITAKE CHICKEN NOODLE SOUP

Here, a nourishing chicken stock combines with
the sweetness of sweetcorn and satisfying vermicelli
to create a soothing meal in a bowl.

1 Place the dried shiitake mushrooms in a heatproof bowl, pour
over 300ml (10fl oz) boiling water, and leave to stand for 30 minutes.
Reserving the mushrooms, strain the soaking water into a large
saucepan and add the stock. Bring the pan to the boil.

2 Slice the mushrooms and cut or shred the chicken breasts into
bite-sized pieces or thin strips. Break the rice vermicelli into short
lengths and stir into the pan. Bring to a simmer and cook for 2 minutes.

3 Add the mushrooms, chicken, and sweetcorn kernels to the pan, bring
back to the boil, and simmer for a further 2 minutes, or until the
chicken is cooked and vermicelli are tender. Spoon into bowls and
serve at once.

SERVES 4–6
PREP 10 MINS
COOK 1 HR
FREEZE UP TO 3 MONTHS

4 chicken drumsticks

1.25kg (2¾lb) mixed vegetables, e.g. carrots (diced), kohlrabi (diced), green beans (topped and tailed; strings removed), cauliflower or broccoli (small florets), leeks (sliced), courgettes (sliced), peas

100g (3½oz) soup vermicelli

sea salt and freshly ground black pepper

2 tablespoons chopped parsley

CHICKEN SOUP WITH PASTA

The pasta and the liberal quantities of vegetables ensure that this chicken soup goes a long way. You can use whatever fresh vegetables are available.

1 Put the chicken drumsticks in a large saucepan, cover with 1.2 litres (2 pints) cold water and bring to the boil. Cover and cook over medium heat for about 40 minutes, skimming occasionally with a slotted spoon. Remove from the heat and strain into a clean pan, then allow the stock to cool slightly before skimming the fat from the surface with a spoon.

2 Remove and discard the skin from the chicken drumsticks, strip the meat from the bones, shred and set aside.

3 Bring the stock back to the boil again, then add the vegetables. Add those with longer cooking times first, cover and simmer for 5 minutes; then add the remaining vegetables and the soup vermicelli and cover and cook for a further 5 minutes.

4 Season the soup with salt and pepper to taste. Add the reserved meat and heat it through. Ladle into bowls, garnish each with a little chopped parsley, and serve piping hot.

SERVES **6**
PREP **20 MINS**
COOK **1½ HRS**
FREEZE **UP TO 3 MONTHS**
WITHOUT THE RICE

2 chicken leg and thigh portions

200g (7oz) smoked lardons
    or diced pancetta

2 boneless belly pork slices,
    rinded and diced

900ml (1½ pints) chicken stock

1 bay leaf

2 red peppers

30g (1oz) butter

1 onion, chopped

1 garlic clove, chopped

1 celery heart, sliced

3 tbsp plain flour

2 beefsteak tomatoes, skinned
    and chopped

2 tbsp tomato purée

115g (4oz) thin green beans,
    trimmed and cut in short
    lengths

150g (5½oz) okra, cut in short
    lengths

2 large sprigs of fresh thyme,
    chopped, plus a little extra
    to garnish

2 tsp sweet paprika

1 tsp smoked paprika

1 tsp light brown sugar

a few drops of Tabasco

salt and freshly ground black
    pepper

225g (8oz) long-grain rice,
    boiled

RECIPE BY
CAROLYN HUMPHRIES

CHICKEN AND PORK GUMBO

You can vary this dish by substituting smoked pork sausage for pancetta or using duck instead of chicken. You may wish to add a little filé powder, if you have it.

1 Put the chicken, lardons or pancetta, and belly pork in a saucepan with the stock and bay leaf. Bring to the boil, reduce the heat, cover, and simmer gently for 1 hour. Meanwhile, roast the peppers under a hot grill for 10–15 minutes until blackened. Put in a plastic bag, leave to cool then peel off the skin, discard the stalks and seeds, rinse, and dice the flesh.

2 Strain the stock through a sieve and set aside. Lift the chicken out of the sieve and place on a board. Remove all the meat from the bones and cut into neat pieces, discarding the skin. Add to the pork and set aside.

3 Melt the butter in the pan. Fry the onion, garlic, and celery for 2 minutes, stirring. Stir in the flour and cook for 3 minutes, stirring, until golden. Remove from the heat and blend in the stock. Return to the heat and bring to the boil. Add the remaining ingredients except the meat and rice. Bring back to the boil, reduce the heat, partially cover and simmer for 30 minutes. Stir in the meats, taste and season with Tabasco, salt and pepper. Remove the bay leaf. Spoon the rice into bowls, ladle the gumbo over, and garnish with thyme.

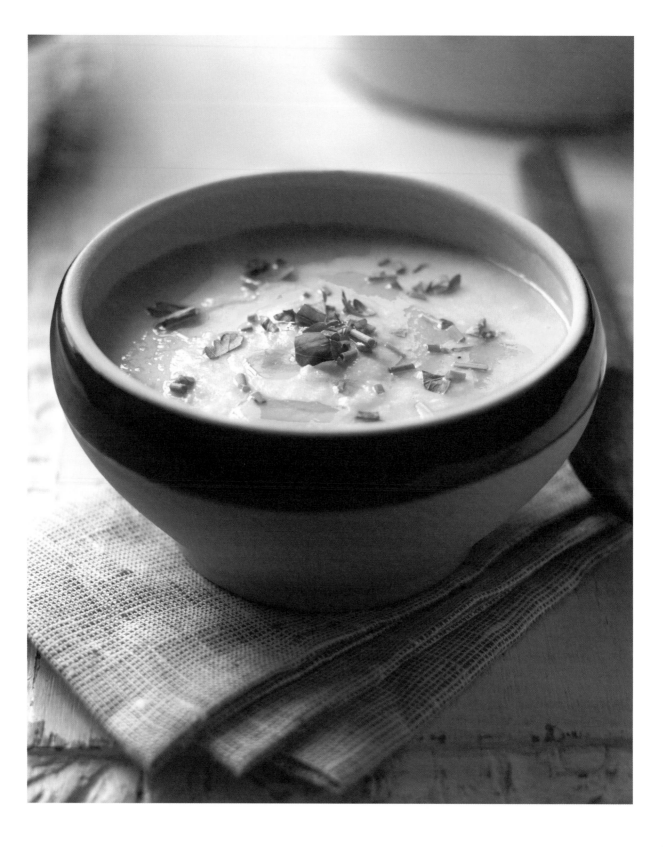

SERVES 6
PREP 15 MINS
PLUS OVERNIGHT SOAKING
COOK 1 HR 40 MINS
FREEZE UP TO 3 MONTHS

RECIPE BY
SHAUN HILL

CHICKEN AND CHICKPEA SOUP

Shaun Hill of The Walnut Tree, near Abergavenny, says,
"The drumstick makes this a questionable dish for your
vegetarian friends – unless you are an accomplished liar."

200g (7oz) chickpeas, soaked in
water overnight, then drained

2.5 litres (4¼ pints) cold water

1 chicken drumstick

4 tbsp olive oil

2 celery stalks, chopped

1 medium onion, chopped

1 medium leek, chopped

3 garlic cloves, finely sliced

salt and freshly ground
black pepper

100ml (3½fl oz) dry white wine

1 tbsp lemon juice

6 tbsp extra virgin olive oil,
to serve

2 tbsp chopped chives and
parsley, to garnish

1 Put the chickpeas in a saucepan with plenty of cold water and bring
to the boil. Skim away any foam with a slotted spoon, then drain and
return to the pan. Add the cold water and chicken, bring to the boil,
and skim again. Cover with a lid and simmer for 1½ hours or until the
peas are done. Lift out the chicken after 45 minutes, remove the meat,
and set to one side.

2 Heat 1 tbsp of the oil in a frying pan, add the celery, onion, and leek,
and cook for 5–10 minutes or until soft. Add the garlic, season with
salt and pepper, then fry for another minute. Add the contents of the
frying pan to the chickpeas, then stir in the cooked chicken. Pour in
a little water if the mixture seems too thick to blend.

3 Transfer the soup to a blender and whizz in batches until smooth, adding
the wine, lemon juice, and the remaining 3 tbsp olive oil in three or four
stages. Season with salt and pepper, then return to the pan and heat
through. Divide the soup among six bowls, drizzle 1 tbsp of extra virgin
olive oil on the top of each one, then serve garnished with the chopped
chives and parsley.

SERVES **4**
PREP **20 MINS**
COOK **30–35 MINS**
FREEZE **UP TO 3 MONTHS**

RECIPE BY
ERIC TREUILLE

SAUSAGE AND BEAN SOUP

Eric Treuille of Books for Cooks, a cookery mecca in Notting Hill, London, writes, "We use chicken, honey, and herb sausages in this dish, but other types work just as well."

250g (9oz) cherry tomatoes, halved

4 tbsp olive oil, plus extra to serve

salt and freshly ground black pepper

1 tbsp balsamic vinegar

1 onion, finely chopped

200g (7oz) organic chicken or other good-quality pure-meat sausages or chorizo, skinned and roughly crumbled

4 garlic cloves, finely chopped

½–1 tsp crushed chilli flakes (according to taste)

400g can cannellini beans, drained, rinsed, and drained again

750ml (1¼ pints) hot chicken stock or vegetable stock

1 handful flat-leaf parsley or basil, chopped

1 Preheat the oven to 180°C (350°F/Gas 4). Place the tomatoes on a baking tray, drizzle with half the oil, sprinkle with a couple of pinches each of salt and pepper, then turn to coat well. Roast for 15 minutes or until softened and slightly wilted, then remove from the oven and drizzle with the balsamic vinegar.

2 Meanwhile, heat the remaining oil in a heavy-bottomed pot over a medium heat. Add the onion and cook for 5 minutes or until soft. Stir in the sausagemeat, garlic, and chilli flakes, and cook, stirring, for 5–10 minutes or until the onion is pale yellow. Stir in the beans and stock, bring to the boil, adjust the heat to a steady simmer and cook for 10 minutes. Add the tomatoes and their juices and stir in half the parsley or basil.

3 Ladle out a cupful of the beans and tomatoes without too much liquid, and whizz until smooth in a blender. Stir back into the pot, then simmer the soup steadily for 10 minutes. If it is too thick, thin with a little hot stock or water. Stir in the rest of the herbs and adjust the seasoning, adding salt and pepper, chilli flakes, and balsamic vinegar to taste. Ladle into warmed bowls, drizzle with a little more olive oil, and serve.

SERVES **4**
PREP **10 MINS**
COOK **1½ HRS**
FREEZE **UP TO 3 MONTHS**

450g (1lb) chicken breasts
   and thighs, skinned

2 bay leaves

1 litre (1¾ pints) chicken or
   vegetable stock

60g (2oz) long-grain rice

2 leeks, thinly sliced

2 carrots, grated

pinch of ground cloves

1 tsp sea salt

1 tbsp chopped fresh parsley

COCK-A-LEEKIE SOUP

This version is quicker than the traditional method
of slow-simmering a whole chicken. Some recipes use
prunes – try adding a few with the vegetables in step 2.

1 Place the chicken in a large pan with the bay leaves and pour over
the stock. Bring to the boil, then reduce the heat, cover the pan, and
simmer for 30 minutes.

2 Skim the surface of the soup and discard any scum that has formed.
Add the rice, leeks, carrots, cloves, and salt. Bring back to the boil, reduce
the heat, cover the pan, and simmer for a further 30 minutes.

3 Remove the bay leaves and discard. If you wish, lift out the chicken,
remove the meat from the bones, then return the meat to the soup. Ladle
the soup into a warm tureen or divide between individual serving bowls,
and serve hot, garnished with parsley.

SERVES **4**
PREP **15 MINS**
COOK **20 MINS**
FREEZE **UP TO 1 MONTH**
AT THE END OF STEP 2

1 litre (1¾ pints) chicken stock

5cm (2in) piece galangal or
    ginger, sliced

8 makrut (kaffir) lime leaves,
    shredded

5 garlic cloves, roughly chopped

2 tbsp chopped coriander
    stems

2 lemongrass, split lengthways
    and lightly bruised (see p25)

salt and freshly ground black
    pepper

2 chicken breasts, about 125g
    (4½oz) each, skinned and
    thinly shredded

2–3 bird's eye chillies, finely
    sliced

2 tsp sugar

3 small shallots, sliced

juice of 2 limes

3 tbsp fish sauce

2 tbsp sweet chilli sauce

2 small pak choi, roughly
    chopped

handful of bean sprouts

RECIPE BY
ROOPA GULATI

HOT AND SOUR CHICKEN BROTH

This broth is crammed with contrasting sweet, sour, hot,
and salty flavours, and can be made in minutes. Instead of
chicken, you could try using fish stock and shelled prawns.

1 Pour the chicken stock into a large pan and add the galangal or ginger,
lime leaves, garlic, coriander stems, and lemongrass. Season, bring the stock
to the boil, turn down the heat and simmer for 10 minutes.

2 Strain the stock into a clean pan and stir in the chicken, chillies, sugar,
shallots, lime juice, fish sauce, and chilli sauce. Simmer for 4–5 minutes,
until the chicken is cooked.

3 Add the pak choi and cook the broth for a further minute. Stir in the
bean sprouts and serve straight away.

SERVES **4**
PREP **15 MINS**
PLUS CHILLING
COOK **1 HR 20 MINS**
FREEZE **NOT SUITABLE**

RECIPE BY
SHAUN HILL

CHICKEN CONSOMMÉ

Consommé regularly has some garnish or herb to lend interest, but it is the quality and clarity of the soup itself that is at its heart.

2 large egg whites

1 tbsp passata or 1 tsp tomato purée

1 chicken leg, boned and minced or finely chopped

1 onion, chopped

1 carrot, chopped

1 leek, chopped

1 garlic clove, chopped

1 tbsp chopped parsley

2 litres (3½ pints) cold chicken stock

salt and freshly ground pepper

chervil, to garnish

1 To make the clarification mixture, whisk the egg whites just enough to loosen them and form a few bubbles. Add the passata or tomato purée, and mix thoroughly.

2 Place the chicken, vegetables, garlic, and parsley in a bowl, add the egg white mixture, and mix thoroughly – use an electric mixer with paddle attachment if need be. Refrigerate until well chilled.

3 Combine the stock with the clarification mixture in a deep, narrow saucepan. Heat slowly, uncovered, until the stock comes to the boil. Gently stir to stop the egg sticking. Once the stock reaches boiling point, turn the heat right down and leave to simmer gently for at least an hour, or until a white crust forms. When it is hard, poke a gap through it to check on the clarity.

4 When the consommé is clear and the clarification ingredients cooked, widen the gap and strain the consommé through a muslin-lined sieve into a clean container. Season, garnish with chervil, and serve.

SERVES **4**
PREP **2½ HRS**
COOK **30 MINS**
FREEZE **UP TO 3 MONTHS**
BEFORE CREAM IS ADDED

FOR THE STOCK

1 small to medium free-range chicken

1 large carrot, chopped

1 leek, cut into segments

3 garlic cloves, unpeeled

20g (¾oz) dried mushrooms

3 celery stalks, chopped

2–3 sprigs each of parsley and thyme

sea salt and freshly ground black pepper

FOR THE SOUP

100g (3½oz) short grain rice or pearl barley

1½ tbsp vegetable oil plus 10g (¼oz) butter

½ large red onion, finely chopped

2 garlic cloves, crushed

250g (9oz) button mushrooms, thinly sliced

4 tbsp single cream

2 tbsp finely chopped parsley

2 tsp finely grated zest of an unwaxed lemon

RECIPE BY
MARIE-PIERRE MOINE

TRADITIONAL CHICKEN SOUP

A universal favourite, this soup has a zingy lemon and parsley finish. It can also be made with leftover meat and the carcase of a roasted chicken.

1 For the stock, put the chicken in a large saucepan over a low heat. Cover with water and bring slowly to boiling, skimming the surface as needed. Add the carrot, leek, garlic, dried mushrooms, celery, and herbs. Season lightly. Bring back to a simmer, partly cover, and cook for 1 hour.

2 Remove from the heat. Once cool, lift out the chicken, strip the meat from the carcase, and set aside. Return the carcase to the pan and boil for 1 hour. Strain through a sieve into a bowl and allow the stock to cool.

3 Soak the rice or barley in cold water for 30 minutes. Rinse and drain. Skim the fat from the stock. You'll need 750ml (1¼ pints) of stock for the soup recipe but you can add boiling water if needed.

4 Put the oil and butter in a sauté pan over a medium heat. Add the onion, garlic, and mushrooms and fry for 3–5 minutes. Add the rice or barley and cook, stirring, for 2 minutes. Add the stock and cook for 15–20 minutes. Shred about 200g (7oz) of the reserved chicken and add to the soup. Taste, season if required, and return to a simmer. Stir in the cream, parsley, and lemon zest, and serve hot.

SERVES **4**
PREP **20 MINS**
COOK **45 MINS**
FREEZE **UP TO 3 MONTHS**

40g (1¼oz) butter

1 large onion, chopped

5cm (2in) fresh root ginger, finely chopped

2 garlic cloves, finely chopped

1 cox apple, unpeeled, diced, with peel

1 carrot, sliced

1 celery stick, sliced

1 heaped tbsp mild curry powder

1 tbsp gram flour or plain flour

4 tomatoes, roughly chopped

2 tsp tomato purée

500ml (16fl oz) hot chicken stock

2 bay leaves

salt and freshly ground black pepper

200ml (7fl oz) coconut milk or single cream

175g (7oz) cooked chicken meat, shredded

juice of ½ lime

2 tbsp chopped fresh coriander

RECIPE BY
ROOPA GULATI

MULLIGATAWNY

An Anglo-Indian soup from colonial days, mulligatawny has many variations. For extra heat, pop a split red chilli in the pan when you pour over the stock.

1 Melt the butter in a large pan and soften the onion, ginger, and garlic for 10 minutes, without colouring. Add the apple, carrot, and celery to the pan and continue cooking, covered, for 5 minutes.

2 Stir in the curry powder and fry for 1 minute, stirring all the time. Sprinkle over the flour and continue cooking for another 20 seconds.

3 Add the tomatoes and tomato purée followed by the chicken stock. Add the bay leaves and season with salt and pepper. Bring to the boil, stirring, then reduce the heat and simmer, half-covered for 20 minutes.

4 Remove the bay leaf and blend until smooth, using a stick blender or liquidizer. Sieve the soup to remove any fibres and skin. Reheat, stir in the coconut milk or cream, and add the shredded chicken. Sharpen with a squeeze of lime and add the chopped coriander.

SERVES **4**
PREP **10 MINS**
COOK **45 MINS**
FREEZE **NOT SUITABLE**

RECIPE BY
SHAUN HILL

THAI CHICKEN SOUP

Although this recipe uses coconut milk as its base and key Thai flavourings, it makes no pretence at authenticity. No extra salt should be necessary as nam pla is salty.

4 stalks lemongrass, bruised and cut into 1cm (½in) lengths

200g (7oz) galangal, peeled and diced

5 makrut (kaffir) lime leaves, bruised

1 chicken leg

2 small chillies

1 litre (1¾ pints) coconut milk

1 tbsp nam pla

juice of 3 limes

3 spring onions, finely chopped

2 tbsp chopped coriander leaves

1 Put the lemongrass, galangal, lime leaves, chicken, and 500ml (16fl oz) water in a pan and bring to the boil. Simmer, uncovered, for 30 minutes or until the chicken is cooked. Remove with a slotted spoon, dice the flesh, discarding the skin and bones, and set aside.

2 Add the chillies to the pan and bring the soup back to the boil. Pour in the coconut milk and heat slowly – you want the soup to become hot enough for the flavours to infuse the coconut milk without coming to the boil.

3 Strain the soup into a clean pan or tureen. Remove the chillies from the sieve and cut into slivers. Add the nam pla, lime juice, spring onions, coriander, and chicken to the soup, then taste to check the seasoning. Serve garnished with the chilli slivers.

SERVES **4**
PREP **40 MINS**
COOK **2 HRS**
FREEZE **NOT SUITABLE**

a few beef bones, if possible

1kg (2¼lb) braising steak cut
into 5–6cm (2–2½in) pieces

salt and freshly ground black
pepper

1 large carrot, thickly cut on
the diagonal

2 turnips, thickly sliced

1 medium-to-large waxy
potato, cut into 8 pieces

1 Spanish onion, halved

2 garlic cloves, crushed

3 cloves

1 large leek, thickly sliced

3 celery sticks, chopped

3 bay leaves

several sprigs each of thyme
and parsley

RECIPE BY
MARIE-PIERRE MOINE

POT AU FEU

This classic French soup takes time to make, but is well
worth waiting for. Try serving this with coarse-grained
mustard, gherkin, and creamed horseradish.

1 Put any bones in a large, deep, heavy casserole pan. Place the meat on
top of the bones. Cover with plenty of cold water, at least 6cm (2½in)
above the meat, and very slowly bring to a simmer over a low heat.
Season lightly. Skim off any scum that rises to the surface with a slotted
spoon. Cover and let simmer very gently for 1 hour, while you prepare the
vegetables. Cut one half of the onion into slices and push the cloves into
the other half.

2 Skim the meat again. Add the vegetables to the pan with the bay leaves,
thyme, and parsley. Bring back to a simmer and skim again. Season lightly.
Reduce the heat, partially cover, and cook gently for at least 45 minutes,
until the meat and vegetables are tender.

3 Skim again if necessary then lift out the meat and vegetables and put
in a large shallow bowl or in individual bowls. Discard the bones, the
clove-studded onion half, bay leaves, thyme, and parsley.

4 Strain the stock into a saucepan through a muslin-lined sieve. Bring
to a simmer and season if required. Ladle sufficient stock over the meat
and vegetables to cover, and serve. Leave the remaining stock to cool,
then refrigerate or freeze for use in other recipes as needed.

SERVES **4**
PREP **10 MINS**
COOK **35 MINS**
FREEZE **UP TO 3 MONTHS**

1 tbsp olive oil

1 onion, chopped

225g (8oz) lean minced beef

½ tsp crushed dried chillies

1–2 fresh red chillies, seeded and chopped

1 tsp ground cumin

1 tsp dried oregano

450ml (15fl oz) passata

450ml (15fl oz) beef stock

400g can red kidney beans, drained and rinsed

1 tbsp tomato purée

½ tsp caster sugar

salt and freshly ground black pepper

1 tbsp chopped fresh coriander or parsley

grated Manchego or Cheddar cheese, to serve

RECIPE BY
CAROLYN HUMPHRIES

BEEF CHILLI SOUP

Warming and hearty, this soup is great served with tortillas and with some guacamole on hand to spoon in.

1 Heat the olive oil in a large saucepan, add the onion and fry for 4–5 minutes or until softened but not coloured. Add the mince and fry, stirring, until the grains of meat are separated and no longer pink.

2 Stir in the chillies and cumin and fry for 30 seconds, stirring. Add the oregano, passata, stock, red kidney beans, tomato purée, sugar, and salt and pepper. Bring to the boil, stirring. Reduce the heat, partially cover, and simmer gently for 30 minutes, stirring occasionally. Taste and adjust the seasoning if necessary.

3 Ladle into warm soup bowls and sprinkle with the coriander or parsley. Serve topped with grated Manchego or Cheddar cheese.

SERVES **6–8**
PREP **15 MINS**
COOK **2 HRS**
FREEZE **UP TO 3 MONTHS**
AT THE END OF STEP 2

120ml (4fl oz) olive oil

675g (1½lb) onions, thinly sliced

2 garlic cloves, crushed

675g (1½lb) chuck steak, cut into 5cm (2in) cubes

salt and freshly ground black pepper

2 tbsp paprika

1 tsp caraway seeds

1 tsp cayenne pepper, plus extra to garnish

4 tbsp tomato purée

1 litre (1¾ pints) beef stock

soured cream, to garnish

HUNGARIAN GOULASH SOUP

The warming flavours of steak and onions make this soup a rich and satisfying meal. For an authentic touch, use Hungarian paprika.

1 Heat 3 tbsp of the olive oil in a large casserole over a medium heat, add the onions, and cook, stirring occasionally, for 10 minutes or until they are golden brown. Add the garlic for the final 2 minutes, then remove the casserole from the heat.

2 Heat the remaining oil in a frying pan, add the steak, and cook, stirring often, for 5 minutes or until brown on all sides. Season with salt and add to the onions, along with the spices and tomato purée. Return the casserole to the heat and cook for 5 minutes, stirring all the time, then pour in the stock. Cover with a lid and simmer gently for 1¾ hours.

3 Season to taste with salt and pepper, then serve the soup garnished with soured cream, a sprinkling of cayenne, and some more pepper.

SERVES **6**
PREP **20 MINS**
PLUS I HR CHILLING
COOK **4 HRS 45 MINS**
FREEZE **UP TO 3 MONTHS**
BEFORE THE SHERRY IS ADDED

OXTAIL SOUP

Enriched with sherry, this slow-cooked soup is a classic for
flavourful comfort eating. If you prefer a chunky texture,
the soup also tastes good unblended.

2 tbsp vegetable oil

salt and freshly ground black
    pepper

600g (1lb 5oz) ox tails,
    disjointed, available from
    your butcher

1 onion, sliced

2 carrots, diced

2 celery sticks, diced

400g tin chopped tomatoes

¼ bunch of parsley

1 bay leaf

2 sprigs of fresh thyme

1 tbsp plain flour

1 tbsp butter

150ml (5fl oz) dry sherry

1 Heat the oil in a large saucepan, season the ox tails with salt and pepper,
add them to the hot oil, and fry until golden on all sides. Add the onion
and fry until softened slightly. Add 2 litres (3½ pints) water, season with
salt and pepper, and simmer, uncovered, for about 2 hours. Cover and
continue to simmer for a further 2 hours. Check to see if the liquid needs
topping up during cooking.

2 Add the carrots, celery, and tomatoes. Tie the parsley, bay leaf, and thyme
sprigs together with kitchen string, and place in the pan. Bring to the boil
and simmer for 30 minutes, or until the vegetables are tender.

3 Remove the herb bundle and discard. Scoop out the meat, remove from
the bones, and discard the skin and bones. Strain the stock, reserving the
vegetables. Refrigerate the stock for an hour or more. Using a blender,
whizz the meat and vegetables and set aside.

4 Once the stock is chilled, remove the fat from the top and discard.
Reheat the stock. In a large, dry frying pan, brown the flour over a high
heat. Cool slightly. Add the butter and blend. A little at a time, stir in the
stock and the meat–vegetable purée. Season with salt and pepper to taste,
and add the sherry just before serving.

SERVES **6**
PREP **30 MINS**
COOK **1 HR 10 MINS**
FREEZE **UP TO 3 MONTHS**

SPLIT PEA AND BACON SOUP

Be careful when seasoning this hearty soup, as the bacon
means that little, if any, extra salt will be needed. Try this
dish with olive oil croûtons.

250g (9oz) dried split green
   peas, rinsed and drained

250g (9oz) piece smoked
   streaky bacon

¼ celeriac, peeled and diced

1 large carrot, diced

1 small leek, diced

1 medium floury potato, peeled
   and diced

1 tsp dried marjoram

15g (½oz) butter

1 onion, diced

freshly ground black pepper

3–4 tsp chopped chives,
   to garnish

1 Put the peas in a large saucepan with 1.5 litres (2¾ pints) water and bring to the boil. Add the bacon, cover, and cook for about 40 minutes over a medium heat. Add the celeriac, carrot, leek, and potato, and stir in the marjoram. Bring to the boil again, cover, and cook for another 20 minutes.

2 Melt the butter in a pan, and add the onion. Brown slightly, stirring continuously, then set aside.

3 Remove the bacon from the soup. Discard the excess fat and rind. Shred the meat and return it to the soup together with the fried onion. Season it with pepper. Sprinkle with chopped chives to serve.

SERVES **6**
PREP **35 MINS**
PLUS OVERNIGHT CHILLING
COOK **3 HRS**
FREEZE **UP TO 3 MONTHS**
WITHOUT THE GARNISH

6 dried red chillies

650g (1½lb) boneless pork belly with rind, cut into 2.5 x 5cm (1 x 2in) chunks

1 tsp cumin seeds

½ tsp black peppercorns

6 garlic cloves, roughly chopped

5cm (2in) fresh root ginger, peeled and roughly chopped

1 tsp sweet paprika

3 tbsp tamarind pulp

3 tbsp white wine vinegar

4–6 tbsp vegetable oil

5cm (2in) cinnamon stick

2 star anise

3 onions, finely chopped

175ml (6fl oz) white wine

1.7 litres (3 pints) chicken stock

2–3 tsp date palm sugar or dark muscovado sugar, to taste

salt

1 red chilli, deseeded and cut into strips, to serve

2 tbsp fresh coriander leaves, to serve

RECIPE BY
ROOPA GULATI

PORK VINDALOO BROTH

A favourite from Goa in southern India, the vindaloo is Portuguese in heritage and notable for its garlicky masala, spiked with wine vinegar and softened with sugar.

1 Soak the chillies in hot water for 10 minutes (for a mild flavour, remove the seeds first). Put the pork in a pan, cover with boiling water, bring to the boil, and simmer for 5 minutes. Drain, discard the liquid, and set aside.

2 Dry-roast the cumin and peppercorns (see p25) and grind using a mortar and pestle. In a small food processor, process the ground spices, drained red chillies, garlic, ginger, paprika, tamarind, and vinegar. Set aside.

3 Heat the oil in a pan. When hot, fry the cinnamon and star anise for 30 seconds. Add the onions and fry for 10–15 minutes. Add the spice paste and cook for 1 minute. Pour in the wine and stock and bring to the boil. Add the pork, turn the heat down low, and simmer for 2 hours. Chill overnight.

4 Next day, scoop out the meat, strip away the rind, and dice. Skim the fat from the stock and strain the liquid into a clean pan. Bring to a fast boil over a high heat and cook for 5–10 minutes. Sweeten with sugar and season with salt. Before serving, stir in the pork and garnish with the chilli strips and coriander leaves.

WINTER

WINTER
SEASON'S BEST

Although we no longer live from the storecupboard alone in winter, it is still a season that traditionally lends itself to comforting, warming soups fortified with pulses and grains. The vegetable plot continues to offer fresh produce, such as kale, celeriac, and leeks, and winter can still offer a wide range of flavours, from a delicate Jerusalem artichoke and scallop soup to a robust, filling potato and kale soup. Creamy curried parsnip soup or chestnut soup deliver earthy, wintry flavour, while chunky Zuppa di verdure or a puff-crusted game soup provide a hearty meal in a bowl.

SERVES **4**
PREP **20 MINS**
COOK **35 MINS**
FREEZE **UP TO 3 MONTHS**

LENTIL SOUP

This hearty vegetarian soup has just a touch of spice and
is quick and easy to prepare. Serve with plain yogurt
and good crusty bread.

1 tbsp olive oil

2 onions, finely chopped

2 celery sticks, finely chopped

2 carrots, finely chopped

2 garlic cloves, crushed

1–2 tsp curry powder

150g (5½oz) red lentils

1.4 litres (2½ pints) vegetable
    stock

120ml (4fl oz) tomato juice or
    vegetable juice

salt and freshly ground black
    pepper

1 Heat the oil in a large pan over a medium heat, then add the onions,
celery, and carrots. Cook, stirring, for 5 minutes, or until the onions are
soft and translucent.

2 Add the garlic and curry powder and cook, stirring, for a further
1 minute, then add the lentils, stock, and tomato juice.

3 Bring to the boil, then lower the heat, cover, and simmer for 25 minutes,
or until the vegetables are tender. Season to taste with salt and pepper,
and serve hot.

SERVES **4**
PREP **5 MINS**
COOK **30 MINS**
FREEZE **UP TO 3 MONTHS**
AT THE END OF STEP 3

RECIPE BY
MARIE-PIERRE MOINE

GREEN LENTIL SOUP WITH LIME

Lime gives a distinctive, vibrant twist to this clean-tasting, healthy soup from New Mexico. It has the added advantage of being very quick and easy to prepare.

1 litre (1¾ pints) light chicken stock

2–3 sprigs fresh thyme

300g (10oz) green lentils

sea salt and freshly ground black pepper

grated zest and juice of 1 organic lime

1 Pour the stock into a saucepan over a medium heat. Add the thyme and bring to a simmer.

2 Add the lentils, and season lightly. Return to a simmer, cover, and reduce the heat a little. Cook for 20–25 minutes until the lentils are very soft.

3 Turn off the heat and leave to cool for several minutes. Transfer to a blender or food processor, and whizz until just smooth.

4 Pour the soup back into the saucepan and stir in the lime zest and juice. Reheat gently, taste, and adjust the seasoning. Serve very hot.

SERVES 6–8
PREP 15 MINS
COOK 50 MINS
FREEZE UP TO 3 MONTHS
WITHOUT THE LIME AND CORIANDER

RECIPE BY
ROOPA GULATI

KHICHDI

This vegetable and lentil dish is best served piping hot, in cavernous bowls. You can find pink lentils (*masoor dal*) in Asian food stores.

1 butternut squash, about 700g (1lb 9oz)

½ tsp garam masala

salt and freshly ground black pepper

2 tbsp olive oil

100g (3½oz) basmati rice

100g (3½oz) pink or red lentils

5cm (2in) ginger, peeled and finely grated

2 tbsp ghee or clarified butter

2 tsp cumin seeds

½ tsp red chilli flakes

juice of 1 lime

3 tbsp chopped coriander

2 tbsp unsalted butter

1 Preheat the oven to 200°C (400°F/Gas 6). Halve the squash lengthways and scoop out the seeds and fibres. Put it in a roasting tin, cut side up, sprinkle with the garam masala, season, and drizzle with the oil. Cover with foil and roast for 45 minutes, or until meltingly tender. Leave to cool slightly then scoop out the flesh, lightly crush it with a fork, and set aside.

2 Meanwhile, combine the rice and lentils in a large saucepan and cover with 2 litres (3½ pints) of water. Add the ginger, bring to the boil, then reduce the heat and simmer for about 30 minutes until the rice grains have lost their texture and broken down. Add more hot water to loosen the texture if needed. Stir in the lightly crushed squash.

3 Heat the ghee in a separate pan and fry the cumin and chilli for about 30 seconds, until aromatic and darker in colour. Tip the spices and ghee into the rice and lentils and stir well, seasoning with plenty more salt and pepper. Stir in the lime juice and coriander.

4 Divide between deep bowls and finish with a generous dollop of butter in the centre of each helping.

SERVES **4**
PREP **15 MINS**
COOK **1 HR 20 MINS**
FREEZE **UP TO 3 MONTHS**
AT THE END OF STEP 2

TUSCAN BEAN SOUP

This hearty, substantial soup improves with reheating, so it benefits
from being made a day in advance. Reheat gently over a low heat.

4 tbsp extra virgin olive oil,
    plus extra for drizzling

1 onion, chopped

2 carrots, sliced

1 leek, sliced

2 garlic cloves, chopped

400g can chopped tomatoes

1 tbsp tomato purée

900ml (1¾ pints) chicken stock

salt and freshly ground black
    pepper

400g can borlotti beans,
    flageolet beans, or cannellini
    beans, drained and rinsed

250g (9oz) baby spinach leaves
    or spring greens, shredded

8 slices ciabatta bread

grated Parmesan cheese, for
    sprinkling

1 Heat the oil in a large saucepan and fry the onion, carrot, and leek over a low heat for 10 minutes, or until softened but not coloured. Add the garlic and fry for 1 minute. Add the tomatoes, tomato purée, and stock. Season to taste with salt and pepper.

2 Mash half the beans with a fork and add to the pan. Bring to the boil, then lower the heat and simmer for 30 minutes. Add the remaining beans and spinach to the pan. Simmer for a further 30 minutes.

3 Toast the bread until golden, place two pieces in each soup bowl, and drizzle with olive oil. To serve, spoon the soup into the bowls, top with a sprinkling of Parmesan, and drizzle with a little more olive oil.

SERVES **8**
PREP **15 MINS**
COOK **40 MINS**
FREEZE **UP TO 3 MONTHS**

2 tbsp olive oil

2 onions, finely chopped

salt and freshly ground
    black pepper

1 tbsp finely chopped fresh
    rosemary leaves

a few fresh sage leaves,
    finely chopped

4 celery stalks, finely chopped

3 garlic cloves, grated or
    finely chopped

2 tbsp tomato purée

2 x 400g cans borlotti
    beans, drained, rinsed, and
    drained again

1.2 litres (2 pints) hot chicken
    stock

2.5kg (5½lb) potatoes, cut into
    chunky pieces

BEAN AND
ROSEMARY SOUP

Robust, garlicky, and fragrant with rosemary and sage, this
is a hearty, satisfying soup. Serve it with some fresh crusty
bread and a drizzle of good-quality olive oil.

1 Heat the oil in a large pan, add the onions, and cook over a low heat
for 6–8 minutes or until soft and translucent. Season well with salt and
pepper, then stir in the rosemary, sage, celery, and garlic and cook over
a very low heat, stirring occasionally, for 10 minutes.

2 Stir in the tomato purée and beans and cook gently for 5 minutes. Pour
in the stock, bring to the boil, then add the potatoes and simmer gently
for 15 minutes or until cooked. Taste, season with salt and pepper, if
needed, and serve.

SERVES **4–6**
PREP **15 MINS**
COOK **40 MINS**
FREEZE **UP TO 3 MONTHS**

1 tbsp virgin rapeseed oil or
   sunflower oil

3 leeks, cleaned and sliced

1 small red pepper, chopped

1 small yellow pepper, chopped

3 garlic cloves

5cm (2in) piece fresh ginger,
   peeled and grated or roughly
   chopped

1 small red chilli

1 tsp cumin seeds

sea salt and freshly ground
   black pepper

2 x 400g cans black-eyed
   beans, drained, rinsed, and
   drained again

400ml (14fl oz) coconut milk

500ml (16fl oz) hot vegetable
   stock

1 tsp brown sugar

fresh coriander leaves, to
   garnish

lime wedges, to serve

RECIPE BY
CELIA BROOKS BROWN

BLACK-EYED BEAN SOUP

If you can, make this soup in advance and let it stand for a while before reheating – it will be even better. It's also good made with overgrown runner beans (podded).

1 Heat the oil in a saucepan over a medium heat, add the leeks and peppers, cover, and cook, stirring frequently, for 5–7 minutes or until soft. Meanwhile, put the garlic, ginger, chilli, cumin, and 1 tsp salt in a blender with 4 tbsp water and whizz until completely smooth. Add to the pan, using a little more water to rinse out every last bit. Cook, stirring, for 2–3 minutes or until most of the liquid has evaporated.

2 Add the beans, coconut milk, stock, sugar, and a good grinding of black pepper and bring to the boil. Reduce the heat to a simmer and cook gently for 30 minutes, stirring frequently. Taste for seasoning, then serve each bowlful garnished with fresh coriander and a lime wedge.

SERVES 4
PREP 10 MINS
PLUS 20 MINS SOAKING
COOK 15–20 MINS
FREEZE UP TO 3 MONTHS
WITHOUT CHEESE CRISPS

RECIPE BY
ANGELA NILSEN

ROSEMARY'S BEAN SOUP WITH ITALIAN CHEESE CRISPS

Flageolet beans give texture while rosemary and dried mushrooms provide plenty of flavour in this rustic Italian-style soup.

12g (½oz) dried porcini mushrooms

50g (1¾oz) Grana Padano, pecorino, or Parmesan cheese, grated

1½ tsp very finely chopped rosemary

2 tbsp olive oil

1 onion, chopped

2 garlic cloves, chopped

3 rosemary sprigs

2 × 400g (14oz) cans flageolet beans, drained and rinsed

600ml (1 pint) vegetable stock

extra virgin olive oil, for drizzling

ciabatta loaf cut into chunks, to serve

1 Preheat the oven to 200°C (400°F/Gas 6). Soak the mushrooms in water for 20 minutes. Make the cheese crisps. Line a baking sheet with parchment. Scatter the cheese and half the rosemary in a thin, even layer on the sheet in an 18cm (7in) circle. Bake for 8 minutes or until it starts to turn golden round the edges. Remove and leave to cool and firm on the sheet. Strain the mushrooms, reserving the liquid, and chop them.

2 Heat the oil in a large saucepan, add the onion, and soften for 4–5 minutes. Stir in the garlic, chopped mushrooms, and rosemary. Fry for 2–3 minutes. Add the beans, stock, and 6 tbsp of the reserved mushroom liquid. Simmer for 10 minutes. Remove the rosemary. Roughly purée about three-quarters of the soup. Pour this back into the pan with the rest of the soup. Season to taste then warm through.

3 Break the cheese crisp into large pieces. For each serving, sprinkle with the rest of the chopped rosemary, drizzle with the oil, and accompany with the cheese crisps and ciabatta.

SERVES **6**

PREP **20 MINS**

COOK **3¼ HRS**

OR 40 MINS WITH A PRESSURE COOKER

FREEZE **UP TO 3 MONTHS**

AT THE END OF STEP 3

225g (8oz) dried kidney beans, soaked overnight in cold water

2 red onions, diced

400g can chopped tomatoes

1 tbsp tomato purée

5 garlic cloves, halved

5cm (2in) fresh root ginger, roughly chopped

3 large green chillies

salt and freshly ground black pepper

150ml (5fl oz) single cream

squeeze of fresh lime juice, to taste

FOR THE GARNISH

1 small mouli, coarsely grated, or 4–6 red radishes, sliced

1 large green chilli, finely chopped

2 tbsp chopped fresh coriander leaves

squeeze of fresh lime juice, to taste

RECIPE BY

ROOPA GULATI

CREAMY KIDNEY BEAN SOUP

This hearty, wholesome soup takes the edge off chilly winter weather. It's worth using dried beans, which have a much fuller flavour than the canned variety.

1 Drain the kidney beans, discarding the soaking liquid. Put the beans in a very large heavy-bottomed pan and cover with 1.7 litres (3 pints) of water. Add the onions, tomatoes, tomato purée, garlic, ginger, and chillies.

2 Cover the pan and simmer for about 3 hours, until the beans are just breaking up. Top up the liquid during cooking if required. Alternatively, use a pressure cooker – the beans will be tender in about 30 minutes.

3 Once the beans have cooled slightly, scoop out the chillies. Using a blender, whizz the soup until smooth in batches, then sieve to remove the skins. Season well with salt and pepper, then stir in the cream and reheat. Add lime juice to taste.

4 For the garnish, combine the grated mouli or sliced radish with the green chilli and coriander leaves. Sharpen with a squeeze of lime, then top each bowl of soup with a small heap of the herby mouli.

SERVES **4**
PREP **10 MINS**
COOK **40 MINS**
FREEZE **UP TO 3 MONTHS**
AT THE END OF STEP 2

2 tbsp sunflower oil

1 onion, chopped

1 small red pepper, deseeded
  and finely chopped

2 garlic cloves, finely chopped

400g (14oz) lean minced beef

1 tsp ground cumin

2 tsp medium or hot chilli
  powder

½ tsp dried oregano

400g can chopped plum
  tomatoes

2 tbsp tomato purée

750ml (1¼ pints) hot vegetable
  stock or chicken stock

400g can red kidney beans,
  drained, rinsed, and drained
  again

handful of chopped flat-leaf
  parsley

salt and freshly ground black
  pepper

soured cream or natural yogurt,
  to serve

grated Cheddar, to serve

4 warm tortillas (optional),
  to serve

RECIPE BY
ANGELA NILSEN

MEXICAN CHILLI BEAN SOUP

This is so thick and hearty it is a meal in itself – a real family soup. For children, try topping it with some broken-up tortilla chips.

1 Heat the oil in a large saucepan, add the onion, and fry for 5 minutes. Add the pepper and garlic and stir-fry for 2 minutes. Add the mince and stir-fry for 5 minutes or until it has broken up and browned. Stir in the cumin, chilli powder, and oregano and fry for another minute or so.

2 Stir in the tomatoes, tomato purée, and stock, then simmer for 20–25 minutes or until reduced slightly and a good soupy consistency. Add the beans and simmer for another 5 minutes. Stir in half the parsley and season with salt and pepper.

3 Ladle into bowls and serve topped with a spoonful of soured cream or yogurt, a scattering of Cheddar, and the rest of the parsley.

SERVES 4–6
PREP 10 MINS
COOK 1 HR
FREEZE UP TO 3 MONTHS

1 tbsp olive oil

20g (¾oz) butter

3–4 leeks, finely sliced

410g tin cannellini beans,
   drained and rinsed,
   then drained again

3 medium carrots, finely
   chopped

salt and freshly ground black
   pepper

1 tsp medium curry powder
   (optional)

750ml (1¼ pints) cold water

extra virgin olive oil, to serve

RECIPE BY
LIVIA FIRTH

CANNELLINI BEAN AND CARROT SOUP

Livia Firth, wife of actor Colin, is founder of the ethical consultancy company Eco-Age. "I use leeks as the base of my soups as they are sweeter than onions."

1 Warm the oil and melt the butter in a large, deep pan over a very low heat. Add the leeks and cook for at least 10 minutes, adding a tiny bit of water when the leeks start to stick to the bottom of the pan.

2 Add the cannellini beans and carrots, then turn up the heat and stir well with a wooden spoon to mix the vegetables and flavours together. Allow it to simmer for 5–6 minutes. Season the soup with salt, and stir in the curry powder, if using. Add the water and bring to the boil. Cover with a lid, and simmer for 45 minutes.

3 Transfer the mixture to a blender and whizz till smooth, then ladle into serving bowls. Encourage your guests to add a bit of olive oil and some pepper to their soup – it makes a wonderful finishing touch.

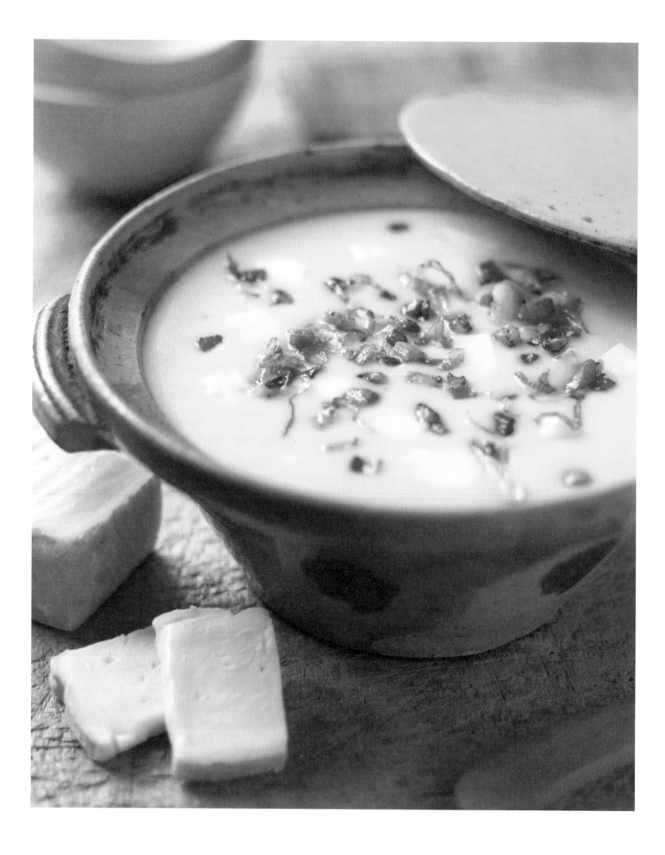

SERVES **4**
PREP **30 MINS**
COOK **2 HRS**
FREEZE **UP TO 3 MONTHS**
AT THE END OF STEP 3

3 tbsp olive oil

2 onions, finely chopped

2 garlic cloves, crushed

225g (8oz) dried cannellini
beans, soaked overnight

1 celery stick, chopped

1 bay leaf

3–4 parsley stalks, without
leaves

1 tbsp lemon juice

1.2 litres (2 pints) vegetable
stock

salt and freshly ground black
pepper

3 shallots, thinly sliced

60g (2oz) pancetta, chopped
(optional)

85g (3oz) fontina cheese or
Taleggio cheese, chopped
into small pieces

WHITE BEAN SOUP

This thick soup from northern Italy is guaranteed to
keep out the winter chills. Soak the beans overnight
to rehydrate them and cut down on the cooking time.

1 Heat 2 tbsp olive oil in a saucepan, add the onions, and fry over a low
heat for 10 minutes, or until softened, stirring occasionally. Add the garlic
and cook, stirring, for 1 minute.

2 Drain the soaked beans and add to the pan with the celery, bay leaf,
parsley stalks, lemon juice, and stock. Bring to the boil, cover, and simmer
for 1½ hours, or until the beans are soft, stirring occasionally.

3 Remove the bay leaf and liquidize the soup in batches in a blender,
or through a hand mill. Rinse out the pan. Return the soup to the pan
and season to taste with salt and pepper.

4 Heat the remaining olive oil in a small frying pan, and fry the shallots
and pancetta (if using) until golden and crisp, stirring frequently to stop
them sticking to the pan. Reheat the soup, adding a little stock or water
if it is too thick. Stir the fontina into the soup. Ladle into individual bowls,
and sprinkle each serving with the shallots and pancetta.

SERVES **4**
PREP **25 MINS**
COOK **30 MINS**
FREEZE **UP TO 3 MONTHS**
BEFORE CREAM IS ADDED

RECIPE BY
SOPHIE GRIGSON

CURRIED PARSNIP SOUP

This is the original curried parsnip soup recipe created by
Jane Grigson in the 1970s. Radical at the time, it has now
become part of the general range of British soups.

1 heaped tbsp coriander seeds

1 tsp cumin seeds

1 dried red chilli or ½ tsp chilli
   flakes

1 rounded tsp ground turmeric

¼ tsp ground fenugreek

1 medium onion, chopped

1 large garlic clove, split in half

675g (1½lb) parsnips, cored
   and diced

30g (1oz) butter

1 tbsp plain flour

1 litre (1¾ pints) vegetable
   stock, beef stock, or
   chicken stock

salt and freshly ground black
   pepper

150ml (5fl oz) single cream

chopped chives or parsley,
   to garnish

1 Whizz the first five ingredients in a coffee mill, or pound the whole
spices in a mortar, then mix with the ground spices. Put the mixture into
a small jar – you will not need it all for this recipe.

2 Cook the onion, garlic, and parsnips gently in the butter, lid on the pan,
for 10 minutes. Stir in the flour and 1–2 tbsp of the spice mixture. Cook
for 2 minutes, giving the whole thing a turn round from time to time.
Pour in the stock gradually, stirring constantly. Bring to the boil and leave
to simmer gently for 10–15 minutes or until the parsnips are really tender.

3 Purée until smooth in a blender, then dilute to taste with water. Season
to taste with salt and pepper, then reheat. Add the cream and serve
scattered with the chives or parsley.

SERVES **4**
PREP **20 MINS**
COOK **30 MINS**
FREEZE **UP TO 3 MONTHS**
BEFORE CREAM IS ADDED

RECIPE BY
MARIE-PIERRE MOINE

PARSNIP AND APPLE SOUP

The sweetness of parsnip is balanced by mild curry powder and sharp green apple in this warming, smooth, easy-to-prepare winter soup.

1 tbsp olive oil

10g (¼oz) butter

½ Spanish onion, finely chopped

1 garlic clove, crushed

2 tsp mild curry powder

1kg (2¼lb) parsnips, chopped

sea salt and freshly ground black pepper

1 large Bramley apple, peeled, cored, and chopped

1 litre (1¾ pints) hot vegetable stock or light chicken stock

6 tbsp single cream

2 tbsp lemon juice

1 Heat the oil and butter in a large sauté pan over a gentle heat. Add the onion, garlic, and curry powder and sweat gently, stirring frequently, for 2–3 minutes or until the onion has softened. Add the parsnips and season lightly with salt and pepper. Turn up the heat a little and fry, stirring frequently, for 5 minutes or until the parsnips are golden.

2 Add the apple, stir for 1 minute, then pour in the stock and bring to the boil. Lower the heat and simmer for 10–12 minutes or until the parsnips are tender. Take off the heat and leave to cool for several minutes, then transfer to a blender or food processor and whizz until smooth and creamy.

3 Pass the soup through a sieve placed over the pan, then rinse out the blender or food processor with 100ml (3½fl oz) hot water and stir this into the soup. Reheat gently, then stir in the cream and lemon juice. Adjust the seasoning and serve piping hot.

SERVES 4

PREP 15 MINS

PLUS CHILLING

COOK NONE

FREEZE UP TO 3 MONTHS

1 large orange

2 heads white chicory

2 slices bread, crusts removed

1 garlic clove, roughly chopped

4 spring onions, trimmed and roughly chopped

1 large beefsteak tomato, skinned, quartered, and deseeded

450ml (15fl oz) cold vegetable stock

2 tbsp olive oil, plus extra for garnish

2 tbsp white balsamic vinegar

4 large basil leaves

salt and freshly ground black pepper

RECIPE BY

CAROLYN HUMPHRIES

CHICORY GAZPACHO

This chilled soup is a reminder of summer in the midst of winter. If you would prefer to make the recipe during the warmer months, use watercress instead of chicory.

1 Thinly pare the zest of half the orange. Cut in thin strips and boil in water for 1 minute. Drain, rinse with cold water, and drain again. Set aside for garnish. Finely grate the zest from the remaining orange, squeeze the juice, and set aside.

2 Cut a cone shape out of the base of each head of chicory and discard. Separate the heads into spears. Reserve four of the smallest spears for the garnish. Roughly chop the remainder.

3 Soak the bread in water for 2 minutes. Squeeze out some of the moisture then put the bread in a blender with the chopped chicory, garlic, spring onions, tomato, stock, olive oil, white balsamic vinegar, basil leaves, and the orange juice and finely grated zest. Purée the soup in a blender or food processor then season to taste. Chill until ready to serve.

4 Ladle into four shallow soup plates, and drizzle with a little olive oil. Garnish each with a tiny chicory spear and a few strands of blanched orange zest. Serve cold.

SERVES **4**
PREP **15 MINS**
COOK **20 MINS**
FREEZE **UP TO 3 MONTHS**
BEFORE CREAM IS ADDED

1 tbsp olive oil

1 large onion, sliced

200g (7oz) leeks, cut into
   2.5cm (1in) lengths

150g (5½oz) potatoes, diced

1 tsp saffron

1 tsp ground cumin

1 litre (1¾ pints) hot chicken
   stock

salt and freshly ground black
   pepper

2 tbsp dry white wine

2 tbsp double cream

1 tbsp lemon juice

snipped chives, to garnish

RECIPE BY
SHAUN HILL

SAFFRON SOUP

This is a variation on leek and potato soup and was a regular item on the menu at Robert Carrier's restaurant in London, where I worked in the 1970s. It has not dated.

1 Heat the oil in a heavy-based pan and fry the onion gently for 6–8 minutes or until soft. Add the leeks, potatoes, saffron, cumin, and stock, then season with salt and pepper. Cover with a lid and bring to the boil, then lower the heat and simmer for 10 minutes or until the potatoes are tender. Do not let them disintegrate into the soup.

2 Transfer to a blender, add the wine, and whizz until smooth. Stir in the cream and lemon juice and season with salt and pepper. If the soup is too thick, dilute it with more stock or water. If it is too thin, add more olive oil. Garnish with the snipped chives and serve.

SERVES **4**
PREP **15 MINS**
PLUS 3 HRS CHILLING
COOK **45 MINS**
FREEZE **UP TO 3 MONTHS**
BEFORE THE CREAM IS ADDED

30g (1oz) butter

3 large leeks (white parts only), finely sliced

2 potatoes, about 175g (6oz) in total, chopped

1 celery stalk, roughly chopped

1.2 litres (2 pints) hot vegetable stock

salt and freshly ground black pepper

150ml (5fl oz) double cream, plus extra to garnish

2 tbsp finely chopped chives

VICHYSSOISE

Despite its French name, this silky-smooth leek soup actually comes from the USA. Traditionally served cold, it can also be enjoyed hot as a winter warmer; simply add the cream and chives at the end of cooking, then serve.

1 Melt the butter in a heavy pan over a medium heat, add the leeks, and stir to coat well. Press a circle of damp greaseproof paper on top of them, cover with a lid, and cook, shaking the pan gently from time to time, for 15 minutes or until they are soft and golden. Discard the greaseproof paper.

2 Stir in the potatoes, celery, and stock, then season with salt and pepper. Bring to the boil, stirring all the time, then cover with a lid and simmer for 30 minutes or until the vegetables are tender.

3 Remove the pan from the heat and leave to cool slightly, then whizz the soup in a blender until very smooth. You may need to do this in batches. Season to taste with salt and pepper, then chill for at least 3 hours. To serve, pour into bowls, stir a little cream into each, then sprinkle with the chives and some more pepper.

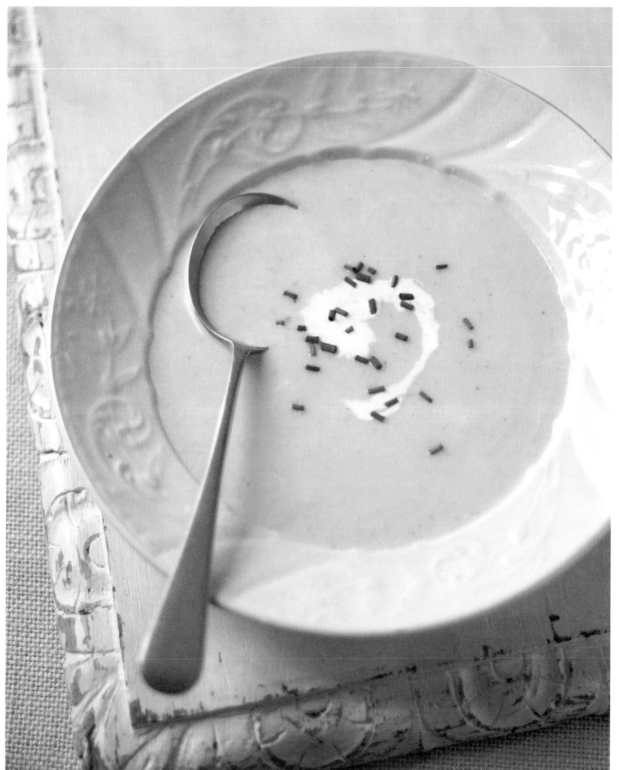

SERVES **4**
PREP **15 MINS**
COOK **30 MINS**
FREEZE **UP TO 3 MONTHS**
WITHOUT THE LARDON GARNISH

RECIPE BY
MARIE-PIERRE MOINE

FRENCH CABBAGE SOUP

This chunky country soup takes minutes to prepare and makes a good supper or lunch dish. For a vegetarian option, leave out the lardons.

1 tbsp olive oil

100g (3½oz) small lardons, or diced bacon

1 Spanish onion, finely chopped

1 garlic clove, crushed

1 large Savoy cabbage, halved, core discarded, and leaves cut into shreds

sea salt and freshly ground black pepper

3 sprigs parsley

croûtons (see p39), to garnish (optional)

1 Heat the oil in a large heavy casserole over a medium heat. Add the lardons (setting aside 2 tbsp to finish), onion, and garlic. Fry, stirring frequently, for 3–4 minutes or until the onion and garlic start to colour. Add the cabbage shreds, reserving a handful to finish. Stir well and season lightly with sea salt and generously with pepper. Continue frying for 2–3 minutes, stirring occasionally.

2 Bring about 850ml (about 1½ pints) water to the boil in a kettle. Pour the boiling water over the vegetables and lardons, stir well, and add the parsley. Cover, lower the heat a little, and simmer gently for about 20 minutes, stirring occasionally.

3 Meanwhile, place a non-stick frying pan over a medium heat. Add the reserved lardons and fry until crisp and golden. Then add the reserved cabbage shreds and fry them until they have wilted, stirring frequently. Season with a little pepper.

4 Taste the soup and adjust the seasoning. Lift out the parsley. Ladle into individual bowls and scatter over the fried bacon and cabbage mixture. A few croûtons scattered across the surface provide a nice finishing touch.

SERVES **4**
PREP **10 MINS**
COOK **30 MINS**
FREEZE **NOT SUITABLE**

SAUERKRAUT SOUP

Sauerkraut is an excellent source of vitamin C. This hearty
soup is redolent of Eastern Europe, though Chinese cooks
were pickling cabbage in wine as early as 200BCE.

2 tablespoons vegetable oil

1 onion, finely chopped

100g (3½oz) bacon, diced

400g jar or can sauerkraut,
roughly chopped

400g can chopped tomatoes,
peeled

2 tsp sugar

600ml (1 pint) hot vegetable or
chicken stock

200ml (7fl oz) double cream

freshly ground black pepper

1 Heat the vegetable oil in a large saucepan over a low heat. Add the
chopped onion and fry gently until softened but not browned. Then add
the diced bacon and fry for another 3 minutes. Finally add the chopped
sauerkraut, cover, and continue to cook for another 5 minutes, stirring
from time to time.

2 Increase the heat under the saucepan slightly and add the chopped
tomatoes, sugar, hot stock, double cream, and pepper and stir well. Bring
to a simmer over a medium heat for 15 minutes until the sauerkraut is
tender. Ladle the soup into bowls to serve and eat with toasted rye bread.

SERVES **4**
PREP **15–20 MINS**
COOK **20–25 MINS**
FREEZE **UP TO 3 MONTHS**

RECIPE BY
SOPHIE GRIGSON

PORTUGUESE POTATO AND KALE SOUP

Potato and kale soup (caldo verde) is ubiquitous in Portugal, where cooks use incredibly finely shredded cabbage. Kale, cavolo nero, or winter greens can all be used in this soup.

450g (1lb) potatoes, peeled
  and sliced

4 garlic cloves, sliced

1 small onion, finely chopped

salt and freshly ground black
  pepper

225g (8oz) curly kale, or cavolo
  nero or Savoy cabbage

110g (4oz) chorizo, skin
  removed and sliced

extra virgin olive oil, to serve

1 Place the potato slices in a large saucepan with the garlic and onion. Season with salt and pepper and add enough water to cover generously. Simmer until tender. Pass through the fine blade of a mouli-legume, or mash to a smooth purée. Add a little more water if necessary to thin to a soupy consistency. Return to the pan and adjust the seasoning, adding plenty of pepper.

2 While the potatoes are cooking, cut the stalks from the kale, then roll up the leaves and shred very thinly – the resulting threads of kale should be around 3mm (⅛in) wide. Bring the soup back to the boil. Stir in the kale and sausage. Simmer for 5 minutes. Ladle into four soup bowls, pour a little olive oil onto each, and serve.

SERVES **4–6**
PREP **20 MINS**
COOK **1 HR 10 MINS**
FREEZE **UP TO 3 MONTHS**
WITHOUT THE SOURED CREAM

RECIPE BY
SOPHIE GRIGSON

BRUSSELS SPROUTS SOUP

This is an unexpectedly good soup, with all the fresh,
nutty flavour of Brussels sprouts tempered by the
sweetness of the onion.

450g (1lb) onions, sliced

30g (1oz) butter

1 tbsp caster sugar

450g (1lb) Brussels sprouts, trimmed and halved

1 generous sprig thyme

1.2 litres (2 pints) light chicken or vegetable stock

salt and freshly ground black pepper

soured cream, crème fraîche, or Greek-style yogurt, to serve

paprika or cayenne pepper, to serve

1 Put the onions into a pan with the butter. Cover and sweat over a gentle heat for about 30–40 minutes until the onions are incredibly tender and soft. Sprinkle over the sugar and cook, uncovered, for another 10–15 minutes or so until the onions are lightly coloured and jammy-looking, stirring occasionally.

2 Add the sprouts and the thyme and stir. Pour in the stock and season with salt and pepper. Bring up to the boil and simmer for about 10–15 minutes until the sprouts are just tender. Cool slightly, remove the thyme, and liquidize in two batches. Reheat gently if needed, then taste and adjust the seasoning. Serve piping hot, with a spoonful of soured cream, crème fraîche, or yogurt in each bowlful, and a light dusting of paprika or cayenne.

SERVES **4**
PREP **15 MINS**
COOK **20 MINS**
FREEZE **UP TO 3 MONTHS**
WITHOUT THE CHILLED BUTTER

RECIPE BY
MARIE-PIERRE MOINE

CELERY AND CELERIAC SOUP

This earthy soup combines mildly nutty celeriac and more assertive celery to create a fragrant, satisfying winter warmer.

1 tbsp sunflower, groundnut, or mild-flavoured olive oil

30g (1oz) butter

500g (1lb 2oz) celeriac, peeled and chopped

1 large head celery, cored and chopped

1 medium floury potato, peeled and chopped

sea salt and freshly ground black pepper

1 litre (1¾ pints) light vegetable or chicken stock

30g (1oz) chilled butter, diced

4 slices walnut bread, lightly toasted, to serve

1 Put the oil and butter in a large sauté pan over a medium heat. Add the celeriac, celery, and potato. Stir well for 2–3 minutes then reduce the heat a little. Add 3–4 tbsp water, and season lightly. Partly cover and leave to stew gently until very soft. Stir the vegetables from time to time and keep the heat low.

2 Transfer the cooked vegetables to a food processor and purée. Return to the pan and add the stock. Season, stir briskly to blend, and bring to a simmer over a medium heat, stirring frequently. Reduce the heat a little and leave to simmer gently for 10–15 minutes, still stirring occasionally. Taste and adjust the seasoning.

3 Just before serving, whisk in the chilled diced butter. Serve hot with toasted walnut bread.

SERVES **4**
PREP **10 MINS**
COOK **25 MINS**
FREEZE **UP TO 3 MONTHS**
BEFORE CREAM IS ADDED

RECIPE BY
CAROLYN HUMPHRIES

CELERIAC AND CAMEMBERT SOUP WITH CRANBERRY SWIRL

A great way to use up any white-rinded soft cheese, even if it's smelling a bit strong. If you don't have celeriac, use a large potato and season with celery salt.

knob of butter

1 onion, chopped

½ small celeriac, about 225g (8oz) prepared weight, roughly diced

450ml (15fl oz) chicken or vegetable stock

1 bouquet garni

salt and freshly ground black pepper

450ml (15fl oz) milk

115g (4oz) ripe Camembert, diced

4 tbsp double cream

4 tsp cranberry sauce

4 tsp orange or cranberry juice

4 tsp sunflower oil

1 Melt the butter in a saucepan. Add the onion and fry gently, stirring, for 2 minutes, or until softened but not browned. Add the celeriac, stock, bouquet garni, and a little seasoning (go easy on the salt). Bring to the boil, reduce the heat, cover, and simmer gently for 15 minutes, or until the celeriac is tender. Remove and discard the bouquet garni.

2 Purée in a blender or food processor, adding the milk and cheese. Return the soup to the rinsed-out pan, stir in the cream, and reheat, but do not boil. Taste and adjust the seasoning.

3 Meanwhile, whisk the cranberry sauce with the juice and oil until thoroughly blended. Ladle the soup into warm, shallow soup plates. Whisk the cranberry mixture again and, using a teaspoon, swirl a little of the cranberry mixture in the centre of each bowl and quickly draw a cocktail stick from the centre to the edge all round to form a Catherine wheel shape. Serve immediately.

SERVES **6**
PREP **15 MINS**
COOK **40 MINS**
FREEZE **UP TO 3 MONTHS**
BEFORE THE CREAM IS ADDED

100g (3½oz) shelled hazelnuts

45g (1½oz) butter

1 medium/large celeriac,
  roughly diced

1 onion, chopped

2 tbsp long-grain rice or
  pudding rice

1 litre (1¾ pints) hot chicken
  stock

salt and freshly ground black
  pepper

juice of ½ lemon

90ml (3fl oz) double cream

RECIPE BY
SOPHIE GRIGSON

CELERIAC AND HAZELNUT SOUP

Make the effort to brew up your own chicken stock (see pp18–19), as it complements the flavour of the celeriac and hazelnuts in this soup in a way that shop-bought stock cannot.

1 Preheat the oven to 190°C (375°F/Gas 5). Spread the hazelnuts out on a baking tray and roast for 5–10 minutes or until they turn a shade darker and the skins flake off easily. Check regularly to prevent burning. Allow to cool slightly, then rub off the skins.

2 Melt the butter in a large pan over a low heat. Add the celeriac, onion, rice, and hazelnuts and turn to coat well, then cover with a lid and leave to sweat gently for 10–15 minutes, stirring once or twice. Pour in half the stock, season well with salt and pepper, and bring to the boil. Simmer gently for 15 minutes or until the celeriac and rice are good and tender.

3 Let the soup cool for a few minutes, then whizz until completely smooth in a blender, adding the remaining stock to thin the soup down. Return to the pan, stir in the lemon juice and then the cream, and reheat, being sure to taste and balance the seasoning. Serve totally hot and steaming.

SERVES **6**
PREP **30 MINS**
COOK **50 MINS**
FREEZE **UP TO 3 MONTHS**
AT THE END OF STEP 2

675–900g (1½–2lb) winter squash (such as onion squash, red kuri, crown prince, or pumpkin), peeled and cut into chunks

450g (1lb) good tomatoes

6 garlic cloves, unpeeled

1 sprig of rosemary

2 sprigs of thyme

1 red onion, cut into 8 wedges

4 tbsp extra virgin olive oil

1.2 litres (2 pints) hot vegetable stock or chicken stock

salt and freshly ground black pepper

12 croûtes (see p39)

freshly grated Comté or Gruyère, to serve

FOR THE ROUILLE

small pinch of saffron

1 garlic clove, chopped

1 red chilli, deseeded and roughly chopped

salt

1 egg yolk

1 tbsp red wine vinegar

90ml (3fl oz) sunflower oil

4 tbsp extra virgin olive oil

RECIPE BY
SOPHIE GRIGSON

ROAST SQUASH SOUP

Roasting the squash concentrates and develops its flavour beautifully, and leaves you free to get on with making a chilli-hot rouille sauce, which gives this soup its vigour.

1 Preheat the oven to 220°C (425°F/Gas 7). Put the first seven ingredients into a roasting tin and turn to coat in oil. Roast, turning occasionally, for 45 minutes or until everything is very tender. Discard the herb stalks, and scrape the rest of the roasted ingredients into a blender. Add the stock and whizz until smooth. You may need to do this in batches. Pour into a large pan and season with salt and pepper.

2 Meanwhile, make a rouille. Soak the saffron in 1 tbsp warm water. Pound the garlic, chilli, and a pinch of salt to a paste in a mortar, then work in the egg yolk and vinegar. Mix the two oils, then drip them in, whisking constantly. When one-third of the oil has been incorporated, increase the flow to a slow trickle. Stir in the saffron in its water, then adjust the seasonings.

3 To serve, reheat the soup, then ladle into bowls. Pass the croûtes, the rouille, and the grated cheese around separately, so everyone can smear the croûtes liberally with rouille, float them in the steaming soup, and then finish with a flurry of grated cheese.

SERVES **6–8**
PREP **25 MINS**
COOK **35 MINS**
FREEZE **UP TO 3 MONTHS**
WITHOUT BASIL AND LIME CREAM

RECIPE BY
SOPHIE GRIGSON

WINTER SQUASH SOUP WITH BASIL AND LIME CREAM

The sharp basil and lime cream melting into this soup is a perfect finish for smart occasions, but for a more everyday supper, you can leave it out.

5 garlic cloves

1 large onion, chopped

2.5cm (1in) piece root ginger, peeled and chopped

3 tbsp sunflower oil

1.5kg (3lb 3oz) winter squash (such as onion squash, red kuri, crown prince, or pumpkin), seeds and rind removed, roughly cubed

2 sprigs of parsley

1 sprig of thyme

1 bay leaf

3 star anise

350g (12oz) tomatoes, skinned, deseeded, and roughly chopped

2 litres (3½ pints) hot vegetable stock or chicken stock

salt and freshly ground black pepper

300ml (10fl oz) whipping cream

juice of 1–2 limes

a small handful of basil leaves, chopped, to serve

1 Chop two of the garlic cloves, but leave the rest whole. Put the chopped garlic and the whole garlic into a large pan with the onion, ginger, oil, and squash. Tie the herbs together in a bundle and throw those in too. Cover with a lid and sweat over a low heat for 10 minutes, stirring once or twice.

2 Add the star anise, tomatoes, and stock, then season with salt and pepper and bring to the boil. Simmer for 20 minutes or until the squash is tender. Pick out and discard the bundle of herbs and the star anise. Whizz the soup in a blender until smooth and then pass it through a sieve. Alternatively, you can work it through a food mill. Taste and adjust the seasoning, then reheat gently.

3 Meanwhile, pour the cream into a bowl, add the lime juice, and whisk. Once the cream holds its shape loosely, fold in the basil. As you ladle the soup into bowls, top with a dollop of basil and lime cream.

SERVES **4–6**
PREP **10 MINS**
COOK **40–50 MINS**
FREEZE **UP TO 3 MONTHS**
BEFORE CREAM IS ADDED

RECIPE BY
CELIA BROOKS BROWN

CREAMY SWEDE SOUP

As a strictly cold-season vegetable, swede stores up lots of starch in the edible root base. It is this that gives this rich, wintry soup its velvety texture.

25g (scant 1oz) butter

2 medium onions, chopped

750g (1lb 10oz) swede (trimmed weight), cut into cubes

sea salt and freshly ground black pepper

1 litre (1¾ pints) hot vegetable stock

1 tbsp honey

½ nutmeg

150ml (5fl oz) single cream, plus extra to garnish

1 Melt the butter in a large pan over a medium heat. Add the onions, and fry for 6–8 minutes or until lightly golden. Stir in the swede and a pinch of salt, cover with a lid, and cook for 10 minutes, stirring frequently. Pour in the stock, add the honey, and bring to the boil, grating in the nutmeg as you do so. Simmer for 20–30 minutes or until the swede is completely soft.

2 Cool briefly, then whizz in a blender until smooth and velvety. You may need to do this in batches. Season with salt and pepper, then stir in the cream. Serve each bowlful with a swirl of cream and a good grinding of black pepper.

SERVES **4–6**
PREP **20 MINS**
COOK **40 MINS**
FREEZE **UP TO 3 MONTHS**

RECIPE BY
ALICE WATERS

TURNIP SOUP

Alice Waters of Chez Panisse restaurant in California writes:
"Young turnips with their greens are in the markets in spring
and fall. Together they make a delicious soup." Through the
winter you could substitute kale for the turnip greens.

2 bunches of young turnips with
   greens, about 675g (1½lb)
   total in weight

3 tbsp butter or olive oil

1 onion, thinly sliced

1 bay leaf

2 sprigs of thyme

salt

1.2 litres (2 pints) well-
   flavoured chicken stock

grated Parmesan, to serve

1 Remove the greens from the turnips, then trim and discard the stems. Rinse and drain the leaves and cut into 1cm (½in) strips. Trim the roots from the bases and, if the skins are tough (taste one to see), peel before slicing thinly. Heat the butter or oil in a heavy pot over a low heat, add the onion, and cook very gently for 12 minutes or until soft.

2 Stir in the turnip bases, along with the bay leaf and thyme, and season with salt. Cook for 5 minutes, stirring occasionally, then pour in the stock and bring to the boil. Lower the heat to a simmer, cover, and cook for 10 minutes. Add the turnip greens and cook for another 5–10 minutes or until tender. Remove the bay leaf, check the seasoning and serve. This is excellent with a little grated Parmesan on top.

SERVES **4–6**
PREP **10 MINS**
COOK **30 MINS**
FREEZE **UP TO 3 MONTHS**
AT THE END OF STEP 1

RECIPE BY
CAROLYN HUMPHRIES

TURNIP SOUP WITH PIMENTO, CHILLI, AND NOODLES

A light, colourful soup with quite a chilli kick. Larger turnips have a stronger flavour, which is perfect for this dish. Don't use the delicate baby ones.

4 spring onions, chopped

2 good-sized turnips, diced

½ tsp crushed dried chillies

1 green jalapeño chilli, deseeded and cut into thin rings

2 star anise

2 tsp tomato purée

900ml (1½ pints) hot vegetable stock or light chicken stock

1 slab dried thin Chinese egg noodles

1 preserved pimento, drained and diced

soy sauce

freshly ground black pepper

small handful of coriander leaves, torn

1 Put the spring onions, turnips, chillies, jalapeño, star anise, tomato purée, and stock in a saucepan and bring to the boil. Lower the heat, part-cover, and simmer gently for 30 minutes or until the turnips are really tender.

2 Meanwhile, put the noodles in a bowl, cover with boiling water, and leave to stand for 5 minutes, stirring to loosen, then drain. Stir the noodles into the soup, along with the pimento. Season to taste with soy sauce and pepper, then stir in half the coriander. Ladle into warm soup bowls, top with the remaining coriander, and serve.

SERVES **4**
PREP **20 MINS**
COOK **40 MINS**
FREEZE **UP TO 3 MONTHS**

RECIPE BY
MARIE-PIERRE MOINE

POTATO SOUP WITH BROCCOLI, SHALLOT, AND MASCARPONE

Broccoli and shallot add colour and freshness to this rich combination of potato and cheese. You can use Caerphilly or Wensleydale in place of the mascarpone if you prefer.

1 tbsp olive oil

10g (¼oz) butter

2 large banana shallots, finely chopped

350g (12oz) floury potatoes, chopped into 2.5cm (1in) chunks

sea salt and freshly ground black pepper

1 large head of broccoli, cut into florets

4 tbsp mascarpone

4 croûtes (see p39)

30g (1oz) creamy, strong-flavoured blue cheese, such as Roquefort, fourme d'Ambert, or Gorgonzola piquante

1 Heat the oil and butter in a sauté pan over a moderate heat, add the shallots and potatoes, and cook for 5 minutes, stirring often. Meanwhile, boil 1.5 litres (2¾ pints) water in the kettle.

2 Pour 1.35 litres (2½ pints) of the boiling water into the pan and stir well. Season lightly with sea salt and pepper and bring to a simmer. Lower the heat, cover with a lid, and simmer for 10 minutes. Add the broccoli, stir, cover again, and continue cooking for 10–15 minutes or until the vegetables are tender. Leave to cool for several minutes, then transfer the contents of the pan to a blender and whizz until smooth. Strain the soup back into the pan through a sieve, using a wooden spoon to push as much of the mixture through as possible.

3 Pour in the rest of the hot water. Place the pan over a moderate heat, stir in the mascarpone, and keep stirring until it has blended in. Season with salt and pepper. Spread the croûtes with the blue cheese, ladle the soup into bowls, and float a piece in the centre of each one.

SERVES 4
PREP 15 MINS
COOK 1 HR 15 MINS
FREEZE UP TO 3 MONTHS
BEFORE ONION AND BACON ARE ADDED

RECIPE BY
ANGELA NILSEN

ROAST POTATO SOUP

Combined with just a few simple ingredients, roast potatoes can quickly be transformed into a luxuriously smooth, rich, and comforting winter soup.

450g (1lb) floury potatoes, such as King Edward, cut into 5cm (2in) chunks

2 tbsp olive oil

salt and freshly ground black pepper

3 large shallots, roughly chopped

2 garlic cloves, halved

1 large parsnip, cut into small chunks

900ml (1½ pints) hot vegetable stock

4 rashers streaky bacon, cut into thin strips and rinds discarded

1 onion, halved lengthways and thinly sliced

100ml (3½fl oz) double cream

large knob of butter

1 Preheat the oven to 200°C (400°F/Gas 6). Put the potatoes and 1 tbsp of the oil into a small roasting tin and toss to coat well. Season with pepper, then roast for 45 minutes or until golden. Turn occasionally to ensure even roasting. Transfer to a large pan and add the shallots, garlic, and parsnip. Add the stock, bring to the boil, then cover with a lid and simmer for 20 minutes or until the parsnip is tender.

2 Meanwhile, heat the remaining oil in a frying pan, add the bacon, and fry for 5 minutes or until crisp. Remove with a slotted spoon and drain on kitchen paper. Add the onion to the pan, along with a pinch of salt, and fry over a medium heat for 8–10 minutes or until dark golden brown and well caramelized. Set to one side and keep warm.

3 Remove the soup from the heat, add the cream and butter, and stir until the butter has melted. Whizz in a blender or food processor until smooth. You may need to do this in batches. Add a little more stock if the soup is too thick. For an extra smooth soup, press the mixture through a fine sieve. Season to taste with salt and pepper, then reheat gently and serve topped with the crispy onion and bacon.

SERVES **6**
PREP **25 MINS**
COOK **45 MINS**
FREEZE **UP TO 3 MONTHS**
WITHOUT THE FRIED ONION
OR CHANTERELLES

GERMAN POTATO SOUP

If you can't get hold of fresh chanterelle mushrooms for this,
you can use jarred or canned. Drain, rinse, and then drain
them again before you fry them.

75g (2½oz) butter

¼ celeriac, diced

250g (9oz) carrots, diced

675g (1½lb) floury potatoes,
diced

1 onion, studded with a bay leaf
and a clove

1.5 litres (2¾ pints) hot
vegetable stock

200g (7oz) leeks, sliced

1 onion, diced

200g (7oz) chanterelles, large
ones halved

120ml (4fl oz) whipping cream
or 150g (5½oz) crème
fraîche

salt and freshly ground black
pepper

pinch of dried marjoram

pinch of freshly grated nutmeg

2 tbsp chopped flat-leaf parsley,
chervil, or chives

1 Melt two-thirds of the butter in a large pan, add the celeriac and carrots, and cook, stirring frequently, for 6–8 minutes or until light brown. Add the potatoes, onion, and stock and bring to the boil. Lower the heat, cover with a lid, and simmer for 20 minutes or until tender. Add the leeks, cover again, and cook for 10 minutes more.

2 Meanwhile, melt the rest of the butter in a frying pan, add the diced onion, and fry, stirring continuously, for 4–5 minutes or until soft but not brown. Add the chanterelles and fry, stirring frequently, for 5 minutes.

3 Remove the whole onion from the soup and discard. Transfer about one-third of the contents of the pan to a blender and whizz until smooth. Stir in the cream and return to the pan. Season with salt and pepper, then add the marjoram, nutmeg, and the fried onion and chanterelles, and reheat gently. Serve sprinkled with the herbs.

SERVES **4**
PREP **5 MINS**
USING COOKED CHESTNUTS
COOK **1 HR 55 MINS**
FREEZE **UP TO 3 MONTHS**
BEFORE RICE IS ADDED

225g (8oz) fresh chestnuts or 180g (6oz) cooked peeled chestnuts

2 sprigs thyme

1 bay leaf

1.2 litres (2 pints) chicken stock

salt and freshly ground black pepper

60g (2oz) risotto rice

30g (1oz) butter

300ml (10fl oz) milk

a little truffle oil, to serve

RECIPE BY
SOPHIE GRIGSON

PIEDMONT CHESTNUT SOUP

You can use vacuum-packed cooked chestnuts for this Italian soup, but fresh ones have a more velvety texture. If you do use fresh, remember to allow time for peeling.

1 If using fresh chestnuts, score a deep cross in the skin of each one with a small sharp knife, then put half a dozen at a time into a microwave-proof bowl. Cover tightly with cling film and cook on full power for 20–30 seconds or until the skins have split, then peel off the outer and inner skins with your fingers. Put the peeled chestnuts in a pan with the herbs, stock, and a little salt and pepper, bring to the boil, then simmer for 1½ hours.

2 Add the rice and simmer for 10 minutes. Stir in the butter and the milk and simmer for a final 10 minutes. Remove the bay leaf and thyme, taste, and adjust the seasonings, if necessary. Serve, with a few drops of truffle oil in each bowlful to turn this peasant soup into a major treat.

SERVES **6**
PREP 15 MINS
COOK **40–55 MINS**
FREEZE **UP TO 3 MONTHS**
WITHOUT THE CREAM AND MILK

45g (1½oz) butter

2 carrots, sliced

1 leek (white part only), sliced

2 parsnips, sliced

1 onion, sliced

1 small turnip, sliced

3 celery stalks, sliced

1 potato, sliced

1.2 litres (2 pints) hot vegetable
stock

2 tsp fresh thyme leaves

1 bay leaf

pinch of grated nutmeg

salt and freshly ground black
pepper

3 tbsp single cream

3 tbsp milk

bunch of chives, snipped,
to garnish

RECIPE BY
ROOPA GULATI

CREAM OF VEGETABLE SOUP

Simple, affordable, and immensely satisfying, this hearty soup makes a warming meal when accompanied with some freshly baked crusty bread.

1 Melt the butter in a large pan, add the carrots, leek, parsnips, onion, turnip, celery, and potato, and stir to coat well. Cover the pan with a lid and cook for 10–15 minutes or until the vegetables have softened.

2 Add the stock, thyme, bay leaf, and nutmeg, then season with salt and pepper. Bring to the boil and simmer, uncovered, for 30–40 minutes or until the vegetables are meltingly soft. Scoop out the bay leaf and discard.

3 Whizz the soup in a blender until smooth. You may need to do this in batches. If you like the texture of your soups very smooth, strain it through a fine sieve, otherwise leave it as it is. Stir in the cream and milk, adding more milk if the consistency is still too thick. Season with salt and pepper, then reheat gently. Garnish with the chives and serve.

SERVES **4–6**
PREP **20 MINS**
PLUS 8 HOURS SOAKING
COOK **1¾ HRS**
FREEZE **UP TO 1 MONTH**
AT THE END OF STEP 2

100g (3½oz) dried white
    cannellini beans

2 tbsp olive oil

2 celery stalks, finely chopped

2 carrots, finely chopped

1 onion, finely chopped

400g can chopped tomatoes

750ml (1¼ pints) hot vegetable
    stock or chicken stock

salt and freshly ground black pepper

60g (2oz) small short-cut pasta

4 tbsp chopped flat-leaf parsley

40g (1½oz) Parmesan, finely grated

MINESTRONE SOUP

A substantial soup that is a meal in itself. Mix and match
whatever vegetables are in season.

1 Put the dried beans in a large bowl, cover with cold water, and leave
to soak in the fridge for at least 8 hours or overnight. Drain the beans,
then place them in a large saucepan and cover with cold water. Bring
to the boil, then boil hard for 10 minutes, skimming the surface of any
scum with a slotted spoon. Lower the heat, part-cover the pan, and
simmer for 1 hour or until the beans are tender. Drain and set aside.

2 Heat the oil in the rinsed-out pan over a medium heat. Add the celery,
carrots, and onion, and fry, stirring occasionally, for 5 minutes or until
tender. Stir in the cooked beans, then add the tomatoes and their juice,
the stock, and some salt and pepper. Bring to the boil, stirring all the time,
then cover with a lid and simmer for 20 minutes.

3 Add the pasta and simmer for 10–15 minutes or until it is al dente. Stir
in the parsley and half the Parmesan, then adjust the seasoning. Serve hot,
sprinkled with the remaining Parmesan.

SERVES **6**
PREP **25 MINS**
PLUS OVERNIGHT SOAKING
COOK **2–3 HRS**
FREEZE **UP TO 3 MONTHS**
BEFORE CAVOLO NERO IS ADDED

200g (7oz) dried cannellini
    or haricot beans, soaked
    overnight in water

1 bouquet garni made from a
    sprig of rosemary, a sprig
    of thyme, and 2 bay leaves
    (see p24)

4 tbsp extra virgin olive oil, plus
    extra to serve

1 onion, chopped

3 carrots, diced

2 celery stalks, diced

2 leeks, very thinly sliced

3 garlic cloves, chopped

1 dried red chilli, finely chopped

3 tomatoes, skinned, deseeded,
    and chopped

2 tbsp tomato purée

salt and freshly ground black
    pepper

4 cavolo nero or curly kale
    leaves, or the outer leaves of
    a Savoy cabbage, tough stalks
    removed and the leaves
    coarsely chopped

6 slices stale bread

1 garlic clove, cut in half

RECIPE BY
SOPHIE GRIGSON

ZUPPA DI VERDURE

Leftovers of this big warming soup from Tuscany are
never thrown away, but used to make the sturdy Ribollita
(see p302). Both are frugally filling, and very good.

1 Drain the beans and place them in a large pan with the bouquet
garni and twice their volume of cold water. Bring to the boil, then boil
hard for 10 minutes. Lower the heat, and simmer gently for 1–2 hours
or until tender, adding more water if needed. Remove the pan from
the heat, discard the bouquet garni, and leave the beans to cool in their
cooking water.

2 Heat the oil in a large heavy pot, then add the onion, carrots, celery,
leeks, garlic, and chilli. Cover with a lid and sweat over a low heat for
10 minutes, stirring once or twice. Add the tomatoes and tomato purée
and cook over a moderate heat for 3–4 minutes. Add the beans, their
cooking water and enough water to cover the vegetables generously.
Season generously. Bring to the boil and simmer gently for 20 minutes
or until the vegetables are tender. Purée half the soup in a blender, then
return to the pan. Add the cavolo nero and simmer for 10 minutes or
until tender. Adjust the seasonings.

3 Rub the bread with the garlic and arrange in a warm shallow dish or
tureen. Spoon in the soup and serve with a bottle of best olive oil out
on the table for people to help themselves.

SERVES **4–6**
PREP **10 MINS**
COOK **40 MINS**
FREEZE **NOT SUITABLE**

RECIPE BY
SOPHIE GRIGSON

RIBOLLITA

Ribollita means "reboiled" in Italian, and that is more
or less what this soup is – reboiled Zuppa di verdure
(see p300). It is wonderful, heart-warming comfort food.

I quantity day-old Zuppa di
verdure, made up to the
point just before the cavolo
nero is added (see p300)

6 cavolo nero or curly kale
leaves, or the outer leaves of
a Savoy cabbage, tough stalks
removed and the leaves
coarsely chopped

6 slices good-quality stale bread

I garlic clove, halved

2–3 tbsp extra virgin olive oil,
plus extra to serve

½–I red onion, very finely
sliced

4 tbsp freshly grated Parmesan
(optional)

I Preheat the oven to 190°C (375°F/Gas 5). Bring the soup to the boil
in a large pan, stir in the cavolo nero, and simmer for 10 minutes or until
tender. Meanwhile, rub the stale bread with garlic.

2 Oil a large gratin dish or similar ovenproof dish with olive oil, then
spoon about a quarter of the soup into the dish, spreading it over the
base. Now, lay half the slices of bread over the soup, then spoon over half
the remaining soup. Repeat these two layers one more time. Lay the red
onion over the top, then scatter with the Parmesan, if using. Drizzle over
a little olive oil, then bake for 30 minutes. Serve sizzling hot, with extra
olive oil out on the table for those who want it.

SERVES **4**
PREP **15 MINS**
COOK **45 MINS**
FREEZE **UP TO 3 MONTHS**
AT THE END OF STEP 2

RECIPE BY
MARIE-PIERRE MOINE

FRENCH COUNTRY SOUP

A mixed vegetable potage (soup) like this is traditional French
family fare. It is ladled out of a tureen into wide shallow bowls
as a starter all over the country.

1 tbsp sunflower oil or
   groundnut oil

30g (1oz) butter

3 large leeks, cleaned and
   chopped

1 large floury potato, roughly
   cubed

2 large carrots, chopped

750ml (1¼ pints) light vegetable
   stock or chicken stock

2 bay leaves

sea salt and freshly ground
   black pepper

100ml (3½fl oz) hot water

1 Put the oil and half the butter in a large sauté pan over a very moderate
heat. Add the leeks, potato, and carrots and cook, stirring frequently, for
5 minutes. Reduce the heat a little, add the stock and bay leaves, then season
lightly with salt and pepper. Cover and cook gently, stirring occasionally, for
30 minutes or until the vegetables are very soft.

2 Leave to cool for several minutes, then lift out the bay leaves. Transfer
the soup to a blender and whizz until smooth. Strain back into the pan
through a sieve, using the back of a wooden spoon to push through as
much as possible. Pour the hot water through the sieve to extract
as much as you can from the vegetables.

3 Reheat gently, stirring frequently. Taste and adjust the seasoning, then
stir in the remaining butter and serve very hot.

SERVES **4**
PREP **15 MINS**
COOK **30 MINS**
FREEZE **UP TO 3 MONTHS**
WITH ALL VEGETABLES PURÉED

1 leek

300g (11oz) potatoes

250g (9oz) large carrots

175g (6oz) small sweet
    potatoes

1 tbsp olive oil

15g (½oz) butter

600ml (1 pint) hot vegetable
    stock

1 tbsp chopped flat-leaf parsley

salt and freshly ground black
    pepper

"PENNY" SOUP

Mounded together in the centre of the bowl, the
vegetables in this soup resemble coins – which is one
of the reasons it got its name. The other is that it is
very inexpensive to make.

1 Slice the vegetables into 3mm (⅛in) rounds. Heat the oil and butter
in a large saucepan, add the leeks, and cook over a medium heat, stirring
frequently, for 3–4 minutes or until soft. Add the potatoes, carrots, and
sweet potatoes and cook, stirring, for 1 minute.

2 Pour in the stock, then bring to the boil, cover with a lid, and simmer for
20 minutes or until the vegetables are tender but not soft. Transfer about
one-third of the vegetables to a blender or food processor with a little of
the liquid and blend to a smooth purée, then return to the pan. Stir in the
parsley, season to taste with salt and pepper, and serve, with the vegetables
in a little mound in the centre.

SERVES **4–6**
PREP 15 MINS
COOK 35–45 MINS
FREEZE UP TO 3 MONTHS

RECIPE BY
CELIA BROOKS BROWN

JERUSALEM ARTICHOKE SOUP WITH SAFFRON AND THYME

Use whatever proportion of carrots and Jerusalem artichokes you have, adding up to 700g (1lb 9oz) in total. The carrots enhance the colour and sweetness of the soup.

2 tbsp virgin rapeseed oil or olive oil, plus extra to garnish

2 medium onions, chopped

3 garlic cloves, chopped

350g (12oz) Jerusalem artichokes, scrubbed and roughly chopped

350g (12oz) carrots, scrubbed and roughly chopped

sea salt and freshly ground black pepper

1.2 litres (2 pints) hot vegetable stock

1 tbsp fresh thyme leaves or 1½ tsp dried thyme

large pinch (about 30 strands) of saffron

juice of ½ lemon

1 Heat the oil in a large pan over a medium heat, add the onions, and fry for 5–10 minutes or until soft and translucent. Add the garlic and fry for 30 seconds or until fragrant. Stir in the artichokes, carrots, and a little salt, then cover with a lid and sweat, stirring frequently, for 10–15 minutes or until the vegetables are softened.

2 Add the stock, thyme, and saffron, bring to the boil, then lower the heat to a simmer and cook for 20 minutes or until the vegetables are thoroughly soft. Cool briefly, then whizz until smooth in a blender. Stir in the lemon juice and season to taste with salt and pepper. Serve in warm bowls, with a drizzle more oil on top.

SERVES **4**
PREP **20 MINS**
COOK **25 MINS**
FREEZE **UP TO 3 MONTHS**
AT THE END OF STEP 2

RECIPE BY
SHAUN HILL

SCALLOP AND ARTICHOKE SOUP

The scallops are a counterpoint to the distinctive taste of the
Jerusalem artichoke purée in this traditional soup menu pairing.

100g (3½oz) unsalted butter

1 onion, chopped

1 garlic clove, chopped

1kg (2¼lb) Jerusalem
    artichokes, peeled or
    scrubbed and cut into
    small dice

1.5 litres (2¾ pints) hot chicken
    stock or water

100ml (3½fl oz) double cream

salt and freshly ground black
    pepper

a pinch of freshly grated
    nutmeg

4 rashers streaky bacon,
    cut into small dice, rinds
    discarded

4 scallops (white part only)

2 tbsp sunflower oil

few drops of lemon juice

snipped chives, to garnish

1 Melt half the butter in a large pan and fry the onion gently. Add the garlic and artichokes and sweat over a low heat for 3 minutes. Add the stock or water, cover with a lid, and simmer until the artichokes are completely cooked and soft. Purée in a blender with the cream and the remaining butter. You may need to do this in batches. Return to the pan and season with salt and pepper, then sprinkle in the nutmeg and keep warm.

2 Fry the bacon in a frying pan until crisp, then spoon on to kitchen paper to drain. Cut the scallops into large discs, season with salt and pepper, then fry in the sunflower oil – they will be ready almost as soon as they are sealed by the heat. Squeeze over a few drops of lemon juice.

3 Divide the artichoke purée among four bowls, spoon the bacon and scallops on top, then garnish with the chives and serve.

SERVES **4**
PREP **20 MINS**
COOK **40 MINS**
FREEZE **NOT SUITABLE**

RECIPE BY
MARIE-PIERRE MOINE

CREAMY SCALLOP BISQUE

A rich broth sets off the sweetness of the scallops while the chorizo (or black pudding) adds a spicy contrast. Serve as the first course of a dinner party menu.

300ml (10fl oz) dry white wine

15g (½oz) butter

1 small onion, finely chopped

1 small shallot, very finely chopped

1 medium-sized ripe tomato, chopped

200g (7oz) prawns, shelled

100g (3½oz) cod or pollock, skinned and cut into chunks

12 small scallops (or 6 large), white parts and corals

2 tbsp chopped parsley

2 tsp dill seeds

3 tbsp brandy

sea salt and freshly ground black pepper

100ml (3½fl oz) single cream

75g (2½oz) chorizo, diced, or black pudding, minced

1 tbsp finely chopped chives, to finish

1 Boil 700ml (1¼ pints) water with the wine. Put the butter in a sauté pan over a medium heat. Add the onion and shallot and soften until golden. Add the tomato, prawns, fish, corals, parsley, and dill seeds. Stir, and cook for 5 minutes. Stir in the brandy, and cook for a minute. Pour in the boiling wine mixture and season lightly. Reduce the heat, and simmer gently for 10 minutes. Take off the heat and leave to cool. Stir and mash down the soup with the back of a spoon. Then gently heat the cream in another pan until hot.

2 Transfer the soup to a blender and purée. Strain through a sieve back into the pan and stir in the hot cream. Return to a simmer. Remove from the heat and adjust the seasoning. Cover and keep warm.

3 Put a non-stick frying pan over a medium heat. Add the chorizo or black pudding and fry for 3–5 minutes until cooked through and crispy. Set aside on a plate lined with kitchen paper and keep warm.

4 Add the scallops to the pan. Cook for 2 minutes, turn over and cook for a minute. Remove from the heat. Ladle the soup into four bowls and add the scallops. Scatter over the chorizo or black pudding and chives and serve immediately.

SERVES **4**
PREP **20 MINS**
COOK **20 MINS**
FREEZE **UP TO 2 MONTHS**
WITHOUT FISH

RECIPE BY
MARIE-PIERRE MOINE

PORTUGUESE HADDOCK SOUP

The strong flavours of cavolo nero and smoked haddock develop
in minutes, making this soup very satisfying. If you want to freeze
it, do so before adding the fish.

300g (10oz) leaves of cavolo
  nero, kale, or savoy cabbage

2 tbsp mild olive oil

1 Spanish onion, finely chopped

3 garlic cloves, peeled and
  crushed

1 large waxy potato, peeled and
  diced

250ml (8fl oz) full-fat or
  semi-skimmed milk

salt and freshly ground black
  pepper

300g (10oz) smoked haddock
  fillet, skinned and flaked

1 Rinse the greens, cut out and discard the large ribs and shred the leaves
finely. Put a sauté pan over a moderate heat and add the oil. Once it is hot,
add the onion and garlic and stir for 4–5 minutes, or until softened.

2 Add the potato and milk, then pour in enough water to cover everything
by 2–3cm (¾–1¼in). Season generously, bring to a simmer and cook for
5 minutes, then add the cabbage and continue cooking for 10–15 minutes
until the vegetables are tender.

3 Stir in the haddock and simmer for a minute, then take off the heat and
cover. Leave to stand for 5 minutes before serving.

SERVES **4**
PREP **15 MINS**
COOK **1 HR 10 MINS**
FREEZE **UP TO 3 MONTHS**
BROTH ONLY

1 chicken leg and thigh portion

1 onion, finely chopped

1 leek, thinly sliced

1 large carrot, finely diced

1 litre (1¾ pints) water

1 sprig of fresh thyme

1 tsp celery salt

salt and freshly ground black
    pepper

FOR THE MATZO BALLS

1 potato, about 115g (4oz),
    cooked and mashed

45g (1½oz) fine matzo meal

½ tsp baking powder

½ tsp grated fresh root ginger

1 tbsp chopped fresh thyme

1 tbsp chopped fresh parsley

1 garlic clove, finely chopped

salt and freshly ground black
    pepper

1 tbsp sunflower oil

1 egg, beaten

4 small sprigs of fresh thyme,
    to garnish

RECIPE BY
CAROLYN HUMPHRIES

MATZO BALL SOUP

This is a traditional soup with a modern twist. Adding baking powder and mashed potato to the balls gives them a really light, fluffy texture.

1 Put the soup ingredients in a large saucepan. Bring to the boil, reduce the heat, cover, and simmer gently for 1 hour, topping up with water if it gets low. Meanwhile, mix the mashed potato with the matzo meal, baking powder, ginger, thyme, parsley, garlic, and a little salt and pepper. Add the oil then mix with the beaten egg to form a soft, slightly sticky dough. Shape into eight balls.

2 Discard the thyme sprig from the soup. Carefully lift out the chicken and remove all meat from the bones, discarding the skin. Chop the flesh and return to the soup. Taste and adjust the seasoning, if necessary.

3 Bring the soup back to a simmer, drop in the balls, cover, and simmer gently for about 10 minutes until the balls are fluffy and cooked through. Ladle into warm soup bowls and garnish each with a small sprig of fresh thyme.

SERVES **4**
PREP **25–30 MINS**
PLUS SOAKING TIME
COOK **25 MINS**
PLUS SITTING TIME
FREEZE **NOT SUITABLE**

1.2 litres (2 pints) chicken stock, preferably home-made

6 slices unpeeled root ginger

½ tsp coriander seeds

4 star anise

2 stalks lemongrass, sliced

2 skinless, boneless chicken breasts

100g (3½oz) rice noodles

2 pak choi, very thinly sliced

thai fish sauce

100g (3½oz) bean sprouts

small bunch coriander, about 20g (¾oz), roughly chopped

small handful mint leaves, finely shredded

2 spring onions, thinly sliced

1 large fresh red chilli, deseeded (unless you like it hot) and thinly sliced

lime wedges

RECIPE BY
ANGELA NILSEN

VIETNAMESE NOODLE SOUP

Start off with a good-quality stock for this fragrant, light, refreshing soup, then serve it piled high with fresh herbs and chillies.

1 Pour the stock into a large saucepan, and tip in the ginger, coriander seeds, star anise, and lemongrass. Simmer gently for 10 minutes. Lower the chicken breasts into the stock and continue simmering for 15 minutes. Remove from the heat and let sit for 5 minutes. Meanwhile, break the noodles (so they are easier to eat) into a large heatproof bowl and cover with boiling water. Leave to soak for the time suggested on the packet.

2 Lift the chicken from the stock with a slotted spoon and transfer it to a board. Slice the chicken into very thin bite-sized strips. Strain and discard the flavourings from the stock and return the stock to the pan. Remove the pan from the heat, drop in the pak choi, and let it wilt in the warmth of the stock. Return the chicken to the stock along with a dash of fish sauce.

3 Drain the noodles and divide between four big bowls. Lay the bean sprouts on top. To serve, ladle the chicken and hot stock over the noodles and top each bowl with a generous scattering of the coriander, mint, spring onions, chilli, and another splash of fish sauce. Offer lime wedges for squeezing over.

SERVES **4**
PREP **40 MINS**
COOK **2 HRS**
FREEZE **UP TO 3 MONTHS**

A small Savoy cabbage,
    cored, ribs removed,
    leaves shredded

salt and freshly ground black
    pepper

500g (1lb 2oz) sauerkraut,
    drained

100g (3½oz) smoked bacon,
    cubed

200g (7oz) smoked Polish
    sausage, sliced

200g (7oz) duck breast or lean
    venison, cubed

1 large red onion, diced

1 clove garlic, crushed

150g (5½oz) brown
    mushrooms, sliced

½ tsp smoked paprika

1 bay leaf

½ tsp juniper berries

1 tsp dried marjoram

½ tsp caraway seeds, crushed
    using a pestle and mortar

200ml (7fl oz) red wine

250ml (8fl oz) beef stock

RECIPE BY
MARIE-PIERRE MOINE

BIGOS

Many variations on this Polish dish exist. Duck or venison
are the traditional choices but you could try lamb or beef
instead. Bacon, sauerkraut, and smoked Polish sausage are,
however, essential.

1 Put a large casserole over a medium heat. Add the cabbage, and cover with
boiling water. Season lightly. Return to a simmer and cook for 10 minutes.
Drain and reserve. Repeat with the sauerkraut but simmer for only
5 minutes. Drain, reserving the sauerkraut as well as the cooking liquid.

2 Put a non-stick frying pan over a medium heat. Fry the bacon until crisp.
Spread over a platter lined with kitchen paper. Fry the sausage and duck
or venison for 5 minutes, stirring, then add to the platter with the bacon.
Set aside. Now fry the onion, garlic, and mushrooms in the same pan until
softened. Add to the casserole, along with all the fried meats.

3 Put the casserole over a medium heat. Stir in the paprika, bay leaf, juniper
berries, marjoram, and caraway seeds. Pour in the wine and stock. Bring to
a simmer, stirring. Cover, reduce the heat a little, and simmer for 1 hour,
stirring from time to time.

4 Add the boiled cabbage, stir, cover, and cook for 10 minutes, and then
stir in the sauerkraut. Add some or all of the reserved cooking liquid
(the mixture should be a thick soup rather than a stew). Simmer for
a further 15 minutes. Taste, adjust the seasoning, and serve very hot.

SERVES **4–6**
PREP **40 MINS**
COOK **I HR**
FREEZE **UP TO 3 MONTHS**

100g (3½oz) lardons or diced
   pancetta

I Spanish onion, finely chopped

3 garlic cloves, crushed

I leg confit of duck

1.5 litres (2¾ pints) chicken
   stock

I small Savoy cabbage, core
   removed and leaves cut into
   2.5 x 7.5cm (1 x 3in) strips

I large carrot, sliced

I celery stalk, diced

I leek, cleaned and sliced

I large floury potato, cubed

sea salt and freshly ground
   black pepper

I tsp pimentón picante or hot
   smoked paprika

½ tsp ground cumin

2–3 sprigs of fresh thyme

2–3 sprigs of flat-leaf parsley,
   plus I tbsp finely chopped
   parsley to garnish

250g can haricot beans,
   drained, rinsed, and drained
   again

8–12 croûtes (see p39), rubbed
   with garlic and brushed with
   olive oil, to serve

RECIPE BY
MARIE-PIERRE MOINE

GARBURE

This one-pot meal of slowly cooked vegetables flavoured with pork and confit of duck comes from southwest France. It is best made the day before and reheated.

I Put a large, deep, heavy-based casserole pan over a moderate heat, add the lardons or pancetta, and fry, stirring frequently, for 2–3 minutes or until crisp and cooked through. Remove with a slotted spoon and drain on kitchen paper. Add the onion and garlic to the pan, reduce the heat a little, and cook, stirring frequently, for 5–8 minutes or until softened.

2 Pick the meat from the duck leg, discarding the skin and bones but reserving the fat, and cut into shreds. Stir into the onion and garlic, then add the stock, cabbage, carrot, celery, leek, and potato. Season lightly with salt and more generously with pepper, then add the pimentón or paprika, cumin, thyme, and parsley. Bring to a simmer, cover, reduce the heat a little, and cook, stirring occasionally, for 30 minutes.

3 Lift out the thyme and parsley. Lightly mash the beans in a bowl, then stir them into the soup and continue cooking until the vegetables are tender. Taste and adjust the seasoning. To serve, stir in the reserved lardons or pancetta along with I tbsp of the duck fat, then sprinkle with the parsley. Place a croûte in each bowl and ladle the piping hot soup on top.

SERVES **4**
PREP **15 MINS**
COOK **30 MINS**
FREEZE **UP TO 3 MONTHS**

1 tbsp olive oil

50g (1¾oz) butter, softened

1 onion, chopped

1 large potato, peeled, cut into
small chunks

2 carrots, cut into small chunks

1 leek, cut into small chunks

2 bay leaves

1 litre (1¾ pints) turkey or
chicken stock, preferably
home-made

25g (scant 1oz) plain flour

50g (1¾oz) frozen peas

200g (7oz) cooked turkey, cut
in chunks

big handful of roughly chopped
parsley

salt and freshly ground black
pepper

hot garlic bread, to serve

RECIPE BY
ANGELA NILSEN

CHUNKY TURKEY SOUP

This thick and creamy soup is perfect for using up
leftover turkey, and tastes even richer if you have
some home-made turkey stock to hand.

1 Heat the oil and half of the butter in a large sauté pan. Add the
onion and fry for 4–5 minutes until just starting to turn golden. Add
the potato, carrots, leek, and bay leaves and fry for a few more minutes
over a high heat until the vegetables are going golden and sticky on the
base of the pan. With the heat still high, pour in the stock, scraping
the bottom of the pan so you have a lovely golden-coloured stock.
Lower the heat, cover with a lid and simmer for 15 minutes.

2 Work the rest of the butter into the flour with a spoon. Drop this in
small pieces into the pan, whisking all the time after each addition with
a wire whisk, until you have a thin sauce consistency. Simmer for about
10 minutes to finish cooking the vegetables, adding the peas for the last
2 minutes. Remove the bay leaves.

3 Stir in the turkey and parsley, grind in lots of black pepper and add
salt if needed. Warm through then serve with slices of hot garlic bread.

SERVES **6**
PREP **20 MINS**
COOK **25 MINS**
FREEZE **UP TO 3 MONTHS**
BEFORE CREAM IS ADDED

1 litre (1¾ pints) turkey stock
    or chicken stock

120ml (4fl oz) dry white wine

1 carrot, finely diced

1 parsnip, finely diced

2 celery stalks, finely diced

1 leek (white part only), finely
    diced

1 small turnip, finely diced

salt and freshly ground black
    pepper

225g (8oz) cooked turkey meat,
    finely diced

100ml (3½fl oz) single cream

2 tbsp chopped parsley

crusty bread, to serve

RECIPE BY
ROOPA GULATI

TURKEY BROTH

Make thrifty use of leftover turkey by simmering your own
stock with the carcase after a roast dinner. This broth is
every bit as appealing when made with chicken.

1 Bring the stock and wine to the boil in a large pan, then stir in the carrot,
parsnip, celery, leek, and turnip. Season with salt and pepper, half-cover
with a lid, and simmer for 20 minutes.

2 Stir in the cooked turkey, cream, and chopped parsley and reheat gently.
Serve the soup with plenty of crusty bread.

SERVES **4–6**

PREP **20 MINS**

COOK **1 HR 15 MINS**
PLUS REHEATING

FREEZE **UP TO 3 MONTHS**
WITHOUT THE CREAM

RECIPE BY
CAROLYN HUMPHRIES

PHEASANT AND APPLE SOUP

This spicy soup is equally delicious made with other game birds, but if they are small, such as pigeon or partridge, use the whole bird including the breasts.

1 small pheasant

15g (½oz) butter

1 onion, roughly chopped

1 small sweet potato, roughly chopped

1 small cooking apple, peeled and diced

500ml (16fl oz) medium-sweet cider or apple juice

450ml (15fl oz) chicken stock

5cm (2in) cinnamon stick

1 bay leaf

salt and freshly ground black pepper

150ml (5fl oz) single cream

4 small fresh parsley sprigs, to garnish

1 Cut the breasts off the pheasant and reserve to cook for a separate dish. Cut the rest of the bird in pieces using a large sharp knife or poultry shears.

2 Melt the butter in a saucepan. Add the onion and fry gently, stirring, for 2 minutes until softened but not browned. Add all the remaining ingredients except the cream and parsley. Bring to the boil, reduce the heat, cover, and simmer gently for 1 hour.

3 Remove the pheasant and leave to cool slightly. Discard the bay leaf and cinnamon stick and purée the remaining soup in a blender or with a stick blender. Return to the rinsed-out pan and stir in the cream. Taste and adjust the seasoning if necessary.

4 Take the pheasant meat off the bones, discarding the skin, and shred it. Add half to the soup. Reheat the soup but do not boil. Ladle into shallow soup plates, put a small pile of the remaining diced pheasant in the centre, and garnish each with a small sprig of parsley.

SERVES **4**
PREP **25 MINS**
COOK **1 HR 20 MINS**
FREEZE **UP TO 3 MONTHS**
WITHOUT THE PASTRY LID

RECIPE BY
CAROLYN HUMPHRIES

PUFF-CRUSTED GAME SOUP

You can buy ready-diced mixed game, which includes furred
game and pigeon, or use diced venison, rabbit, or hare.
Well-hung beef is another option.

a large knob of butter

175g (6oz) diced game meat,
   thawed if frozen, cut into
   small pieces

1 red onion, chopped

2 tbsp plain flour

900ml (1½ pints) beef stock

1 tbsp redcurrant jelly

3 chestnut mushrooms, halved
   and sliced

1 tbsp chopped fresh sage

4 tbsp ruby port

salt and freshly ground black
   pepper

1 sheet ready-rolled puff pastry,
   thawed if frozen

1 egg, beaten

1 Melt the butter in a saucepan and fry the meat and onion for 5 minutes,
stirring, until browned.

2 Blend in the flour and cook for 1 minute. Remove from the heat,
gradually stir in the stock, add the redcurrant jelly, and bring to the boil,
stirring. Add the mushrooms, sage, port, and some seasoning. Bring back
to the boil, reduce the heat, cover, and simmer very gently for 1 hour,
stirring occasionally until rich and really tender. Taste and adjust the
seasoning if necessary.

3 Meanwhile, preheat the oven to 220°C (425°F/Gas 7). Cut four circles
from the pastry slightly larger than deep oven-proof soup cups and brush
with beaten egg. Stand the soup cups on a baking sheet. Brush the edges
of the cups with beaten egg. Ladle in the soup. Top with the circles of
pastry, pressing down lightly with a fork around the edge to secure. Make
a small slit in the top of each pie lid with a sharp knife to allow the steam
to escape. Bake in the oven for about 15 minutes or until puffy, crisp, and
golden brown. Allow to cool for 3–5 minutes before serving.

SERVES **4**
PREP **20 MINS**
COOK **65 MINS**
FREEZE **UP TO 3 MONTHS**
WITHOUT THE SHERRY

1 tbsp sunflower oil

1 partridge, quartered

1 onion, unpeeled and
  quartered

900ml (1½ pints) chicken stock

1 bouquet garni

salt and freshly ground black
  pepper

1 potato, diced

1 carrot, diced

1 small turnip, diced

2 tbsp plain flour

4 tbsp water

200g (7oz) cooked peeled
  chestnuts, quartered

2 tbsp amontillado sherry

a few drops of soy sauce

a little chopped fresh parsley

RECIPE BY
CAROLYN HUMPHRIES

PARTRIDGE SOUP

This is a substantial soup that is a great way to make one partridge feed four people. You could use any other small game bird in exactly the same way.

1 Heat the oil in a saucepan and brown the partridge pieces all over. Add the onion, stock, bouquet garni, and a little salt and pepper. Bring to the boil, reduce the heat, cover, and simmer gently for 1 hour.

2 Strain the stock and return to the saucepan. Add the potato, carrot, and turnip. Bring back to the boil, partially cover and simmer gently for about 20 minutes until the vegetables are really tender. Meanwhile, take all the meat off the partridge, discarding the skin, and shred the meat.

3 Remove the bouquet garni from the soup and discard. Blend the flour with the water and add to the soup. Bring to the boil, stirring, until lightly thickened and simmer for 2 minutes.

4 Add the shredded meat, chestnuts, and sherry to the soup and simmer for 2 minutes. Add a few drops of soy sauce to taste. Ladle into warm soup bowls and garnish with a little chopped parsley.

SERVES **4**
PREP **40 MINS**
COOK **I HOUR**
FREEZE **UP TO 3 MONTHS**
SOUP AND MEATBALLS SEPARATELY

FOR THE MEATBALLS

I garlic clove, crushed

½ Spanish onion, finely
    chopped

½ tsp hot smoked paprika

½ tsp ground cumin

I tsp dried thyme (or fresh
    leaves)

2 tbsp freshly grated Parmesan
    cheese

breadcrumbs made from
    2 slices bread

400g (14oz) minced steak

I large egg

sea salt and freshly ground
    black pepper

3 tbsp plain flour

3 tbsp vegetable oil

15g (½oz) butter

FOR THE SOUP

2 tbsp vegetable oil

½ Spanish onion, coarsely
    chopped

I garlic clove, crushed

250g (9oz) tomatoes, deseeded
    and chopped

I large Savoy cabbage, halved,
    core and ribs discarded,
    and leaves sliced into
    bite-sized pieces

I litre (1¾ pints) light beef
    stock

sea salt and freshly ground
    black pepper

2 tbsp finely chopped parsley,
    to finish

3 tbsp grated or shaved
    Parmesan cheese

RECIPE BY

MARIE-PIERRE MOINE

CABBAGE AND TOMATO SOUP WITH MEATBALLS

Both soup and meatballs can be prepared ahead of time, but should be stored separately. Allow approximately 30 minutes to reheat and finish off the cooking.

I For the meatballs, put the first nine ingredients in a bowl, season, and mix well. Shape into walnut-sized balls and refrigerate for 30 minutes.

2 Put a large deep pan over a medium heat. Add the oil. Tip in the onion, garlic, and tomatoes. Fry for 3–5 minutes, stirring. Add the cabbage and stir for 3 minutes. Stir in the stock, season, and simmer for 15–20 minutes.

3 Meanwhile, sift the flour onto a plate and coat the meatballs. Heat the oil and butter in a pan over a medium-high heat. Add the meatballs and cook for 3 minutes until they are a rich brown all over. Add to the soup and simmer for 15–20 minutes. Serve scattered with parsley and Parmesan.

SERVES 4–5
PREP 10 MINS
COOK 1 HR 40 MINS
FREEZE 3 MONTHS

150g (5½oz) stewing beef, diced

1 boneless belly pork slice, rinded and diced

115g (4oz) piece of salami, diced

1 chicken portion

1 large onion, chopped

1 litre (1¾ pints) beef stock

1 sprig of fresh rosemary

1 bay leaf

salt and freshly ground black pepper

¼ head spring greens or 4–6 cavolo nero leaves, shredded

1 head of green or red chicory

60g (2oz) soup pasta shapes

freshly grated Parmesan cheese

crusty bread, to serve

RECIPE BY
CAROLYN HUMPHRIES

ITALIAN WEDDING SOUP

The Italian name for this soup is *Minestra Maritata*, which simply means the flavours marry well together. Recipes vary, but it is always a robust, rustic mixture.

1 Put all the meats in a large pan with the onion, stock, rosemary, and bay leaf. Season well. Bring to the boil, skim the surface, reduce the heat, cover, and simmer very gently for 1½ hours until the meat is meltingly tender. Discard the herbs.

2 Lift out the chicken, discard the skin, remove all flesh from the bones, cut into neat pieces, and return to the pot. Add the greens, chicory, and pasta. Bring back to the boil, reduce the heat, and simmer for 10 minutes. Taste and adjust the seasoning, if necessary. Ladle into large open soup plates, sprinkle with grated Parmesan cheese, and serve with crusty bread.

SERVES **4**
PREP **20 MINS**
COOK **45 MINS**
FREEZE **UP TO 3 MONTHS**
AT THE END OF STEP 2

RECIPE BY
MARIE-PIERRE MOINE

PUY LENTIL SOUP WITH GAMMON

Small, dark green, and with a distinctive earthy flavour,
puy lentils are less floury than paler or red lentils, and
they cook quickly without disintegrating.

3 tbsp fruity olive oil, plus extra
 for serving

1 Spanish onion, finely chopped

1 garlic clove, crushed

400g (14oz) puy lentils, rinsed
 and drained

salt and freshly ground black
 pepper

2 thick gammon steaks,
 100g (3½oz) each

2 sprigs of fresh thyme

2 sprigs of flat leaf parsley,
 plus 1 tbsp, finely chopped,
 to serve

1 tsp grated zest of an unwaxed
 lemon, to serve

1 Put 1½ tbsp oil in a large, heavy saucepan over a moderate heat. Fry the onion and garlic for 2–3 minutes until golden and softened, stirring frequently. Stir in the lentils and season with salt and pepper. Put one of the gammon steaks on top of the lentils and add the thyme and parsley. Pour in enough cold water to cover the lentils and gammon with an extra 3cm (1¼in) water on top. Bring gently to a simmer, partially cover and cook for 25–30 minutes until the lentils are cooked through.

2 Lift out the cooked gammon and chop into small pieces. Discard the parsley and thyme. Reserving three ladlefuls of soup, put the contents of the pan with the chopped gammon in a blender or food processor and whizz until smooth. Return to the pan and stir in the reserved mixture.

3 Gently reheat until piping hot. Meanwhile, using the rest of the oil, fry the second gammon steak in a non-stick frying pan over a moderately high heat for 4–5 minutes, turning after 3 minutes, until cooked through and crisp and golden on both sides. Cut into small chunky pieces.

4 Taste and adjust the seasoning. Stir the soup and ladle into warmed bowls. Scatter the crispy gammon over the top and add a drizzle of extra virgin olive oil. Finish with a little chopped parsley and lemon zest, mixed together.

SERVES **4**
PREP **20 MINS**
PLUS OVERNIGHT SOAKING
COOK **1¾ HRS**
FREEZE **UP TO 3 MONTHS**

RECIPE BY
CAROLYN HUMPHRIES

CUBAN BLACK BEAN SOUP WITH HAM

This soup contains annatto. If you've never used the spice before, it has a sweet peppery flavour and an orangey red colour. It is widely used in Latin America.

225g (8oz) dried black beans, soaked in cold water overnight

1 bay leaf

450ml (15fl oz) chicken stock or ham stock

1 tbsp sunflower oil

1 large onion, finely chopped

1 garlic clove, crushed

½ tsp ground cumin

½ tsp ground annatto

pinch of ground cloves

1 beefsteak tomato, skinned and chopped

1 tsp white wine vinegar

115g (4oz) cooked ham, diced

1½ tsp light brown sugar

salt and freshly ground black pepper

a few torn coriander leaves, to garnish

corn tortilla chips, crushed, to serve

grated Cheddar, to serve

1 Drain the soaked beans and put in a large saucepan with enough water to cover by 5cm (2in). Add the bay leaf, bring to the boil, then boil rapidly for 10 minutes. Reduce the heat, cover loosely with a lid, and simmer gently for 1 hour or until really tender. Drain, reserving the liquid. Add enough stock to the cooking liquid to make 900ml (1½ pints) in all.

2 Discard the bay leaf and coarsely purée the beans and some of the stock in a blender – the mixture should not be completely smooth. Alternatively, crush with a potato masher, then set aside.

3 Heat the oil in the rinsed-out pan, add the onion, and fry gently, stirring, for 3–4 minutes or until softened but not browned. Add the garlic and fry for 1 minute, then add the spices and fry for 30 seconds. Add the tomato and vinegar and cook, stirring, for 3–5 minutes or until pulpy.

4 Add the beans, the remaining stock, the ham, and the sugar. Bring to the boil, reduce the heat, and simmer gently for 20 minutes or until thickened. Season with salt and pepper, then ladle into bowls, garnish with the coriander, and sprinkle with tortilla chips and grated Cheddar.

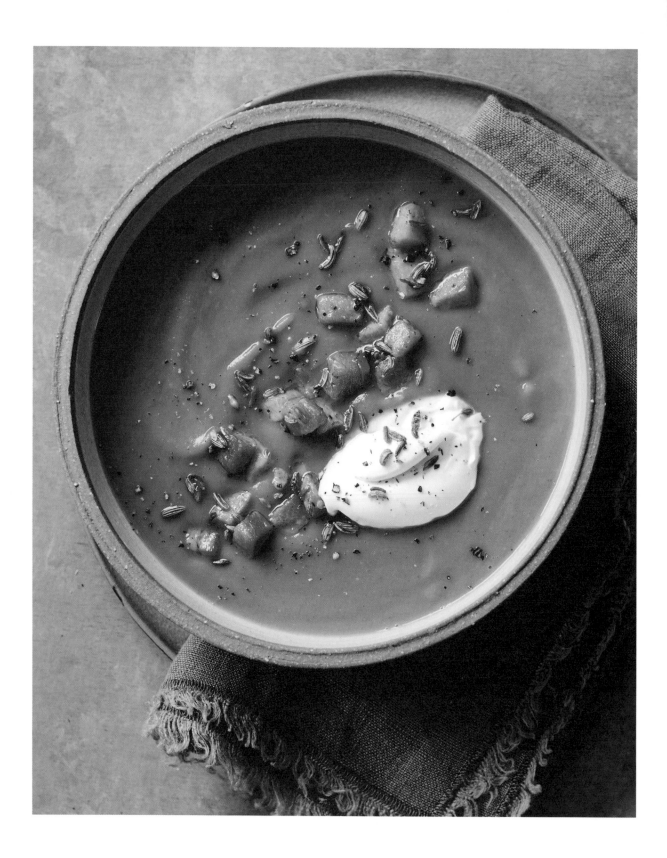

SERVES **4**
PREP **30 MINS**
COOK **45 MINS**
FREEZE **UP TO 3 MONTHS**
WITHOUT THE HAM GARNISH

RECIPE BY
MARIE-PIERRE MOINE

CHESTNUT SOUP WITH HAM

If fresh chestnuts aren't in season, use canned whole unsweetened chestnuts or dried peeled ones. You could also use pancetta or lardons instead of ham.

600g (1lb 5oz) fresh chestnuts

1½–2 tbsp sunflower, groundnut or mild-flavoured olive oil

20g (¾oz) butter

½ Spanish onion, finely chopped

1 garlic clove, crushed

3 bay leaves

2 tsp dried fennel seeds, plus 1 heaped tsp, to garnish

sea salt and freshly ground black pepper

1.2 litres (2 pints) light vegetable stock

100g (3½oz) slice of cooked ham, diced

1½ tbsp mascarpone, to finish (optional)

1 Score each chestnut with a small sharp knife, then place them in a saucepan, cover with cold water, and bring to the boil. Drain, leave until cool enough to handle, then peel and set aside. You could also peel them using the microwave method (see p296).

2 Place a large, heavy-based saucepan over a medium heat. Add the oil and half the butter. Fry the onion and garlic until golden and softened, about 2–3 minutes, stirring frequently. Add the peeled chestnuts, the bay leaves, and the 2 tsp fennel seeds. Stir and season. Pour in the stock. Bring to a gentle simmer, partly cover, and cook for 20–30 minutes, stirring occasionally until the chestnuts are soft.

3 Leave to cool. Discard the bay leaves. Transfer the soup to a blender or food processor and whizz until smooth. Strain the soup through a sieve back into the pan, pushing with the back of a spoon. Gently reheat the soup.

4 Meanwhile, place a non-stick frying pan over a fairly low heat. Add the reserved butter, and then add the diced ham and the extra fennel seeds. Fry gently, stirring a few times. Taste and adjust the seasoning. Stir the soup and ladle it into bowls. Scatter over a little of the diced ham and fennel seeds. If you like, add a small dollop of mascarpone to each serving.

BREAD

MAKES 1 LOAF
PREP 35 MINS
PLUS 1½ HRS RISING
COOK 40 MINS
FREEZE UP TO 6 MONTHS

CRUSTY WHITE LOAF

This basic white loaf is soft on the inside, with a light texture. If you have any left the day after you've baked it, use it for croûtons (see p39).

450g (1lb) strong plain flour, plus extra to dust

1½ tsp fast-action dried yeast

1 tsp salt

1 tsp sugar

1 tbsp vegetable oil, sunflower, or light olive oil, plus extra to oil

300ml (10fl oz) lukewarm water

1 Stir the flour and yeast together in a large bowl, then mix in the salt and sugar. Make a well in the middle and pour in the oil and water. Mix to form a soft dough, adding more water if required. Turn out on to a lightly floured work surface and knead the dough for 5–10 minutes or until smooth and elastic. Shape into a round by tucking the edges into the middle, then place it smooth side up in a large oiled bowl. Cover loosely with oiled cling film and leave in a warm place for 1 hour or until doubled in size.

2 Oil and flour the inside of a 900g (2lb) loaf tin, tapping out any excess flour. Lightly knead the dough and press it into a rough rectangle. Tuck the shorter ends in, followed by the longer edges, then lay it seam side down in the loaf tin. Cover loosely with oiled cling film and leave for 30 minutes or until risen.

3 Preheat the oven to 220°C (425°F/Gas 7). Dust the top of the loaf with a little flour, then slash it with a sharp knife. Bake for 20 minutes, lower the oven temperature to 200°C (400°F/Gas 6), then bake for another 20 minutes or until risen with a golden crust. Turn the loaf out and check that it is cooked – it will sound hollow when tapped on the base. Transfer to a wire rack to cool completely.

MAKES 16
PREP 25 MINS
PLUS 1½ HRS RISING
COOK 20 MINS
FREEZE UP TO 6 MONTHS

SOFT WHITE ROLLS

Use only a small amount of flour on your hands and work surface when you're kneading and shaping the dough for these rolls – too much will make it dry and stiff.

500g (1lb 2oz) strong white flour, plus extra to dust

2 tsp light soft brown sugar

7g sachet fast-action dried yeast

2 tsp salt

250–300ml (8–10fl oz) lukewarm water

a little vegetable oil

1 Sift the flour into a large mixing bowl. Add the sugar, yeast, salt, and enough of the water to form a soft, pliable dough. Dust a work surface lightly with flour and knead the dough for 10 minutes. Transfer to a lightly oiled bowl and cover loosely with oiled cling film. Leave in a warm place to rise for 1 hour or until doubled in size.

2 Turn the dough out on to the floured work surface and knead again briefly. Divide into 16 equal pieces and shape into balls. Smooth the tops and place on two lightly oiled baking trays, leaving enough space between the balls for them to spread out without touching. Leave to rise in a warm place for 30 minutes or until doubled in size.

3 Preheat the oven to 200°C (400°F/Gas 6). Bake the rolls for 20 minutes or until they are light brown on top and sound hollow when tapped on the bottom. Transfer to a wire rack and leave to cool completely.

MAKES 1 LOAF
PREP 35 MINS
PLUS 1 HR 40 MINS RISING
COOK 40 MINS
FREEZE UP TO 6 MONTHS

225g (8oz) strong white flour,
plus extra to dust

225g (8oz) strong wholemeal
flour, plus extra to decorate

1½ tsp fast-action dried yeast

1 tsp salt

1 tbsp vegetable oil, sunflower
oil, or light olive oil, plus
extra to oil

1 tbsp honey

200ml (7fl oz) lukewarm milk

150ml (5fl oz) lukewarm water

1 egg, beaten, to glaze

WHOLEMEAL LOAF

The mix of white and wholemeal flours in this loaf makes it light and moist. The recipe may seem complicated, but it is actually much easier and quicker than it sounds.

1 Mix the flours, yeast, and salt in a large bowl, then make a well in the centre. Stir the oil, honey, milk, and water together in a jug until the honey has dissolved, then pour into the well. Mix to form a slightly sticky dough, then leave to stand for 10 minutes.

2 Dust the work surface lightly with flour, then knead the dough for 5–10 minutes or until it is smooth and springs back when pressed gently. Shape into a ball and place in a large oiled bowl. Cover loosely with oiled cling film and leave in a warm place for 1 hour or until doubled in size. Meanwhile, oil and flour a 900g (2lb) loaf tin, tapping out any excess flour.

3 Turn the dough out on to a lightly floured surface and knead briefly. Shape into a rough rectangle, then tuck the shorter ends in, followed by the longer edges. Lay it seam-side down in the tin, cover loosely with oiled cling film, and leave for 30 minutes or until doubled in size.

4 Preheat the oven to 220°C (425°F/Gas 7). Sift a little wholemeal flour, leaving the bran in the sieve. Brush the top of the loaf with the beaten egg, sprinkle with bran, then slash the surface with a sharp knife. Bake for 20 minutes, then lower the heat to 200°C (400°F/Gas 6) and bake for another 20 minutes or until risen with a dark golden crust. Turn the loaf out on to a wire rack to cool completely.

MAKES 16
PREP 20–25 MINS
PLUS 1½ HRS RISING
COOK 15–20 MINS
FREEZE UP TO 6 MONTHS

225g (8oz) strong white flour, plus extra to dust

225g (8oz) strong wholemeal flour

7g sachet fast-action dried yeast

1 tsp salt

1 tbsp sunflower oil, plus extra to oil

1 tbsp honey

200ml (7fl oz) lukewarm milk

150ml (5fl oz) lukewarm water

1 egg, beaten, to glaze

oats, to decorate

WHOLEMEAL ROLLS

These rolls are perfect with hearty soups. For a special occasion, you could roll each piece of dough into a long rope and then wind it in a spiral or tie it in a figure-of-eight knot.

1 Mix the flours, yeast, and salt in a large mixing bowl, then make a well in the centre. Stir the oil, honey, milk, and water together in a jug until the honey has dissolved. Pour into the well and mix to form a slightly sticky dough. Dust a work surface lightly with flour, then knead the dough for 10 minutes or until no longer sticky. Shape into a ball and place in an oiled bowl. Cover loosely with oiled cling film and leave to rise in a warm place for 1 hour or until doubled in size.

2 Knead the dough lightly again, then divide into 16 equal pieces. Roll each into a ball and place on two oiled baking trays, leaving enough space between the balls for them to spread out without touching. Cover loosely with oiled cling film and leave to rise for 30 minutes or until they have doubled in size.

3 Preheat the oven to 200°C (400°F/Gas 6). Brush the rolls with the beaten egg and scatter a few oats on top. Bake for 15–20 minutes or until they sound hollow when tapped on the base. Transfer to a wire rack to cool.

MAKES **8**
PREP **10 MINS**
PLUS 55 MINS RISING
COOK **40 MINS**
FREEZE **UP TO 6 MONTHS**

EASY FLATBREADS

These simple yeast-raised breads are cooked in a frying pan. If you would like to make them in advance, simply wrap them in foil, then reheat in the oven just before serving.

500g (1lb 2oz) strong white flour, plus extra to dust

2 tsp salt

7g sachet fast-action dried yeast

3 tbsp olive oil, plus extra to oil

250–300ml (8–10fl oz) lukewarm water

1 Mix the flour, salt, yeast, and oil in a large mixing bowl, then add enough of the water to make a soft dough. Dust a work surface lightly with flour and knead the dough well. Place in a lightly oiled bowl, cover loosely with oiled cling film, and leave to rise in a warm place for 45 minutes or until it has doubled in size.

2 Turn the dough out on to the floured surface and knead lightly. Divide into eight equal portions, then flatten them with your hands. Use a rolling pin to flatten them a little more, then place on a lightly floured baking tray and set aside for 10 minutes.

3 Heat a large frying pan over a medium heat, add one of the circles of dough, and fry for 3 minutes or until brown. Turn it over and fry for 2 minutes. Transfer to a wire rack to cool while you cook the rest.

MAKES **2 LOAVES**
PREP **20 MINS**
PLUS 1½ HRS RISING
COOK **35–40 MINS**
FREEZE **UP TO 3 MONTHS**

SEVEN-GRAIN LOAF

Wholesome and healthy, this chewy bread is made from oats, millet, polenta, quinoa, rice, rye, and bulghur. If you don't have one of these grains to hand, substitute it for more of another.

85g (3oz) bulghur

50g (1¾oz) polenta

50g (1¾oz) millet

50g (1¾oz) quinoa

600ml (1 pint) lukewarm water

450g (1lb) strong white flour, plus extra to dust

250g (9oz) strong wholemeal flour

75g (2½oz) rolled oats

75g (2½oz) rye flakes

2 x 7g sachets fast-action dried yeast

2 tsp salt

50g (1¾oz) cooked long-grain brown rice

4 tbsp honey

250ml (8fl oz) milk

2 tbsp sunflower oil, plus extra to oil

1 Mix the first four ingredients in a bowl, stir in 400ml (14fl oz) of the water, cover with a tea towel, and set aside for 15 minutes. Meanwhile, mix the next six ingredients in a bowl. Add the bulghur mixture, then stir in the rice.

2 Heat the honey with the milk until it dissolves, then add to the bowl along with the oil. Gradually add the rest of the water or until a sticky dough forms. Knead on a lightly floured work surface for 10 minutes or until elastic. Shape into a ball, place in a lightly oiled bowl, then cover with oiled cling film. Leave to rise in a warm place for 1 hour or until doubled in size. Meanwhile, oil and flour two 900g (2lb) loaf tins.

3 Turn the dough out on to the floured surface and knead for 1 minute. Divide into two equal pieces and, with a floured rolling pin, roll each into a rectangle as wide as the tins and twice as long. Fold both ends to the centre and pinch the edges to seal. Place in the tins, cover with tea towels, and leave to rise for 30 minutes. Preheat the oven to 220°C (425°F/Gas 7).

4 Brush the tops with oil and bake for 10 minutes, then reduce the heat to 190°C (375°F/Gas 5) and bake for a further 25–30 minutes or until the loaves sound hollow when tapped on the base. Leave to cool on a wire rack.

MAKES **1 LOAF**
PREP **25 MINS**
PLUS 8–12 HOURS FOR STARTER
AND 1½ HRS RISING
COOK **40–50 MINS**
FREEZE **UP TO 3 MONTHS**

300g (10oz) rye flour

150g carton live natural yogurt

1 tsp fast-action dried yeast

1 tbsp black treacle

1 tsp caraway seeds, lightly crushed

250ml (8fl oz) lukewarm water

200g (7oz) strong white flour, plus extra to dust

2 tsp salt

a little vegetable oil

1 egg, beaten, to glaze

1 tsp caraway seeds, to decorate

RYE BREAD

Despite the need for forward planning, this loaf is relatively straightforward to make. The sourdough "starter" gives the bread an agreeably tangy flavour.

1 The day before you want to serve the loaf, make a "starter" by putting half the rye flour in a mixing bowl with the yogurt, yeast, treacle, and caraway seeds. Stir in the water, then cover and leave overnight until the starter is bubbling.

2 The next day, combine the remaining rye flour with the white flour and salt, then add to the mixture you made the day before. Mix to form a dough, adding a little water, if necessary. Turn out on to a lightly floured surface and knead for 5–10 minutes or until the dough is smooth and springy. Shape into a ball, place in an oiled bowl, and cover loosely with oiled cling film. Leave to rise in a warm place for 1 hour or until doubled in size. Meanwhile, flour a baking tray.

3 Lightly knead the dough again, then form into a rugby-ball shape and place on the tray. Cover with oiled cling film and leave to rise for 30 minutes. Preheat the oven to 220°C (425°F/Gas 7).

4 Brush the top with the beaten egg, sprinkle with the caraway seeds, then slash the knife along its length with a sharp knife. Bake for 20 minutes, then reduce the heat to 200°C (400°F/Gas 6) and bake for another 20–30 minutes or until dark golden with a hard shiny crust. Transfer to a wire rack to cool completely.

MAKES **8**
PREP **25 MINS**
PLUS 1 HR 20 MINS RISING
COOK 12–15 MINS
FREEZE **UP TO 6 MONTHS**

500g (1lb 2oz) strong white
    flour, plus extra to dust

1½ tsp fast-action dried yeast

1 tsp caster sugar

1½ tsp salt

45g (1½oz) butter, at room
    temperature

150ml (5fl oz) full-fat milk

150ml (5fl oz) lukewarm water

a little vegetable oil

BUTTERMILK BISCUITS

Favourites in the American South, these biscuits are rather
like English scones. They are delicious with soup and are
best served straight from the oven.

1 Mix the flour and yeast together in a large mixing bowl, then stir in the
sugar and salt. Rub the butter in with your fingertips until the mixture
resembles fine breadcrumbs. Make a well in the centre, pour in the milk
and water, and stir with a wooden spoon to form a dough. Transfer to
a lightly floured work surface and knead for 5 minutes or until smooth.
Place in a bowl, cover with a tea towel, and leave to rise in a warm place
for 1 hour or until doubled in size.

2 Dust the work surface lightly with flour and knead the dough briefly
again. Divide into eight equal portions, then roll each piece out into
a flat round about 10cm (4in) in diameter. Place the rounds on two lightly
floured baking trays. Make a small hole in the centre of each one with the
handle of a wooden spoon, then prick the rounds lightly with a fork. Cover
with oiled cling film and leave in a warm place for 20 minutes or until slightly
risen and puffy. Meanwhile, preheat the oven to 220°C (425°F/Gas 7).

3 Bake the biscuits for 12–15 minutes or until risen and lightly golden.
Transfer to a wire rack to cool for a few moments before serving hot.

MAKES 1 LOAF
PREP 10 MINS
COOK 30–35 MINS
FREEZE UP TO 6 MONTHS

SODA BREAD

To give it a lighter texture, this yeast-free bread is made with
buttermilk rather than plain milk. For brown soda bread,
replace half or all the white flour with wholemeal flour.

450g (1lb) strong white bread
flour, plus extra to dust

2 tsp bicarbonate of soda

2 tsp cream of tartar

1 tsp salt

60g (2oz) butter or lard, diced

300ml (10fl oz) buttermilk

1 Preheat the oven to 220°C (425°F/Gas 7). Sift the flour, bicarbonate
of soda, cream of tartar, and salt into a mixing bowl and stir together.
Add the butter or lard and rub it in with your fingertips until the mixture
forms fine crumbs. Make a well in the centre and pour in the buttermilk,
then mix to form a soft dough.

2 Transfer to a floured work surface and knead lightly, then shape into
a ball and roll around to smooth the surface. Place the ball on a floured
baking tray, flatten slightly, then dust lightly with flour. Use a floured knife
to cut it into six sections, but don't cut all the way through to the bottom.

3 Bake for 30–35 minutes or until the bread is well risen, golden brown,
and sounds hollow when tapped on the bottom. Transfer to a wire
rack and leave to cool completely.

MAKES I LOAF
PREP 10 MINS
COOK 25–30 MINS
FREEZE UP TO 6 MONTHS

CORNBREAD

A golden quick bread that is delicious straight from the
oven. To ring the changes, add a couple of crushed cloves
of garlic, a diced chilli, or some grated Cheddar to the batter.

a little sunflower oil

200g (7oz) cornmeal or
medium-coarse polenta

75g (2½oz) plain white flour

I tsp baking powder

I tsp salt

1½ tbsp caster sugar

300ml (10fl oz) milk

25g (scant 1oz) butter, melted

I egg

I Preheat the oven to 190°C (375°F/Gas 5). Grease a 21 x 16cm (8½ x 6½in) ovenproof dish with oil. Place the cornmeal or polenta in a large bowl and sift in the flour, baking powder, salt, and sugar. Stir together, then make a well in the centre. Whisk the milk, butter, and egg together, then pour the mixture into the well and mix thoroughly to form a batter. Transfer to the ovenproof dish and smooth the surface.

2 Bake for 25–30 minutes or until browned at the edges. To test if the cornbread is cooked, insert a skewer in the centre – it should come out clean. Cut into squares and serve warm.

INDEX

INDEX

ACKNOWLEDGMENTS

THE SOIL ASSOCIATION WOULD LIKE TO THANK:

Darina Allen, Dan Barber, Raymond Blanc, Sarah Canet, Joyce Cellars, Sally Clarke, Jeff Cox, Monty Don, Josephine Fairley, Sophie Grigson, Skye Gyngell, Shaun Hill, Juliet Kindersley, Daphne Lambert, Sofia Larrinua-Craxton, Lorraine Martin, Allegra McEvedy, Clodagh McKenna, Jeanette Orrey, Anna Paszczynska, Arthur Potts Dawson, Thane Prince, Sarah Raven, Eric Schlosser, Charlotte Senn, Rosemary Shrager, Geetie Singh, Rebecca Sullivan, Eric Treuille, and Alice Waters.

DORLING KINDERSLEY WOULD LIKE TO THANK:

For their work on the new photography (see below), DK would like to thank Charlotte Tolhurst (photographer), Kate Wesson (food stylist), Rob Merrett (prop stylist), and Sara Robin (art director). Thanks to William Reavell for his photography work on the first edition of the book. DK would also like to thank Shreya Chauhan and Millie Andrew for editorial assistance and Vanessa Bird for indexing.

TEXT CREDITS:

Sally Clarke's Beetroot and tomato soup recipe first appeared in *Sally Clarke's Book: Recipes from a Restaurant, Shop and Bakery* by Sally Clarke, first published by Macmillan and latterly by Grub Street. Jeanette Orrey's Pumpkin and apple soup recipe first appeared as a variation on her Basic cream of vegetable soup in *Second Helpings from The Dinner Lady* by Jeanette Orrey, published by Bantam Press.

PICTURE CREDITS:

All images © Dorling Kindersley.
For further information see: dkimages.com
New photography for the 2019 edition: p46, p50, p90, p92, p100, p112, p114, p118, p144, p158, p162, p164, p206, p226, p262, p278, p282, p287, p290, p292, p298, p300, p308, p312, p324, p328

USEFUL WEBSITES:

The Soil Association – www.soilassociation.org
Food for Life – www.foodforlife.org.uk

Editor Amy Slack
Editorial assistant Oreolu Grillo
Senior designer Glenda Fisher
Designer Hannah Moore
Jacket designer Nicola Powling
Jackets co-ordinator Lucy Philpott
Senior producer, pre-production Tony Phipps
Producer Samantha Cross
Managing editor Stephanie Farrow
Managing art editor Christine Keilty
Art director Maxine Pedliham
Publishing director Mary-Clare Jerram

DK DELHI
Senior editor Arani Sinha
Assistant editor Rishi Bryan
Managing editor Soma B. Chowdhury
DTP designers Rajdeep Singh, Manish Upreti
Pre-production manager Sunil Sharma

This edition published in 2019
First published in Great Britain in 2009 by
Dorling Kindersley Limited
80 Strand, London WC2R 0RL

A CIP catalogue record for this book is available from the British Library.

ISBN: 978-0-2413-8804-4
Printed and bound in China

A WORLD OF IDEAS:
SEE ALL THERE IS TO KNOW

www.dk.com